Learning, Teaching

Higher Edu

Developing Reflect.

Learning, Teaching and Assessing in Higher Education:
Developing Reflective Practice

Edited by
Anne Campbell
Lin Norton

LearningMatters

First published in 2007 by Learning Matters Ltd.

© 2007 Chris Beaumont, Christine Bold, Anne Campbell, Anthony Edwards, Wendy Hall, Deirdre Hewitt, Pat Hughes, Pat Hutton, Anne Marie Jones, Colleen Loomis, Stephen McKinnell, Moira McLoughlin, Lin Norton, Tessa Owens, John Patterson, Deborah Smith, Moira Sykes and David Walters

British Library Cataloguing in Publication Data

A CIP record for this book is available from the British Library

ISBN–13: 978 1 84445 116 6

The right of Chris Beaumont, Christine Bold, Anne Campbell, Anthony Edwards, Wendy Hall, Deirdre Hewitt, Pat Hughes, Pat Hutton, Anne Marie Jones, Colleen Loomis, Stephen McKinnell, Moira McLoughlin, Lin Norton, Tessa Owens, John Patterson, Deborah Smith, Moira Sykes and David Walters. to be identified as the Authors of this Work has been asserted by them in accordance with the Copyright, Designs and Patents Act 1988.

Cover design by Topics – The Creative Creative Partnership
Project management by Deer Park Productions, Tavistock
Typeset by Pantek Arts Ltd, Maidstone
Printed and bound in Great Britain by Cromwell Press Ltd, Trowbridge, Wiltshire

Learning Matters Ltd
33 Southernhay East
Exeter EX1 1NX
Tel: 01392 215560
info@learningmatters.co.uk
www.learningmatters.co.uk

Contents

Contributors   vii

Preface   xi
Sally Brown

Chapter 1 Introduction   1
Anne Campbell and Lin Norton

Chapter 2 Learning about learning or learning to learn (L2L)   9
Pat Hughes

Chapter 3 Supporting students' critical reflection-on-practice   21
Christine Bold and Pat Hutton

Chapter 4 Problem-based learning in higher education   31
Tessa Owens

Chapter 5 Action learning and research and inquiry methods   44
on postgraduate courses for professional practitioners
Anne Campbell and Moira Sykes

Chapter 6 Who do they think they are? Students' perceptions   56
of themselves as learners
David Walters

Chapter 7 Moving from dependence to independence: the   68
application of e-learning in higher education
Anthony Edwards and Stephen McKinnell

Chapter 8 Beyond e-learning: can intelligent agents really   80
support learners?
Chris Beaumont

Chapter 9 Using assessment to promote quality learning in   92
higher education
Lin Norton

Chapter 10 Formative assessment of the practice-based element   102
of degree work
Deirdre Hewitt and Deborah Smith

Chapter 11 Building on vocational competence: achieving a   111
better workforce by degrees
Moira McLoughlin and Ann Marie Jones

Chapter 12 Combining service learning and social enterprise in   120
higher education to achieve academic learning, business skills
development, citizenship education and volunteerism
John A. Patterson and Colleen Loomis

Chapter 13 Supporting students with disabilities in higher   130
education
Wendy Hall

Chapter 14 The development of reflective practice in higher   140
education: a theoretical perspective
Lin Norton and Anne Campbell

Index   149

Contributors

Chris Beaumont is deputy director of the Write Now Centre for Excellence in Teaching and Learning and Senior Lecturer in the School of Computing at Liverpool Hope University. After graduating as a Senior Scholar in Computer Science from Trinity College Cambridge, he worked in industry with GEC and DEC before returning to higher education. He was awarded a Learning and Teaching award from Liverpool Hope in 2005 and nominated for a National Teaching Fellowship in 2006. He has been practising and researching problem-based learning (PBL) since 1997 and is currently researching how pedagogical agents can promote learning in PBL teams.

Christine Bold is a Senior Lecturer and Programme Leader at Liverpool Hope University. For the past 14 years, she has worked in higher education on a range of undergraduate programmes in education. She focuses on improving the learning environment for students through action research projects. Her current research focuses on the use of e-forums in developing students' critical reflection about their practice.

Anne Campbell is newly appointed to a personal chair at Leeds Metropolitan University and was previously Professor of Education at Liverpool Hope University. Anne also holds a Fellowship at the Moray House School of Education, Edinburgh University. She has a long history of both researching and supporting others in practitioner inquiry and research. She is the co-author of a major text in this area, *Practitioner Research for Professional Development in Education* (Sage 2004), which is used widely in the UK by practitioner researchers. As well as a long-term interest in learning and teaching in school and higher education sectors, she researches narrative approaches and the use of practitioners' stories of professional practice. She is co-editor of *An Ethical Approach to Practitioner Research: Dealing with Issues and Dilemmas in Action Research* (Routledge 2007). Anne is currently a member of the Executive Council of the British Educational Research Association where she supports the advancement of practitioner research. She is a member of the editorial boards of the journals *Teacher Development* and *Educational Action Research*.

Anthony Edwards is currently Head of ICT in the Education Deanery at Liverpool Hope University. He has taught extensively in the secondary sector in the UK and abroad. He has also worked as an education consultant for BP and been a Fellow of the University of Surrey. He has written a technology series for schools and presented papers in India and Croatia on e-learning. His current research interest is the application of new technology to the creative process.

Wendy Hall is an experienced teacher of primary, secondary and adult students. She holds a Masters qualification in assessment and management of special needs as well as post-graduate qualifications in the assessment and teaching of dyslexic students. She has tutored, internationally, teachers studying to qualify as assessors of dyslexic pupils and has written teaching material on the subject of teaching adults who are dyslexic. She has substantial experience of a variety of disabilities and special needs and has been the Deanery Disability Advisor for the Education Deanery at Hope. She has provided input to the TDA on recruiting and retaining students with disabilities.

Deirdre Hewitt is a Senior Lecturer at Liverpool Hope University, lecturing on both the Bachelor of Arts with Qualified Teaching Status (BAQTS) as well as the new Childhood and Youth Studies (BAC) degree pathway. She has 20 years' primary school teaching experience. She is interested in supporting students to develop their reflective learning skills in order to improve their practice. Deirdre is a firm believer in teaching alongside students, trying to demonstrate on a practical, as well as theoretical level, how and why assessment is so vital in teaching and learning. She is currently involved in researching aspects of the teaching of phonics within primary classrooms, as she specialises in primary English.

Pat Hughes is a Senior Lecturer in Primary Education at Liverpool Hope University. After a degree at Durham University, she worked as a social worker, pre-school playgroup supervisor, cleaner, laboratory assistant and FE lecturer before training to be a primary school teacher. She has been a registered Ofsted inspector, a non-executive director of Knowsley PCT (NHS) and an external assessor for performance management. Pat has published many books, articles and training packs with a number of publishers including Heinemann, Hodder, Wayland, Oxford University Press, Nelson Thornes, David Fulton and Scholastic. She has contributed chapters to a variety of books published by Routledge, Paul Chapman, Multilingual Matters and Learning Matters.

Pat Hutton is a lecturer at Liverpool Hope University and is currently involved in the Foundation Degree in Supporting Learning and Teaching, Educational Studies and Inclusive Education degrees. She particularly enjoys developing on-line learning and teaching programmes and has contributed to small-scale research projects at the university. Her experience is varied and in addition to higher education, has included teaching in mainstream and special sectors, most recently as headteacher in a primary school.

Ann Marie Jones trained as a nurse and then as a health visitor, and has worked in London, Latin America and Liverpool. She taught child development and health studies for 12 years in further education. A growing interest in disability studies led to research towards a Masters degree in this area and is still a central aspect of her current post in Liverpool Hope University, where she was instrumental in devising the Disability Studies/Special Needs degree programmes and now leads the Foundation degree. Personal experience of studying part-time whilst working has fuelled her interest in how best to support non-traditional students through their degree.

Colleen Loomis is Assistant Professor of Psychology at Wilfrid Laurier University and Associate Director of the Laurier Centre for Community Service-Learning, in charge of research. She received her PhD in Community-Social Psychology from the University of Maryland Baltimore County (2001), was a Postdoctoral Scholar at Stanford University Medical Centers (2001–2003), and began working at Laurier in 2003. Financial support for preparation of this manuscript came, in part, from the McConnell Foundation and Laurier's Vice President of Academic Funds for teaching release. The views expressed herein are the author's and do not necessarily represent the view of the McConnell Foundation.

Stephen McKinnell is currently Director of the Learning Technology and Web Communications Unit in the Faculty of Medicine at the University of Liverpool. During the mid to late 1990s he developed a growing interest in the use of technology to support his teaching activities at Liverpool Hope and then in 1999 he was seconded to Hope's REACHOut programme, a European funded initiative to broaden access to HE among previously marginalised sections of the community, as its ICT Coordinator. This was followed by a move to Hope's Learning and Teaching Development Centre in 2000 where he took on various roles including supporting the use of Hope's own in-house developed VLE and the implementation of a commercially available VLE as its replacement. In 2004 he was appointed as Hope's first e-Learning Manager. During this time he maintained a hands on approach to supporting colleagues as they developed their use of the VLE at Hope. Always keen for the VLE to be more than just a repository of electronic paper, he worked closely with colleagues from a wide range of subject areas to develop the blended use of the VLE with traditional face-to-face teaching methods. Stephen joined the Faculty of Medicine at the University of Liverpool in September 2006 where he continues to develop the use of a VLE to support learning and teaching activities.

Moira McLoughlin has taught 7–80+ year olds in a range of settings which include primary schools, further education, a secure psychiatric hospital, a secure unit for adolescent offenders, and was headteacher of a residential special school for children with social, emotional and behavioural difficulties. She has been a Senior Lecturer in Special Educational Needs, Special Needs and now Disability Studies for nearly six years, initially at Edge Hill University and now at Liverpool Hope University, having taught at both undergraduate and post-graduate levels. She has also been involved in the training and assessment of learning mentors, higher level teaching assistants and teaching students on school experience and has a particular interest in the work of para-professionals in schools. Moira is a lay representative for the North Western Deanery for Postgraduate Medicine and Dentistry.

Lin Norton is Professor of Pedagogical Research and Dean of Learning and Teaching at Liverpool Hope University, where she has worked for the last 20 years. In her present role, she leads the Centre for Learning and Teaching (**www.hope.ac.uk/learningandteaching/**), whose aim is to encourage continuing professional development through reflective practice and through choice. A chartered psychologist and psychology lecturer for many years, her research interests include pedagogical action research, student assessment, meta-learning and lecturers' beliefs and behaviours. She has published extensively in journals and books. She currently holds the position of research director in the collaborative Centre for Excellence in Teaching and Learning on writing for assessment (**www.writenow.ac.uk**) and is Editor of *Psychology Teaching Review*.

Tessa Owens began her career in the Financial Services sector working in Banking and Insurance. She held a variety of posts from Branch Official, to Systems Analyst in Organisation and Methods, Administration Management and Management Development. She began teaching Business and

Management Studies in 1992 and joined Liverpool Hope University in September 1999, as a senior lecturer to co-develop the university's first uundergraduate pathway in Business Studies.

Tessa has now moved into the Centre for Learning and Teaching where she has a university-wide staff development remit particularly to promote good pedagogical design when using new technologies.

John A. Patterson is head of Primary Physical Education for Initial Teacher Training at Liverpool Hope University, teaching on qualified teacher training pathways and the new Inclusive Education degree. John received his BEd (Hons) from Liverpool Hope (1989) having retrained after some years as an engineer. John's teaching career took him across his native Liverpool, ending up as deputy headteacher and curriculum co-ordinator in a challenging inner-city school. John was employed to pilot his ideas to raise standards across developing learning networks by a Liverpool City Council Objective One programme, leaving to develop the SIGNAL process with the Dark Horse Venture charity. Employed by Liverpool Hope since 2002, John has developed this project, securing an MSc in Education (2006) focusing on citizenship education and community partnerships in social enterprise.

Deborah Smith is a Senior Lecturer at Liverpool Hope University, lecturing on both the Bachelor of Arts with Qualified Teaching Status (BAQTS) degree as well as the Early Childhood Studies (BAC) degree pathway. She has 17 years of primary teaching experience, working across Key Stage 1 and the Foundation Stage. Her passion is Early Years education. She is currently involved as an assessor for the Early Years Professional Status following Liverpool Hope University's successful bid to be one of the first training providers. Her recently achieved Masters degree focused on the 'fitness for purpose' of assessments within the BAQTS degree.

Moira Sykes worked as a history teacher in secondary schools for 20 years. During this time she worked closely with higher education in teacher training including the implementation of the National Curriculum for ICT for teacher training. She is currently the Director of Partnerships for the Education Deanery in Liverpool Hope. Her research interests are in mentoring and teachers' professional learning and development. She teaches on the masters courses and is developing an interest in teacher research in schools.

David Walters studied music at the Royal Scottish Academy of Music and at the Royal Northern College of Music. An experienced piano accompanist, he has spent much time teaching musical performance skills and coaching students preparing for performance assessments, concerts and recitals. He has been a member of the Music Department of Liverpool Hope University for many years and has worked variously as piano tutor, lecturer, Head of Performance and Music Course Leader – frequently, all at the same time. In addition to these roles, he spent a number of years working across a variety of subject areas as a Learning and Teaching Fellow.

Preface

What really matters in assessment, learning and teaching? And how can we prioritise competing demands on our time as busy academics and learning support staff who want to do the best by our students? In the UK, our views of what we need to concern ourselves with have been shaped and directed in the last couple of decades both by external quality drivers and internal imperatives. The Quality Assurance Agency set us an agenda to work with, firstly through *Teaching Quality Assessment*, then through *Subject Review* and more recently through a range of *Quality Enhancement* initiatives. Additionally, most higher education institutions (HEIs) have themselves garnered student feedback through questionnaires and other forms of review and these have now been supplemented by the National Student Survey (NSS), which has focused attention further on what students really think of the ways we design, deliver, assess and evaluate the curriculum. Legislation too, particularly that related to disabled students, has helped us further to concentrate our endeavours.

This provides us with a number of clear goals for us to work towards in proposing new directions for an ethical approach to higher education. A key starting point is student-centredness, which underpins all the chapters in this book and without which no HEI can be effective in the twenty-first century. Central to the book is a focus on reflective practice for the practitioner in higher education, but also as a powerful way of modelling for students the advantages of taking a reflective approach. The editors and authors stress that reflection on practice and undertaking pedagogical research and practitioner inquiry are necessary to encourage change and improvement of practice. Having selected students from diverse backgrounds who have the capability for higher education study, we need to ensure that the student experience is as positive as possible, enabling all students to use their talents to the full and maximise individual achievement, no matter what their starting points. Whether they study full-time or part-time, we need to be sure that they are effectively guided on their choices, inducted into HE cultures, supported during their studies and sent into the next stage of their lives well prepared for employment or further study; hence the concentration in this volume on the holistic student experience, underpinned by a commitment to inclusivity and social justice. Innovative as well as tried-and-tested approaches are covered here, with both generic and subject-orientated material.

Those who teach and support the learning of our students must be effectively trained and supported themselves, adopting a professional approach which is based on an evidence-based understanding of what research tells us works well in the classroom and the wider learning environment. This book brings together a range of authorial viewpoints, on matters of high relevance and currency including formative assessment, problem-based and action learning, plagiarism and a variety of e-learning and blended learning approaches. Amply illustrated with case studies and practical examples, this research-informed text blends theory and practice to propose an inclusive and developmental approach that is centred clearly on assuring student achievement and success. The editors who have shaped and steered the progress of the book are themselves expert practitioners in assessment, learning and teaching, and the scope and breadth of this book reflects their expertise.

I heartily welcome this book and commend it to you, whether you are just starting out in teaching or learning support, or whether you an experienced 'old-hand' seeking guidance through the newer aspects of HE learning territories.

Sally Brown

Pro-Vice-Chancellor
Assessment, Learning and Teaching, Leeds Metropolitan University

Acknowledgements

The Editors would like to thank Christina Anderson for her preparation of the manuscript, always done with willingness and a smile. In addition, we would like to thank Ian Kane for his helpful and painstaking proof reading and help with the editing, always with a smile and a useful suggestion.

Chapter *1*

Introduction

Anne Campbell and Lin Norton

The time seems ripe for this book. There has been a major focus on learning, teaching and assessment in higher education in recent years evidenced by the work of the Higher Education Academy (HEA), of which many university teachers are members. New postgraduate qualifications in learning and teaching in higher education also evidence the move to enhance and professionalise teaching and learning. A new UK Professional Standards Framework has been developed which informs institutions and enables them to determine their own criteria for application to their provision (**www.heacademy.ac.uk/professional standards.htm**). In addition, the implementation of the UK government's agenda for widening participation has influenced teaching and learning approaches in many institutions, requiring them to adapt and develop strategies to support students. Taken together, these developments require university teachers to actively question existing practice, develop a solid understanding of the pedagogy of their subject and of how students learn, but above all else to become reflective practitioners.

The book covers the current context for teaching and learning in higher education from foundation degrees to postgraduate level. It also uses a range of courses to provide exemplars. These include, for example, initial teacher education students, undergraduate modular combined studies courses in music, business studies and health as well as postgraduate courses for professional practitioners. The chapters are all written by higher education practitioners and are based on 'tried and tested' strategies and materials as well as pedagogical research. Topics range across the following: developing reflective teaching; setting and meeting learning objectives; action and inquiry techniques; strategies for students with disabilities; assessment strategies; teaching generic courses to mixed cohorts of students; use of virtual learning environments and Intelligent Tutor Systems for supporting learning; learning and teaching on Foundation degrees; student perceptions of learning and teaching; and students as volunteers. The book is directly aimed at sharing and developing reflective practice.

The purpose of this book is not to provide a definitive text about learning, teaching and assessing in higher education but to bring an exploratory practitioner perspective to developing practice through a fusion of theory and practice and the use of actual practical activities and strategies. It also addresses issues raised by the new National Professional Standards Framework, previously unexplored by existing texts. Throughout the book reference is made to this framework, so readers can locate their own practice in conjunction with this reference point. The emphasis on reflective practice, on choice and on personal responsibility of the university educator is the underpinning rationale. As such, it is intended to be a stimulus to readers' own reflective practice and, at the same time, provide practical and pragmatic suggestions for developing their own practice. The authors are drawn from across a number of departments in Liverpool Hope University, an acknowledged leader in the field of pedagogical research and practice and the host organisation of the first International Pedagogical Research in Higher Education Conference, Liverpool, May 2006 (**http://hopelive.hope.ac.uk/PRHE/**). Despite focusing on the work of one institution, a breadth of experience is evident which draws on authors' previous experience in a variety of different institutions and settings.

In order to help readers determine how they might approach reading and using the book, each chapter is summarised and discussed in the rest of this Introduction. As already stated, this is a practical book that is meant to be used, as well as hopefully stimulating evaluation, review and reflection. As the editors, this posed us with a difficulty in deciding on the authorial style of the chapters, in particular whether we should insist that everyone should write in the first or the third person to ensure a consistent approach. In the end we decided that it would be more in keeping with the book's purpose to allow both where appropriate. Thus the reader will find that some chapters predominantly use 'I' to indicate where the author is reflecting on her or his practice; others use both the first and the third person, and some of the chapters are written entirely in the third person.

Chapter 2 questions the value placed on learning in higher education (HE) and seeks to broaden the concept of a learner within the HE context. It discusses learning-how-to-learn (L2L) strategies. By helping students to see themselves as learners it hopes to aid the development and acquisition of new skills and knowledge. It draws on the fields of health and social marketing to illustrate these ideas.

Pat Hughes begins with a look back at her own experiences of learning in university and suggests that selling or marketing courses will become more important in the future. She also suggests that learning should not be a passive activity and that we should move away from the traditional teacher–student models to one of 'lead learner'. She advocates tutors in higher education considering themselves as learners also and urges us to consider Claxton's (2002) 'Building Learning Power' strategies adapted by Rush (2005) for teachers and students in the tertiary sector. Her first case study is a call to support students in identifying many different ways of learning effectively and to consider that some of these may be different from a student's preferred learning style and provide an appropriate challenge to develop themselves as learners.

Hughes discusses the current foci on accelerated learning, differing learning styles and multiple intelligences and alerts us to the issue of finding a 'recipe' approach to learning, a pitfall which many in the school sector may have failed to avoid. Her second case study builds on De Bono's (1991) work on developing thinking skills and shows how activities can be adapted for students in higher education by designing effective strategies for developing interesting and varied approaches to learning. The chapter identifies the teaching academic as a 'lead learner', with a clear remit to support students in learning to learn (L2L) across the many different ways in which learning now takes place in HE.

Chapter 3 is based on collaborative action research undertaken by its authors, Christine Bold and Pat Hutton, with their part-time students on a Foundation degree. It details their development of students' critical reflection-on-practice, based on Ghaye and Ghaye's (1998) ten principles of reflective practice. It considers five broad areas of activity: a) developing reflective writing; b) self-managed learning agreements; c) developing reflection-on-practice in peer support groups; d) reflection-on-practice in asynchronous e-forums and e) online formative and summative assessment.

Bold and Hutton firmly believe that a capacity for reflection is central to effective learning, in particular deep learning as put forward by Leung and Kember (2003). They take the reader on a journey through a variety of strategies and practices in the development of reflection such as: a portfolio of reflective practice; self-managed learning agreements; asynchronous e-forums and assessment tools. These strategies and practices are illuminated by actual and fictional examples which bring the student voice to the work and provide a sense of reality to the chapter. They also tackle the use of 'I' in academic work and encourage students to draw on their experience and make use of personal reference where appropriate.

Bold and Hutton aim to enhance the quality of learning and teaching for students via increased levels of peer and tutor support and the provision of varied contexts for learning. The authors believe that developing student capability to reflect on practice within their work-based degree programmes is a fundamental requirement before focusing their thoughts on the contributions of other practical and theoretical perspectives. They conclude that not all students are consistent in their approach to learning and a range of factors influences engagement, such as maturity, previous learning experiences, academic qualifications, workplace experience and commitment.

Tessa Owens in Chapter 4 considers the introduction of problem-based learning (PBL) as an increasingly popular learning and teaching pedagogy in UK universities. She examines the claims for PBL's development of transferable skills, in addition to the development of 'deep' learning in diverse curriculum areas and provides a theoretical rationale for PBL referring to the work of Biggs (2003), Yeo (2005) and Ramsden (2004). She espouses constructivist learning theory where learning is conceived as social construction and requires active learning.

Owens provides a case study from research in business studies (Owens and Norton, 2006), which compared students' perceptions and performance on a PBL module with that of a traditionally taught module. The main findings from this study showed that although PBL was initially an unpopular learning and teaching approach, student evaluations ultimately revealed that they enjoyed their experiences and found the curriculum more relevant to real-life business issues. The assessed results following the first module, however, were no better (or worse) than in their traditionally taught modules. However, the research revealed that there was a statistically significant improvement in student grades in their next PBL module, which took place in the following semester.

Examples of PBL activities are provided with a commentary which supports the trialling by others. Owens also highlights the phenomenon of plagiarism and suggests that PBL approaches may help to reduce instances of plagiarism by making students' progress more visible. Owens also provides discussion prompts, questions to support tutor reflection and useful proformas and student resources to support the development of problem-based learning in higher education.

In Chapter 5, Anne Campbell and Moira Sykes focus on the development of action learning and research and inquiry methods in postgraduate courses. They draw on approaches to teaching and learning that combine workplace and university learning contexts, which are based on their current and previous teaching. They tackle the differences between action learning and action inquiry and state that action learning is a process of investigating problems or concerns within a group or set (a small group of people who meet together on a regular basis), which results in new knowledge, insights and practices. Action research or inquiry can be undertaken either by individuals or collaborative groups. It uses previous literature in the field and is generally more rigorous in design and conduct than action learning and results in a form of publication or dissemination.

Practical examples of action learning sets and action inquiry projects are presented and discussed as effective learning activities for practitioners in the professions of education and social and health care. Many of the practices they describe have originated in business courses and are suitable for all subjects with carefully chosen case study examples to customise them for specific professionals. Activities involving critical friendship groups, where collaborative support and challenge for development is the aim, may lead to more specific peer coaching and critical evaluation techniques. The aims of these activities are to build communities of practitioners who continuously engage in the study of their craft and develop a shared language and a set of common understandings for collegial study and investigation of practice (Joyce and Showers, 1982).

The issues and difficulties in assessing reflective and collaborative work are addressed by Campbell and Sykes, who reference Winter *et al.* (1999) and their criteria for assessing reflective writing. Assessing an individual's work within a collaborative group presentation is discussed with an actual example to illustrate the issues involved. The authors conclude their chapter by providing some useful further reading for those interested in developing action learning and inquiry approaches.

David Walters, in Chapter 6, focuses on a study of a group of first-year students in music looking at their perceptions of themselves as learners in order to better understand their attitudes and approaches to study. The research studied student responses to a constructivist questionnaire, a version of the Ideal*** Inventory (Norton, 2001), namely 'The Ideal Self Inventory: A new measure of self esteem', applied at the beginning and end of the first year.

In this chapter Walters attempts to find a manageable method of investigating learners' conceptions of learning (in context), their epistemological beliefs, their understanding of their personal learning processes as well as their understanding, or personal view of their practical and academic skills. He proposes that motivations for learning can be summed up as: academic; vocational; self-development; peer pressure; and family expectations. In considering motivation, he borrows ideas from the world of music, as the study on which this chapter is based focused on work with music students. Walters investigates the process of learning a musical instrument – a process which may not be totally unfamiliar to many readers, either through trying to learn an instrument themselves or through observing the efforts of others.

He addresses confidence, competence and autonomy, which are identified as being essential skills in learning. He uses case studies to illustrate approaches to investigating what makes a 'really good learner' or a 'not very good learner' and uses students' self-reported perceptions at the beginning and end of the year to measure this. The Good Learner Inventory is recommended as a useful research tool for those wishing to investigate the effects of their teaching on student perceptions. Walters identifies the next stage as finding ways of using the inventory as the basis for discussion with students, either in class or one to one, to promote awareness of the meta-learning 'requirements' for truly successful study at this level. Walters concludes with a number of reflective discussion points to develop practice.

In Chapter 7, Edwards and McKinnell explore the vexed question of how new technologies can be applied to teaching and learning in universities. The term 'e-learning' is used in the chapter to apply to activities that involve some form of interaction with information networks such as web-based and virtual learning environments. The authors discuss Heppell's (2006) 13 features of transformation in education and discuss the benefits and challenges involved in applying e-learning. Edwards and McKinnell present a case study illustrating how e-learning can be used to accommodate individual need, support curriculum enrichment and offer a wide variety of opportunities to track student progress.

Four modes of e-learning are presented and evaluated and the authors, to borrow their words, conclude that we are in the age of the learner rather than the digital age, stressing the underlying tenets of this book. They ask the question of where and how the boundary between the virtual and physical classroom in higher education should be established. They state that there are no shortcuts and that all the skills, knowledge and understanding we currently possess in traditional approaches need to be applied with the same vigour to the development of e-learning packages. They see it as essential that tutors employ sound pedagogical reasoning in the design of such packages and warn that inappropriate use of the technology can be highly counterproductive. They urge us to retain balance in teaching and learning, otherwise there is a real danger that the tutor can become marginalised and the only relationship the student has with the institution is two dimensional. Edwards and McKinnell provide 13 points to aid reflection and to avoid lack of balance in curriculum design and learning and teaching approaches for the future.

Chris Beaumont in Chapter 8 examines the development of pedagogical agents as learning companions and explores how artificial intelligence (AI) technology has been applied to assist learning. He traces the development of Intelligent Tutoring Systems (ITS) and the more recent research into learning companions, using agent technology. He critically analyses the relationship between pedagogy and technology in such systems and discusses aspects important for achieving success. The development of ITS/learning companions requires detailed consideration of the context in which the student will be working, and the chapter examines relevant factors, using examples to illustrate the points. Beaumont also discusses if, and how, such technology has a place within higher education

Beaumont offers a brief review of the development of Intelligent Tutor Systems and artificial intelligence in education through agents and learning companions and simulations. With regard to pedagogy and technology, he considers the challenges for developing useful systems such as: epistemological assumptions (social constructivist/ behaviourist); implicit student models and knowledge representation; interactions: student-content; student-agent; student-student. The place of the human tutor in the system is also considered with reference to: affective factors, interaction styles, learning styles; interface design issues and animation and dialogue; student reactions and help-seeking behaviour when using agents. Examples of ITS and pedagogical agents are presented and they cover the domains of use and context, the interaction models and pedagogical assumptions, effectiveness, and research challenges and directions. The chapter concludes with a discussion of how intelligent agents can effectively support learners.

Lin Norton emphasises the centrality of assessment to the learning process in Chapter 9 and urges all who teach and facilitate student learning in higher education to reflect critically on assessment practices. She reminds us that the key area of assessment and feedback scored poorly on the annual National Survey of Student Satisfaction. She argues that if universities are driven down the path of just pleasing the student, through market forces, league tables and an increasingly competitive global market, then the concept of quality learning is under serious threat. Drawing on some of her own practice and research over the past 15 years, she encourages readers to look at their own assessment practices with a fresh eye by exploring what can be done in a practical and pragmatic sense. In so doing, she aims to encourage a reflective approach to assessment and feedback practice, based on an identification of personally held professional values together with a basic understanding of how university students learn.

In the first section of the chapter, Norton identifies appropriate questions to help readers reflect on their own assessment practice before outlining a theoretical background to a systemic approach to assessment. She addresses students' strategic approaches to assessment and warns of the dangers of competitive and cheating behaviour and plagiarism. Norton presents a case study of an account of how she has tried in her own practice, in a counselling psychology module, to address the problem of setting an assessment task which is authentic and discourages students from taking a strategic marks-orientated approach. She illustrates how Psychology Applied Learning Scenarios (PALS) were used to give students the opportunity to apply their theoretical understandings of different psychological theories to a range of counselling cases.

The second big question Norton tackles in this chapter is: 'What part do assessment criteria and feedback play in improving student learning?' and in a similar way to the first section poses reflective questions and provides a theoretical background to locate issues and challenges for tutors. A second case study is focused on the use of a simple tool called the Essay Feedback Checklist (Norton and Norton, 2001; Norton *et al.*, 2002a; Norton *et al.*, 2002b) which is aimed at improving tutor feedback. In the final section of the chapter, Norton reflects on her practice in assessment and encourages others to adapt and develop strategies to support their students, but also to actively question the establishment and institutional policy around assessment.

In Chapter 10, Deirdre Hewitt and Deborah Smith consider the value of work placements to the individual's skills and knowledge base. They explore how successful work placements should involve an element of formative assessment and how all stakeholders can be involved in this process. Good practice is highlighted from the field of teacher education and the issues and relevant transferable skills, principles and/practices are discussed. They consider the value of the practice-based element of degree work. If no value to the learner were to be found or demonstrated, then there would be no need for it to be included, especially since what is required is an expensive investment in terms of financial, personal and professional commitment of time and effort on the part of all stakeholders. The authors refer to the National Committee of Inquiry into Higher Education (NCIHE) which suggested that all undergraduates should be able to access work experience placements, as it gives added value to the learner (NCIHE, 1997). They identify that what has received little attention is the transfer of learning between the placement and the university course which needs to be recognised as important.

Hewitt and Smith's first case study raises the issue of the role of employers in work placements for students and demonstrates the need for consistent collaboration and discussion so that the student can actively construct learning from the formative assessment. A second case study examines a teacher education school-based experience and reports that 100 per cent of the students agreed that the period of school-based experience was 'very useful' or 'useful' for demonstrating knowledge and skills.

Hewitt and Smith conclude from this example that students received verbal and written feedback on lessons taught by them during the placement as well as weekly reviews and a final written report by their placement-based tutor. Throughout, their individual achievements and qualities were acknowledged and celebrated. The authors argue that these written records can then form the basis for future target-setting. This method of assessment, they claim, is respected by students as the purpose of it is clear to them and it has a direct impact upon how they perform in their chosen career, demonstrating how formative assessment can work well in a workplace setting. The chapter concludes with more questions to aid reflection on formative assessment in workplace placements.

Chapter 11 by Jones and McLoughlin explains the nature and purpose of Foundation degrees, which have provided a route to degree level study for practitioners in a wide range of disciplines and employment settings. These degree programmes do not usually draw upon the traditional university entrant group of 18-year-old students but the authors argue that there are many features of Foundation degree study which may well benefit all students.

The chapter draws on materials from the Foundation degree in Special Needs (re-named Disability Studies) at Liverpool Hope University which was specifically developed for students who had some experience with people with special needs and a real interest in the subject. Students study alongside the full honours degree students for all modules, but in addition they study two modules which form the focus for this chapter: these are Developing Learning Skills (DLS) and Work Practice (WP). The course is student-centred and, at the beginning, students are introduced to the concept of meta-learning. One of the first topics of study is learning styles. The students complete questionnaires to ascertain their own style and apply this new-found knowledge to their own learning. The authors identify relevant skills as reading, note taking and note making, time management and conditions for study learned from personal experience of being 'taught' how best to carry out these tasks.

The chapter concludes by echoing Biggs' (2003) consideration of being a reflective teacher. This consists of three elements: these are to use one's experience to find the solution to a problem which has arisen in the classroom; to possess a thorough subject knowledge so that when students question or misunderstand, tutors find a clearer way to explain a concept; to be prepared to consider why learning is not taking place and find a way to engage the students in a more active way. Biggs reminds us that this is an ongoing cycle in which 'one keeps looking at what the students do, what they achieve and link that with one's own work'. Jones and McLoughlin aim to get to know their students as learners very well, which is a fundamental principle of being an effective teacher.

In Chapter 12 Patterson and Loomis comment on the growing concern in the Higher Education Academy (HEA) about how to address the need for educating citizens and developing a capable workforce, while few models exist for simultaneously accomplishing these twin goals. An adult educational model is effective for developing trade-specific skills. The authors discuss one limitation of this approach, an absence of attention to developing an ethic of care for others. They argue that industry and ecclesiastical institutions only partly fulfil society's need to foster youth's vocational and ethical development, facilitating their contributions to political, social, and economic life.

Patterson and Loomis examine why a unifying framework for education delivery is necessary. They claim that not having a framework to deliver the content of various curricula translates into missed opportunities. The course of educational history reflects periods of attention on academic achievement, often without concern for personal outcomes such as social and emotional development (e.g. feelings of empathy, conflict-resolution skills, and helping behaviours). They argue that a narrow focus on individuals' academic outcomes excludes attention on community and social outcome.

The chapter focuses on definitions of service learning in international contexts and links these with citizenship and volunteering and social enterprise initiatives.

The Schools Intergenerational Nurturing and Learning Project (SIGNAL) is used as an example of how citizenship and social enterprise initiatives can be brought together in a worthwhile project which encompasses aspects of the 'Every Child Matters' agenda and combines broader aspects of service-learning and student emotional intelligences with business enterprise. The chapter ends with a call for further research and asks that programme developers work closely with researchers to evaluate the pedagogy of blending service-learning with social enterprise.

Wendy Hall, in the comprehensive Chapter 13, states that while the impetus for her chapter has come from the work that she and other colleagues undertake supporting students with disabilities at Liverpool Hope University, it is intended that the issues raised will also prompt reflection on existing practice. Hall uses the Special Educational Needs and Disability Act (SENDA) of 2001, the Disability Rights Commission in 2006 and the Disability Discrimination Act of 1995 to define her terms, and 'disability' in particular.

The basis of this chapter is that students with disabilities are entering higher education in ever greater numbers and have a right to demonstrate their capabilities as much as other students. Hall states that it is the responsibility of those who work in universities to make sure that students' disabilities do not prevent them from gaining access to learning or prevent them from demonstrating their knowledge and understanding. The challenges she identifies, both institutionally and as tutors, are to ensure support for the transition to higher education; provide for, and support access to, the subjects the students wish to study including analysing assessment strategies to ensure equality of opportunity; use time and other resources efficiently and proportionally, and make best use of the resources available.

Hall addresses all the key issues and more: institutional issues; use of ICT; the role of student support services; the role of the disability adviser; administrative issues; and, of course, assessment issues. She identifies some examples of good practice which comprehensively cover most eventualities encountered by students with disabilities. This discussion of issues constitutes good advice for university departments and schools. Three case studies conclude the chapter, one considering the needs of blind students and the others also considering differing sensory impairments. This chapter gives the reader useful information about organising the learning environment for students who have disabilities.

In the final chapter of the book, Lin Norton and Anne Campbell take an overview of the theoretical underpinnings of the concept of the reflective practitioner. In a personal view of the place of reflection, they argue that given the competing demands on the time and requirements of the role of university educators, reflective practice as operationalised in the form of action research or practitioner inquiry is an effective way forward. They acknowledge the criticisms of both the concept of reflection and action research but suggest that an analytical and rigorous approach is as valid as more positivist empirical science. In arguing this as editors of the book, they have drawn together and highlighted the philosophical rationale which is the common theme running through the chapters. As such, this may, paradoxically, be the first chapter that readers wish to dip into in order to orient themselves to the purpose and aims of the book.

Norton and Campbell begin their chapter with a brief account of the origins of reflective practice, drawing on the work of many experts in the field such as Schön (1983, 1987), Brockbank and McGill (1998) and Moon (2004) who have all written extensively on the place of reflection and reflective practice in higher education. In considering the potential of reflection, they consider the input of the two philosophers who Moon describes as 'backbone philosophers': John Dewey and Jurgen Habermas. In a short chapter, it is not possible to go into the detail that such philosophers merit, but Norton and Campbell are making the point that reflection and reflective practice are not untheorised concepts, an argument that is important when responding to critics. They go on to suggest a pragmatic answer to those who argue that reflective practice is comfortable, introspective and passive, by putting forward the case for action research or practitioner enquiry. In the context of university education where the *status quo* is to preserve the autonomy of the individual and the institution, the authors argue that there is a need for evidence to inform practice and policy decisions. This is very different to the current Quality Assurance Agency's demand for accountability in the form of measurable outcomes. Evidence gathered from practice-based enquiry can be used either to generate new theory and/or, as argued throughout this book, should be a primary source for modifying one's practice. Norton and Campbell end with a plea for personal commitment to change, and thereby refer back to the fundamental goal of the whole book, which is to encourage the development of reflective practice on teaching, learning and assessment in higher education.

References

Biggs, J. (2003) *Teaching for quality learning at university* (2nd edition). Buckingham: Open University Press / SRHE.

Brockbank, A. and McGill, I. (1998) *Facilitating reflective learning in higher education*. Buckingham: SRHE and Open University Press.

Claxton, G. (2002) *Building learning power*. Bristol: TLO.

De Bono, E. (1991) *Teaching thinking*. London: Penguin.

Ghaye, A. and Ghaye, K. (1998) *Teaching and learning through critical reflective practice*. London: Routledge.

Heppell, S. (2006) web log, **http://rubble.heppell.net**

Higher Education Academy (2006) National Professional Standards Framework for Teaching and Supporting Learning in Higher Education. Available online at **www.heacademy.ac.uk/reganaccr/StandardsFramework(1).pdf**.

Joyce, B. and Showers, B. (1982) Improving in-service training: the message from research. *Educational Leadership*, 37 (5), 375–385.

Leung, D.Y.P. and Kember, D. (2003) The relationship between approaches to learning and reflection upon practice. *Educational Psychology*, 23 (1) 62–71.

Moon, J.A. (2004) *Reflection in learning and professional development. Theory and practice*. London: RoutledgeFalmer.

National Committee of Inquiry into Higher Education (NCIHE) (1997) *Higher Education in the Learning Society*. London: HMSO.

Norton, L.S. (2001) The Ideal *** Inventory. A useful tool for pedagogical research in HE. *ILTHE Members resource area; scholarship of learning and teaching*. **www.ilt.ac.uk/1808.asp** (accessed 9 October 2004).

Norton, L.S., Clifford, R., Hopkins, L., Toner, I. and Norton, J.C.W. (2002a) Helping psychology students write better essays. *Psychology Learning and Teaching*, 2 (2), 116–126.

Norton, L.S., Hopkins, L., Toner, I., Clifford, R. and Norton, J.C.W. (2002b) The essay feedback checklist: helping psychology students to write better essays and tutors to give better feedback. Paper presented at the Psychology Learning and Teaching Conference (PLAT 2002), University of York, 18–20 March 2002.

Norton, L.S. and Norton, J.C.W. (2001) The essay feedback checklist: How can it help students improve their academic writing? Paper and workshop given at the first international conference of the European Association for the Teaching of Academic Writing across Europe (EATAW), Groningen, The Netherlands, 18–20 June 2001.

Owens, T. and Norton, B. (2006) Learning about learning: from student learning to the learning organisation. *HERDSA International Conference: Critical Visions Conference*, 9–12 July, Perth, Australia.

Ramsden, P. (2004) *Learning to teach in higher education*. (2nd edition) London: Routledge Falmer.

Rush, L. (2005) Teaching for learning power. INSET presentation to academic tutors. Southport (also available on HEA website).

Schön, D.A. (1983) *The reflective practitioner*. New York: Basic Books.

Schön, D.A. (1987) *Educating the reflective practitioner. Toward a new design for teaching and learning in the professions*. San Francisco: Jossey-Bass.

Winter, R., Buck, A. and Sobiechowska, P. (1999) *Professional experience and the investigative imagination: The art of reflective writing*. London: Routledge.

Yeo, R.K. (2005) Problem-based learning: lessons for administrators, educators and learners. *International Journal of Educational Management*, 19 (7) 541–551.

Chapter 2

Learning about learning or learning to learn (L2L)

Pat Hughes

Introduction

This chapter questions the value placed on learning in higher education (HE) and seeks to broaden the concept of a learner within the HE context. It then draws on work carried out in the Health Promotion field (French and Blair-Stevens, 2005) on social marketing to show how 'selling' learning to learn is necessary to promote learning and also to attract and retain students. The final section looks at some practical strategies to use in helping learners to learn about their own and others' learning. It includes two case studies of work which have been carried out with undergraduates and postgraduates.

Meeting the Standards

This chapter will meet the UK Professional Standards Framework in the following ways:

- **by strengthening the design and planning of learning activities;**
- **by supporting student learning**
  (Areas of activity 1 and 2);
- **by developing appropriate methods for teaching and learning;**
- **by developing understanding of how students learn**
  (Core knowledge 2 and 3);
- **by respecting individual learners;**
- **by demonstrating a commitment to incorporating research and scholarship to teaching;**
- **by engaging in continuing professional development.**

(**www.heacademy.ac.uk/professionalstandards.htm**)

Learning to learn (L2L)

There are several different definitions of learning to learn (L2L) and in this chapter I am using it to mean assisting students in (a) seeing themselves as learners and (b) having confidence that they can improve their learning skills through taking part in specific activities and acquiring new learning skills.

The changing nature of the university and HE (a personal perspective)

A hundred years ago (or maybe it was slightly fewer when I was a student), I attended a Russell Group university (Durham) and had tutorials in groups of five, one-to-one seminars and lectures with 50 (at most). All my tutors knew me by name, I was invited to their houses, provided with food and wine and they were reimbursed by the university. My son's Oxford experience in the 1990s was very little different from mine 20+ years previously.

Today, I am part of higher education which operates within a very different frame. Both new and old universities have taken on their previous incarnations. They are research, teaching or training institutions. The sceptic might say that they offer what their market wants, while visioning what the current political agenda is for HE. The two are not necessarily the same. The university students I see are an essential element of broadening participation in higher education. They have no grants – unlike Tony Blair and Gordon Brown and me. They have seminar groups with far higher numbers, have poorer financial support and mostly need to live at home and work in order to survive. They are not full-time students, despite their registration as such.

This system is well established in the USA, indeed my daughter bought into courses at postgraduate level. They did not run if not enough students bought in; for example, in teacher training four students were enough to buy into a reading course. The tutor did not work if the students did not buy in. Selling yourself and the course will be more important in the future.

The academic as 'lead learner'

This section is designed to raise a question about who are the learners and who are the teachers. It also identifies reasons why learning to learn (L2L) is important.

- **To alert learners to their own and other's learning strategies; it enables them to recognise learning as a skill which can be improved upon.**
- **As an important vocational skill for career.**
- **As a means of dealing with change and reducing stress levels, now and in the future.**

This extract from a fairly typical university student charter makes the role of the student very clear.

The student is 'expected' to do the following.

- *Attend and contribute fully to lectures, seminars, workshops and other learning opportunities.*

- *Behave responsibly in classes and treat lecturers, other staff and fellow students with respect.*

- *Complete assessment requirements and meet assessment submission deadlines.*

- *Treat property with respect.*

- *Abide by the rules and regulations relating to the use of libraries and learning resources.*

- *Abide by rules and regulations relating to the use of computers.*

Discussion point

The good student appears here to be someone who attends and behaves. This is a very passive role and actually counter to the concept of the active learner. There are no details about what to do should the teaching received not be of high quality, or sufficiently personalised to provide the support needed to gain a degree. I have deliberately chosen that particular document, rather than a policy document on learning and teaching, because it is the one given the highest profile in prospectuses. It certainly conveys the message about a promise that provided all this is done, you (the student) will gain a degree.

It might be useful for readers to look at the Student Charter in their own institutions and see exactly what image that throws on the role of the student as learner.

Lead learners

Ironically, many other educational institutions have moved beyond this distinction between teacher and learner. Many schools, for example, have become learning organisations, communities, networks and centres. This attitudinal shift is reflected in their vision statements, their publicity, vacancies and signage (see the Jobs Section of the *Times Educational Supplement* any week). They are also part of a wider learning community, inviting the public to come in and learn with them. One of the Merseyside local authorities, for example, is replacing its 11 secondary schools with nine 'learning centres'. The teachers have become the 'lead learners' modelling, scaffolding and discussing their learning and supporting students in identifying 'how' they learn as well as 'what' they learn (Hughes, 2004). This does not take the place of subject-specific knowledge, skills and concepts, but becomes a means of arriving more successfully at the learning outcomes for these.

The Dearing Report (DfEE, 1997) on HE is now over ten years old. It recognised the need to 'train' new staff in learning, teaching and assessment. The Institute for Learning and Teaching (ILT), and now the Higher Education Academy (HEA), were established with a mission to help institutions, discipline groups and all staff *to provide the best possible learning experience for their students*. Their strategies and aims (2005) include promoting good practice in all aspects of support for the student learning experience.

The HEA website shows a very active research community which is committed to looking at learning to learn in the changing conditions of HE – including technological changes. Many of its publications are for academics to learn how to learn and help others to do so. It provides support for academics interested in how to teach effectively and there has been a distinct move towards much more detailed understanding of the processes of learning and the importance of new developments in neuroscience. Phil Race's work (2001, 2006) provides a good insight into this debate as well as demonstrating, very practically, how today's HE lecturers should be trained and able to demonstrate that they enhance student learning.

Some challenges for the lead learner

Operational practice, however, tends to have different priorities. Performance management (PM), for example, in HE tends to reflect a rather low-key approach to student learning. Strategic and operational policy for PM has to reflect the current issues relevant for HE generally. For academics these obviously include the levels of research and publications; the ability to generate income; to manage projects and programmes; to work on courses which students, at all levels, complete successfully, and take part in some professional development to update themselves within their own disciplines.

There is still surprisingly little on tutors' own ability to learn and to be able to model successful learning. Research, publications and continuing professional development (CPD) do not result in successful learning for others *per se*; even when the subject matter is directly related to learning. Nor does the ability to generate income and manage programmes necessarily enhance learning. Certainly Pickford and Clothier's (2006) *FeFiFoFun* model for lecture design and delivery requires the lecturer to have *enthusiasm, expression, clarity of explanation, and rapport and interaction*. While this is obviously good practice, the operational practice is not that easy. Nor is it part of PM. HE lecturing today is high content. Being able to 'perform' in this way five, six or seven times a week is unrealistic. Large seminar/workshop groups of 20–50 students militate against the personal learning of the past where academics interacted more directly with students.

Student evaluation of learning and teaching tends to be hidden quietly within quality assurance systems and only rarely is seen as a dynamic part of an individual academic's PM. It then becomes all too easy to blame widening participation and inflated A-level results on students' failure to engage and achieve. Direct teaching of students in learning can offer them something to base their new courses on. The nature of student numbers in HE today means that they need to believe that they can adapt, change and challenge prior learning. L2L (Learning to learn) offers them this.

L2L as a future vocational skill

Another reason why providing degree-level students with skills on learning to learn is particularly important, is that so many move from universities and other HE institutions to areas where they are involved in educating (in its widest sense) others. Students going into public services such as social care, health, schools and nurseries are charged with teaching responsibilities. Many of those going into the private sector are also involved *inter alia* in training, mentoring and coaching. If these students emerge, plus a degree, but limited in knowledge and skills in how people learn, they are in danger of failing both themselves and those for whom they work.

L2L and managing change

Learning to learn is also a crucial element in coping with change. Change is taking place within our institutions, in our own personal lives and in the much wider world. Computers and mobile technologies are the most obvious examples of this change at the moment; but so too are the much greater diversity of students and changes within schools and society which also influence the student body. Unless academics see themselves as generic learners, they cannot move forward. Sometimes their voice is one of caution (Seidensticker, 2006), but this caution has to be based on strong evidence.

For the purposes of this chapter, I have been trying and will continue to try to avoid the term 'academic/teacher/lecturer' in favour of 'lead learner'. The terminology may not be so flattering, but it does describe the position more clearly. The fact that it does not seem so high powered is perhaps an indication of the implied assumption that learning is passive whereas teaching/research/programme and team management are active.

Social marketing and selling L2L

Today's UK university students buy a degree. Some also buy a university education. We live in a consumer economy. Education purchases are no different. Those coming into higher education, and those who support them economically, are buying something. They are arguably little different from consumers walking into shops.

Those working in the health sector have recognised that not only do you need to convince people about the relationship between databases and outcomes, e.g. if you smoke you are likely to live fewer years; but also that their own behaviour can influence outcomes.

Social Marketing is *a systematic application of marketing concepts and techniques to achieve specific behavioural goals relevant to a social good* (French and Blair-Stevens, 2005). Anyone who meets students at the start of a programme recognises that 'selling' them the product is essential. This is not just for retention, but also to enhance effective learning. This is more likely to take place if we can sell both ourselves as effective guides (lead learners) and the programme as being achievable. This means selling L2L as a means of transforming lives as well as meeting learning needs. The 'sell' is indeed the vision with the action.

This selling is often harder when the course results in a vocational qualification with a high percentage of workplace experience; for example nursing and teacher training. There is a danger that the course is perceived only as the means to an end and its contents are largely irrelevant because the student believes that they already have most of the skills necessary. They lack only the piece of paper. And they see the work experience as the sole key to learning skills. This information comes from individual interviews with primary PGCE students during profiling sessions at the start of their course. They also rate the hands-on teaching as being the most important element of the placement and have difficulty recognising how improving their observation of practitioners can enhance their own practice (Mitchell and Honore, 2006). Coursework, however practical, is seen – at this stage – as having little relevance to their need for a technical course in 'how to'. The knowledge element is seen as minimal. The links between the course and its practical application and the value of theory–practice interaction need repeatedly to be made explicit and sold to the consumer. L2L within placements has a developing literature and has uses far beyond HE.

Step 1: HE L2L social marketing

The introduction to a course is the advert. It has been marketed on the institutional website, marketed in the prospectus, marketed by personal presentations and now re-marketed for those who actually arrive to do the course. In today's financial climate, retention is a key issue and so this marketing continues throughout the course.

> *Discussion point* |
>
> Think of a course with which you are involved. How is it marketed, prior to student uptake? How is the institution marketed to attract students? Is this ever anti-academic learning? Is learning sold? Is L2L sold?

Step 2: social marketing as a means of achieving improved learning outcomes

Education-related social marketing is much broader than this initial recruitment of students. It involves the systematic application of marketing concepts and techniques to achieve specific behavioural goals relevant to enhancing the students' knowledge, skills, concepts and understandings.

L2L is a key element in this for many students. They arrive in HE with a number of characteristic attributes such as:

- **a specific perception of themselves as a learner – generally based on their academic results to date;**
- **a clear view of what learning is and what it is not – their learning experiences so far;**
- **a belief that gaining a degree will support their life chances;**
- **an experience of what HE 'teaching' involves – based on teaching they have had;**
- **what other things they want to gain from being a student – friends, enjoyment, being away from home.**

Step 3: selling L2L for the wider community

The social marketing model looks at the customer/consumer in the round and identifies other key influences on behaviour such as school, family and peers. It also recognises the influence on behaviour by partners and stakeholders such as industry, media, community and technology.

These influences are often made explicit in student behaviour. Indeed, many of the behavioural outcomes are covered elsewhere in this volume – critical reflection; problem-solving; learning from the practice-based element of degree work; having clear learning objectives; learning from assessment; moving towards more creative approaches to learning; identifying opportunities from having disabilities rather than a deficit model of themselves as learners.

If we take the example of critical reflection, it is not just about teaching a skill called critical reflection. This often ends up only in a template, which the average student follows dutifully and accordingly receives a satisfactory mark. It is about an attitude to learning and indeed to life which is critically reflective. The template is a start, but the social marketing element involves persuading the student into behavioural changes and with that comes a behavioural goal. Initially, this may be an improved mark for an assignment. In the end, this behavioural change has to become a voluntary action. This can be expressed as outlined in Table 2.1.

Table 2.1 Critical reflection

Critical reflection involves:

Behaviour	Incentives	Outcomes
Positive behaviour – researching widely and independently; discussing with fellow students face-to-face or online; engaging in different levels of thinking (Bloom, 2002), time management, dealing with stress, seeking help for writing and IT skills	Increased incentives – greater understanding of the subject matter; self-satisfaction; raising image of themselves as learners, self confidence; less reliance on others to do the assignment, or parts of it, for them: more satisfactory mark for assignment	Removes barriers and blocks to learning; using behavioural goals to learn skills related to positive outcomes
Negative behaviours	Reduces benefits of learning and lowers expectations for both student and teacher	Adds more blocks to learning and fails to challenge existing views about learning

Students have personalised views about learning and being learners themselves. French and Blair-Stevens (2005) writing from a health education perspective describe this as 'audience segmentation'. The Department for Education and Skills (DfES) would describe this as differentiation.

Social marketing of our product 'learning' and 'learning to learn', has three core principles. These are stated below.

1. Behaviour and behavioural goals. These involve achieving something which is tangible and measurable with an impact on actual behaviour. Time management is often the starting point and behavioural goals can initially be directed towards that. Managing stress is another behavioural outcome. There is increasing recognition in society of the risk in identified mental illness; for example, research for the charity Young Minds identifies one in five young people developing a mental illness (2005), with only one in four receiving any support (see website). Social marketing of L2L in HE can incorporate knowledge about stress as well as skills in how to prevent high levels of stress.
2. Voluntary actions. These focus on positive behaviours in relation to learning at university and having strategies to remove barriers and blocks.
3. Audience segmentation/differentiation, which involves looking at a more personalised approach to learning.

There are clearly similarities between this approach in selling changes in learning behaviour to that outlined in Prochaska et al.'s stages of change (1994). See Figure 2.1.

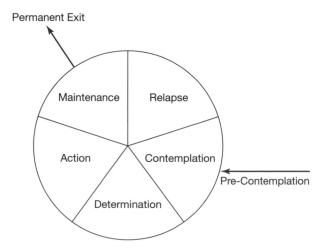

Figure 2.1 Stages of change

Initially, this was used extensively in work with addicts. It is increasingly being found useful to change behaviours in relation to learning (Liverpool Excellence Partnership (LEP) 2003). The National Learning Mentor Training Programme has a section to guide mentors through the cycle, so they in turn can use it to *break down barriers to learning*. Many of us in the university sector work with students who also need to change their behaviour in order to become more effective learners.

Social marketing differs from the approach of Prochaska et al. (1994) because it recognises that behaviours are heavily influenced by key factors outside the situation and these need to be addressed by specific strategies before appropriate learning behaviours can take place, for example, peers, media, friends, family.

Some strategies for HE

This section will examine the practical strategies which experience shows can be used to support students' own L2L.

Case study

Students are encouraged to read Claxton's text prior to the session and have provided for them, on the course CD, a talking-head presentation as part of an e-learning element of the course. There is a heavy sell on this, to ensure they engage in the material, but essentially the time is freed up from the lecture which enables ideas about learning to be followed up.

Most students have already done personal learning profiles and questionnaires based either on the VAK (visual, auditory and kinaesthetic) model of Smith and Call (2000) or on Gardner's multiple intelligences (1983) and are happy to discuss what type of learner this has shown them to be. Hughes (2004) provides a useful overview of learning styles as well as a copy of the Barsch learning style audit. These measuring instruments can be useful as a distance-learning task, which students can do and then try another one (Race, 2001, 2006). This can then be used to reflect critically in terms of (1) how helpful this is to the learner, (2) what strategies can be developed to broaden this, and (3) the methodology of such questionnaires. The critique is also useful because often students have accepted what Ben Goldacre (editor 'Bad Science' column for *The Guardian*) would describe as *bad science without thought*. They can look at the nature of testing and question the methodology behind this simplistic analysis of learning.

We then look at the nature of learning – and do this via one of Claxton's measures. This needs to be done in small groups with support, so that the results are open-ended and remain like that. It is important that students recognise that there is no one right answer. Later, students have the opportunity to look in more depth at the advances in neuroscience in relation to learning. The Oxford Centre for Staff and Learning Development (OCSLD) provides a very useful briefing paper from Lee Dunn (2002) on traditional theories of learning in their Learning and Teaching series.

The next step is to look at each of Claxton's four R's of learning – Resilience, Resourcefulness, Reflectiveness and Reciprocity. All of these are behavioural and sit closely with the need to 'market' behavioural change to enhance learning. Under 'resilience,' for example, Claxton looks at how this involves being 'ready, willing and able to lock on to learning'. Students can then discuss how they manage distractions; if and how they can absorb themselves in a learning activity; how they can sense what is going on in relation to their learning and their own perseverance. Perseverance here is defined as 'stickability'; tolerating the feelings of learning.

Claxton's language is accessible and covering this topic early in the academic year provides a framework for discussing learning at a later stage. Recognising that we are all learners, the lead learner can then move students into questioning how to learn and ways in which they can build up their learning skills. This involves teaching explicit key components, which Claxton summarises as explaining, commenting, orchestrating and modelling. He further defines these with four subheadings: informing, reminding, discussing, training.

Building learning power

This subheading is taken from Guy Claxton's *Building learning power* (2002). This is based on work done in schools, but Rush (2005) has documented its use at HE level and I have used it with some success to alert students to the need to reassess first how they learn and secondly how others learn. This is a challenge and forces some students out of their comfort zone, into a discomfort or challenge zone. It is important that they do not move into the stress or panic zone (Senge, 2002). By the time students enter university, many have fixed ideas about how they learn most effectively. Questioning this discomforts them. Identifying that there are many different ways of learning effectively and that some of these may be different from their chosen one is also challenging.

Discussion point |

Claxton defines 'explaining' as telling students directly and explicitly about learning power. This involves:

- informing – making clear the overall purpose of the learning environment (lecture theatre, workshop, classroom);
- reminding– offering ongoing reminders and prompts about learning power;
- discussing – inviting students' own ideas and opinions about learning;
- training – giving direct information and practice in learning: tips and techniques.

Obviously this approach involves lead learners in learning specific strategis themselves. How easy is this to do within HE?

Accelerated learning

Cavigolioli and Harris (2001) in their book on mind-mapping define accelerated learning as a *considered, generic approach to learning based on research drawn from disparate disciplines and tested with different age groups and different ability levels in very different circumstances*.

It is often termed 'mind-friendly' learning. It is not for a specific group of learners, nor for a particular age group, nor for a particular category of perceived ability. It does not mean doing the same things faster.

It seems to have come originally from Colin Rose's book *Accelerated learning*, written in 1976. At this stage the idea of accelerated learning seems to have largely stayed within the American system and extended particularly into corporation and business management. A quick web search on accelerated learning exemplifies this move into business, where consultants in accelerated learning clearly found business corporations more open to the idea that their employees needed to learn through different processes than had been used in the past. Learning needed to be more personalised and accompanied by an insight into the learning process.

The growth and expansion of accelerated learning in the UK has been largely due to the work of Alistair Smith, the organisation Alite and the publishing house Network Educational Press. In-service provision is of very high quality and uses the philosophy of accelerated learning to ensure that participants engage in the process of learning how to learn and can then plan for others.

The accelerated learning planning cycle

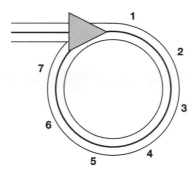

Figure 2.2 Accelerated learning planning cycle

This is one version of the cycle which provides support for lead learners in planning their work. Although this is linked to work with students in schools, it makes for good practice in HE as well. It involves the lead learner planning learning to include a variety of stages.

- **Connect the learning with prior learning.**
- **Review the 'big picture' of what is going to take place.**
- **Describe the outcomes.**
- **Provide input – which utilises visual, auditory and kinaesthetic learning styles.**
- **Activate understanding which utilises these different learning styles.**
- **Provide students with a variety of different ways of demonstrating understanding.**
- **Review what they have learnt and how they have learnt it.**

(Based on Greenhalgh, 2002)

These are particularly challenging tasks when HE is faced with an increasing number of both students and virtual learning environments. One other challenge is not to see these approaches as recipes for learning but to adopt and modify them to the learning and learners' contexts.

Accelerated learning has also looked at other strategies; in particular the physical and emotional health of the learner. Providing a supportive learning environment needs to include such low-level factors as:

- **constant access to water to avoid dehydration, which can lead to drowsiness, inattention and poor learning;**
- **following a good diet;**
- **working in a room with the appropriate temperature;**
- **physical breaks;**
- **teaching specific skills to learners such as listening, paying attention, concentrating.**

Widening participation and relative poverty amongst the student population has meant that some of these factors are really challenging, particularly with those students who do not live at home. Regulations, rooming, timetabling and staff resourcing may also hinder positive learning environments. Providing a good, secure and purposeful working environment is often extremely difficult in today's under-resourced and overcrowded HE institutions.

Discussion point

Imagine that you have unlimited funding. How would you design a learning centre for one of your courses which would truly provide a good, secure and purposeful working environment?

What negative factors about the physical space for learning in your institution may prevent students maximising their learning potential? What does this tell us about L2L?

The CORT Thinking Programme

This programme looked at strategies for generating ideas for lateral thinking and is an essential part of a programme for L2L. De Bono called them 'attention-directing tools' and they are outlined in Table 2.2.

Case study

Thinking tools

This technique has had a recent resurgence of interest and is in use in many schools. I originally used it with postgraduate students working in schools, but then realised that it made a good tool for helping undergraduates. It is particularly useful for those in their first year as it gives them scaffolds for looking at ways of discussing items from the media and later to use in their writing. We used the technique in workshops first, taking current examples from their own lives and interests. It has been particularly successful in broadening responses to assignments and providing a scaffold for organising materials. In some cases thinking tool templates were used to give a visual prompt. The responses to the lost £10 note have been particularly interesting. Thinking tools can be used independently or when students work as small groups of two or three.

Table **2.2** Attention, directing tools

1. PMI

Plus – the good things about an idea, why you like it.
Minus – the bad things, why you don't like it.
Interesting – what you find interesting about an idea.

This is an exploring and evaluation tool. It provides an attention-directing framework to widen thinking. Students can put forward the things they like about something, those they don't like and those they find interesting. It frames the discussion and/or report.

2. CAF

Consider All Factors – look around, explore. What factors should be considered in our thinking? Have we left anything out? PMI is more concerned with judging good and bad. CAF notes all possible factors. This reflects real-life thinking, which is often messy.

3. OPV

Other People's Views – people are doing the thinking and others are going to be affected by this. Who are these people? What views do they have?

4. APC

Alternatives, Possibilities and Choices – What are the alternative courses of action? What can be done? You find a £10 note on the pavement; what choices do you have? Most of my students have said that they would pick it up and put it in their pocket. A few protest vehemently.

5. AGO

Aims, Goals and Objectives – What is the objective of the thinking? What do we want to achieve? If we know exactly where we want to go we will have more chance of getting there.

6. FIP

First Important Priorities – this tool looks to identify what really matters. Not everything is equally important. After generating a number of ideas, students need to decide which are the most important. In running a disco, what are your priorities?

C & S

Consequence and Sequel. If you have chosen one alternative as a possible outcome of thinking, what would happen if we went ahead with the alternative?

Thinking tools are attention-directing tools and different from de Bono's 'thinking hats'. Students have also enjoyed the idea of changing thinking hats, although we have not, as yet, actually had the different coloured hats in the workshops.

De Bono (1991) suggests that the hats can also be used individually and separately or in a sequence. See Table 2.3.

Table **2.3** Thinking hats

White hat (fact-gathering) – Information, data, facts and figures. Linked with CAF, OPV and FIP. 'Oh, if only it was I'd have loads of them!'

Red hat (gut reactions, feelings) – Intuition, hunches, feelings and emotions. Links with OPV.

Black hat (negative points) – Assessment and checking. Relationship to PMI and C & S.

Yellow hat (positive points) – Benefits and advantages of what is proposed. Relationship to C&S and PMI.

Green hat (creativity and new ideas) – Creativity, action, proposals and suggestions; constructive ideas and new ideas links with APC.

Blue hat (organising things) – Overview and control of the thinking process itself. 'What are we doing?'

Adult learning is often not significantly different from children's learning and these techniques can be easily and quickly taught to support discussion, an online forum and for written papers.

Conclusion

This chapter has identified the teaching academic as a 'lead learner', with a clear remit to support students in L2L across the many different ways in which learning now takes place in HE. It looks at the theory of social marketing in terms of selling both L2L and learning. It acknowledges that this needs to be marketed with students, colleagues and the much wider community. Various strategies are suggested for how to approach L2L with students. Some of these, such as Claxton's and De Bono's work, involve focused teaching. Others, such as the accelerated learning planning cycle and creating a positive learning environment, need to permeate all our learning institutions.

References

Caviglioli, O. and Harris, I. (2001) *Mapwise*. Stafford: Network.

Claxton, G. (2002) *Building learning power*. Bristol: TLO.

De Bono, E. (1991) *Teaching thinking*. London: Penguin.

DfEE (1997) *The National Committee of Inquiry into Higher Education (The Dearing Report)*. London: DfEE.

Dunn, L. (2002) *Theories of learning*. Oxford Centre for Staff Learning and Development (**www.brookes .ac.uk/services/ocsd**).

French, J. and Blair-Stevens, C. (2005) *Social marketing*. London: DH.

Gardner, H. (1983) *Frames of mind*. New York: Basic Books.

Greenhalgh, P. (2002) *Reaching out to all learners*. Stafford: Network.

Hughes, P. (2004) Learning and teaching: What's your style, in Bold, C. (ed.) *Supporting learning and teaching*. London. Fulton.

LEP (2003) *Learning Mentor Training. Module 4*. London: EiC/DfES.

Mitchell, A. and Honore, S. (2006) e-Learning: critical for success – the human factor. Session Paper *HEA Annual Conference*.

Pickford, R. and Clothier, H. (2006) The art of teaching: A model for the lecture in the 21st century. Session Paper *HEA Annual Conference*.

Prochaska, J., Norcross, J. and DiClemente, C. (1994) *Changing for good*. London: Morrow.

Race, P. (2001) *The lecturer's toolkit*. Oxford: RoutledgeFalmer.

Race, P. (2006) *Making learning happen: A guide for post-compulsory education*. London: Paul Chapman.

Rose, C. (1976) *Accelerated learning*. Bantam Doubleday.

Rush, L. (2005) Teaching for learning power. INSET presentation to academic tutors. Southport (also available on HEA website).

Seidensticker, B. (2006) *Futurehype: The myths of technological change*. Berrett-Koehler.

Senge, P. (2002) *The dance of change*. Bearley.

Smith, A. and Call, N. (2000) *The ALPS approach*. Stafford: Network.

Websites

www.heacademy.ac.uk/184.htm – The Higher Education Academy website.

www.practicebasedlearning.org/home.htm – Making Practice Based Learning Project website.

www.escalate.ac.uk/1707 Learning to Learn project website. This is promoting innovation in educational practice 'through supported enquiry-based learning (EBL)'.

www.youngminds.org.uk/professionals – Children's and young people's mental health (advice, training and information).

Chapter *3*

Supporting students' critical reflection-on-practice

Christine Bold and Pat Hutton

Introduction

This chapter is the result of collaborative action research conducted by the authors with their students over a period of two years. It is an account of our developing practice and understanding in five broad areas of activity: a) developing reflective writing; b) self-managed learning agreements; c) developing reflection-on-practice in peer-support groups; d) reflection-on-practice in asynchronous e-forums, and e) online formative and summative assessment. Our part-time students, who all have employment in educational settings, are studying for a Foundation degree, which is a work-related higher education programme in England, the equivalent of the first two years of a bachelor with honours degree. However, we believe that our strategies and approaches to supporting critical reflection-on-practice are transferable to many student groups at all levels. Initially, our interest was in supporting students' development as writers and, in particular, reflective writing in their portfolio of reflective practice, a mainly self-managed practice-based module assessment. Over time, we realised that underlying the students' writing capability were issues of confidence, levels of engagement and acceptance of responsibility to become independent learners in higher education. In addition, we further developed our resources in supporting all students' understanding of the nature of reflection-on-practice based on Ghaye and Ghaye's (1998, pp15–19) ten principles of reflective practice. Reflection-on-practice engages participants in:

- **reflective conversations that have the potential to disturb their professional identity;**
- **interrogation of experiences;**
- **returning to look at taken-for-granted values, professional values and understandings – 'a reflective turn';**
- **describing, explaining and justifying practices;**
- **viewing professional situations 'problematically';**
- **creating knowledge of interest to self and others;**
- **asking probing and challenging questions;**
- **decoding a symbolic landscape, e.g. the 'school culture';**
- **linking theory and practice as a creative process;**
- **socially constructing 'ways of knowing'.**

Ghaye and Ghaye's principles build on the work of Schön (1991), who identified reflection in action as core to understanding practice, developing knowledge across a range of professions and theory building. Schön also introduced the notion of the reflective conversation and, in acknowledging the limitations of capturing and understanding what professionals do in action, he introduced the idea of reflection-on-action, where someone would reflect after the event. For many academics supporting students whose practice is located in another context (e.g. a student gaining work experience or who performs in the local dramatic association), a focus on supporting students' reflection-on-action is most appropriate. Hence, we set out to further develop our practice through designing learning activities and assessments that would support student learning. In so doing, we improved the whole learning environment for the students and improved our knowledge of the theory of reflective practice and the use of appropriate e-learning technologies. All of these are key features of professional values within the

National Professional Standards Framework for Teaching and Supporting Learning in Higher Education (Higher Education Academy, 2006) and our work demonstrates our commitment to the continuing development and evaluation of practice.

New students' predominant concern is to learn the process of academic writing. However, our main concern is to establish a common understanding of reflection-on-practice. We believe that a capacity for reflection is central to learning. Involvement of students in reflection about their workplace practice and their academic development underpins programme learning and teaching processes. Students need to understand the nature of reflection and its relationship to deep-learning, identified by Leung and Kember (2003). We aim to support deep-learning through engaging in the five broad areas of activities outlined at the beginning of this chapter.

Developing reflective academic writing

Many new students require support to develop confidence in their reflective writing. In particular, students show concern about their ability to use other sources such as their own experiences, relevant documents and academic texts. New students often have a weak understanding of reflection-on-practice and the nature of reflective writing. They often lack confidence in their writing capability and struggle with referencing conventions. Some have weak grammar, spelling and punctuation in addition to weaknesses in structural elements. Many students tend to focus on product rather than process when writing, which is a common behaviour (Nightingale, 1988). We avoid a rigid focus on academic writing conventions alone, since we believe that such a focus is detrimental to the development of reflective writing.

In any first-year group, we advocate working on many short pieces of writing in which students express their own opinions, values and beliefs with some conviction and evidence. The challenge is to engage students in reflection-on-practice in any practical activity including studying, while developing the ability to evidence this in writing. Bolton (2001) asserts that writing is an explorative process; a vehicle for reflection (reflection in writing) (p135). Many students express reflective thoughts orally, but not necessarily within their assessed writing. In our own research (Bold *et al.*, 2006) we identified lack of confidence as a reason, but another might be the inhibitive nature of summative assessments obstructing reflection in writing.

Engaging students in critical review and reflection on each other's experiences establishes a community of enquiry. Our students share their writing, making critical comment on content and style. They develop their writing skills in supported activities over a period, resulting in varying degrees of reflection exhibited in portfolio tasks. To illustrate this we have constructed fictional examples, in order to preserve anonymity, as typical extracts from students' work. The example below shows limited reflective thought, although there is some exploration of a professional interest and an attempt to explain the discrepancy in the children's test results.

> *Two of the children had very different results in a numeracy test even though they were in the same year. One child had all the answers correct and had clearly learned all the number facts. The other child only had half of it correct. My reflections were that there could be many reasons for the difference. For example, the way they were taught differently or the way they were assessed.*

The second fictional example draws on an expression of opinions or assertions, something we actively encouraged, but fails to provide supporting evidence except for citing government non-statutory guidance as a credible source without questioning it.

> *Schools should provide quality opportunities for Personal, Social and Emotional development. I believe that children need to feel happy and able to choose their own way through the system. In my opinion, happy children will perform better than others do. The DfES (2004) supports this view. The recent* Every Child Matters *document is one we all have to use.*

The final fictionalised example shows characteristics of deepening reflection about practices in the workplace, through reference to experience and relevant reading, and acceptance that one might not be able to make conclusive judgements about a situation.

> *The children show very slow progress in learning number facts. We have to use multi-sensory approaches, to support them. I am not convinced that Bracket and Burke* (2004) were correct in their suggestion to keep the pace brisk. My observations show that they require a slower pace. However, I acknowledge that the multi-sensory approach might be the problem and Bridges* (2004) warns us of this.*

*fictitious

In our experience, students learn to write best in the context of their studies, as suggested by Hurley (2005) and others (see for example, Nightingale, 1988). The perception that all academic writing is depersonalised does not help students, and we support Crème and Lea's (1998) challenge of such conventions as avoiding the use of the first-person 'I'. We actively encourage students to write from their own experiences where appropriate and to make use of personal reference when required. Students are also encouraged to draw on their previous experiences as writers and thus build upon current skill level. The integration of study skills with the content of the programme also provides contextual relevance for the learning of such skills. We propose a range of learning experiences to support students' writing development.

- **Reading and reflection activities.**
- **Tutors' modelling writing and referencing skills.**
- **Focused writing tasks, e.g. to reflect on and refer to a set reading.**
- **Paired sharing and evaluating writing.**
- **Tutor-led editing activities.**

Such activities are formative and set within the context of writing reflectively on short tasks and can occur in any subject discipline. Undertaking several short writing tasks requires tutors to provide clear feedback in support of the students' development as writers. Feedback might be individual, e.g. modelling a reflective style on a submitted formative piece, or to whole cohorts of students, e.g. summarising common issues arising within the tasks and discussing ways to improve. The key to quality feedback is to be specific rather than general and to support it with practical examples. The focus for our first-year students is the production of a portfolio of reflective practice based on the students' workplace experiences. In other subject disciplines that do not have work-related elements, there is potential for early development of critical reflection-on-practice in keeping learning logs, regular oral and written critiques of news articles and recent topical papers. Students should have early opportunity in the academic experience to reflect on their learning practices and the practices of others in the wider local, national and international communities.

Self-managed learning agreements

At the start of the course, encouraging students to be reflective in their thinking, in their writing and in discussion, presents challenge, as most students do not reflect naturally, or with ease. For a minority of students, demonstrating 'being reflective' about workplace practice or academic issues presents a continued anxiety and, for some, remains elusive. We have experienced some final-year students unable to think critically, or to write critically, and we chose this aspect of study as the focus for our pedagogical research.

Within the annual review of the teaching programme, we reflected on teaching practices, approaches to learning and teaching and features of the learning environment. We set out to explore and examine factors and underlying reasons that may suggest why some students were engaging in reflective practice more effectively than others and how we could be more effective in supporting the skills involved. Team discussions included questions such as these below.

- **Do we have a shared understanding of 'reflection', 'being reflective' and 'reflective practice'?**
- **Do we share individual interpretations with tutor colleagues and students?**

- **Is the learning environment supporting students' reflective activity?**
- **Do we teach what is involved in reflection?**
- **Are there opportunities for students to reflect individually, in peer groups and as a class?**
- **Do we provide activities beyond taught sessions, for students to reflect on practice and learned theory?**
- **Are there activities for students to practise these new skills within their writing?**

The aim was to identify features of practice within the programme that supported student engagement from the earliest stages. We introduced learning agreements (see Figure 3.1) to offer students a starting point in their engagement with learning and to provide a meaningful context for personal reflection. Based on a pre-course study-skill audit, students considered previous learning experiences, identified individual needs and developed ways to meet these needs within the study-skill component of the programme. The learning agreement was self-managed and an opportunity for students and tutors to reflect collaboratively on practice over time. In particular, there would be opportunities for reflection on student engagement in the differing aspects of the programme. Within the agreement, the students were presented with a defined route for developing study skills and were able to choose individual targets for personal development.

Based on your initial work in the pre-course study guide, submit your Learning Agreement following these guidelines and headings:

1) Reviewing study skills

Review your confidence and competence in study skills based on your most recent experiences of studying.

2) Reviewing communication skills

Write about your capability to communicate effectively with a range of different people by different means, e.g. orally, in writing, by telephone, email, chat rooms. Identify your strengths and weaknesses.

3) Reviewing time management

Review your time management strategies including planning ahead, using a diary, consideration of work, family and study.

4) Reviewing attendance and time-keeping

Consider work commitments and other regular commitments such as previous study.

5) Reviewing engagement with learning and teaching

What sort of learner are you and how much time do you spend in learning new things? How do you prefer to learn? Might you need to learn new strategies for learning?

Targets:

Set up to five specific targets relating to each element:

Study skills

Communication

Time management

Attendance

Engagement

Figure 3.1 Learning agreement for Year 1 students

In taught sessions and peer group activities, each element was discussed, for example understanding and interpreting 'study skills'. At end of the first month, Student A commented on her study skills as follows:

> *I struggle with written assignments mainly due to the fact that I know what I want to say but feel I do not have the correct vocabulary. After further discussion in peer support groups, I identified targets and discussed these, enabling me to choose targets that were best suited to my present understanding.*

Student A's targets were:

- **essay structure;**
- **extracting information from text;**
- **referencing different styles of academic writing.**

The learning agreement provided opportunity for Student A to reflect on personal experience and to practise 'being reflective' both in thinking and writing and in a non-threatening situation. Since the agreement is not assessed, it creates an opportunity for a student to be involved in self-reflection and in addressing individual developmental needs. Usher (1985, cited in Moon, 1999, p130) supports the notion that students need to have meaningful starting points in their studies and suggests that personal experience offers the means to link these with academic material. Personal target-setting allowed Student A to determine future areas for development and subsequent reviews, offering the opportunity to evaluate progress. For tutors, there is the opportunity to recognise the students' needs and to offer increased support, as necessary. Student A's comments in reviewing her progress at the end of Term 1 demonstrate the value of this approach in developing skills of self-reflection.

> *As each task and assignment is completed and marked, my learning is developing. I have improved my strategies by preparing my tasks through prior research, reading and clear planning. Referencing and citation is becoming easier through discussions with tutor and peer group support. I am confident that I can extract information from texts. Practising different styles of academic writing is a target and one that I want to continue. I still need to improve my understanding of these different types of writing.*

From our experience, the learning agreement allows the student to act on actual rather than perceived needs. Initially, the process is unnerving for some students as they are required to identify aspects for improvement rather than the tutor. Via critical reflection, students consider current levels of engagement within their learning and the agreement provides a context to support this activity in a relevant and developmental way.

Developing reflection-on-practice in peer-support groups

Through exploring the impact of including regular peer-support group activities within our taught sessions, we have evidence to support the benefits of such groups. The type of activity set for the group and tutor intervention is an important factor in the development of reflection-on-practice. We have used peer-support groups in a range of ways to engage students in 'reflective conversations'. Ghaye and Ghaye (1998) describe the reflective conversation as the medium by which practitioners question the assumptions, values and beliefs that guide their work. Such conversations should be public and build knowledge collaboratively, although they might begin as a conversation with oneself. We believe that peer-support groups play an important role in sharing experiences, providing enlightenment and empowerment through increased understanding of practice. However, the principles behind such groups are also relevant for developing understanding of theoretical concepts. Reflective conversations should encourage the sharing of opinions, provide opportunity for participants' identities to be disturbed, while at the same time providing for a collective, mutual sharing of consciousness but not necessarily developing a shared view, since each participant will enter and leave the conversation with a different set of assumptions.

Strong-Wilson (2006) supports the notion of public discussion as part of the reflective process, alongside personal reflection and memory. Her research highlights the importance of *bringing memory forward*; using memory to stimulate personal reflection based on group discussion. Making memory a central feature in developing reflective capacity makes sense, since students engaging in work or other practical experiences will draw on their memories of past events in order to make sense of current and future events in their daily practice. Students who engage in reflective conversations about their experience should also move towards 'self-authorship' (Kegan, 1994, cited in Bristol Business School [BBS], 2006), by which is meant a person's ability to develop and co-ordinate internally her/his own set of values and beliefs. Individual development of reflective skills is important while at the same time ensuring everyone feels valued and involved through collaborative restructuring of experiences and developing new understandings. In addition, self-esteem and metacognitive processes develop through acceptance of responsibility and accountability for actions within and beyond the group.

We have observed peer groups operating in the way that Ashwin (2003) describes, with each of the group having two roles: facilitator and learner, bringing pieces of writing to generate discussion. Our experience shows that students who engage fully with group activities gain most in developing their ability to reflect on practical experiences and theoretical concepts orally and in writing. Such students recognise that peer learning is active and social, described by Topping (2005) as *structured interdependence*, where a group works towards a common goal. In our peer groups, the common goal was to engage in reflective conversations that disturbed deeply held values and beliefs, challenged assumptions and enabled students to develop a capacity for critical reflection. We have noticed that some students are particularly reluctant to share their writing with the group, usually because they feel threatened, but occasionally because they think everyone else will take their ideas for an assignment. If students have different activities to bring to the group, the threat reduces and the sense of working collaboratively, rather than competitively, increases. Our students acknowledged that they did not always understand the expectations and that although they engaged in reflective conversations, they thought they could explore issues more deeply (Bold, 2006). This highlights the need for tutor intervention to maintain the focus, ensure the level of reflection is challenging and ensure everyone takes the responsibility to support each other's learning. Students may feel initial pressure that lessens as they become more confident. Improving students' confidence within the peer group also has an impact on their practical experiences outside university and on students' understandings of the purpose of reflective writing. To quote one student, *Writing is not just for the course but also for my professional development.*

Reflection-on-practice in asynchronous e-forums

As part of blended learning, asynchronous e-forums extend the students' opportunities to engage in reflection-on-practice and increase the criticality of such reflections through a different medium beyond face-to-face sessions. They allow students from different groups and different venues the opportunity to engage with a wider community. From a tutor's perspective, there is a skill to structuring and using the e-learning environment effectively as a learning tool. Allen (2005) believes that online learning offers the potential for Bruner's notion of scaffolding by facilitators, who in our e-forums might be the tutor or peers. The e-forum offers the opportunity for social construction of learning and transformation of knowledge. It is a special kind of dialogue and Table 3.1 aims to compare it with face-to-face opportunities for discussion, considering the advantages and disadvantages of each, based on our experiences and with some reference to relevant reading. In constructing the table, we have omitted common features that exist in either situation (e.g. the tutor can detect those who do not join in the discussion and draw them into it).

Table 3.1 A comparison of online and face-to-face discussions

	Face-to-face discussion	**Asynchronous e-forum discussion**
Potential advantages	A range of group sizes from pairs to whole class Everyone can observe the whole context from an individual perspective Gesture, body language, facial expression are all clear Loudness, tone and speed of discussion are evident Immediate impact	A range of group sizes equal to, or greater than a class Situated across spaces and times Time to read and reflect before replying (Tiene, 2000, cited in Gilbert and Dabbagh, 2005) Opportunity for deeper thinking and challenging assumptions (Ambrose, 2001) People with different learning needs benefit from the opportunity to work at their own pace Loud voices cannot dominate and a record of insightful contributions is maintained (Bird, 2004) Opportunity for formative feedback and peer mentoring (Chapman et al., 2002)
Potential disadvantages	Situated in a particular space and time Limited thinking time before Responding makes it easy to lose the focus People with different learning needs might not engage as easily as others Less confident contributors might say very little, especially if the group includes a more knowledgeable or forceful character The tutor or leader of the group takes over Insightful contributions are often lost	Working in an e-learning environment challenges thinking and learning styles (Bird, 2004) Time consuming Might seem decontextualised and the dialogue flow is less visible (Chapman et al., 2002) No visual or auditory information from others Misunderstanding protocols Misunderstanding postings Inappropriate responses Reluctance to respond to tutors Reluctance to challenge others Contributors may feel vulnerable, exacerbated by permanent written record (van Aalst, 2006) Threatens privacy (Joinson, 2006)

To ensure effective engagement with forums, we must pay attention to choosing relevant activities and providing clear guidelines. We drew on the ten principles (Ghaye and Ghaye, 1998) to create a set of suggestions for maintaining effective dialogue and developing critical thinking. Four key aspects for student development in forums are:

- **drawing together similar points from previous postings;**
- **comparing and contrasting differing ideas;**
- **revisiting taken for granted beliefs and values;**
- **viewing situations problematically.**

We believe groups of less than 30 are most effective for developing critical thinking skills. Each forum requires a clear protocol for reading and responding to postings.

- **To read and think about all previous postings.**
- **To draft a tentative response drawing on a range of points made by others.**
- **To reply to the final posting to maintain the line of discussion.**

Gilbert and Dabbagh (2005) agree that having such a protocol in place has a significant impact on the quality of the discussion, and we suggest that the aim is to maintain a dialogue that enhances critical reflection through peer support and sensitive intervention rather than tutor control of the dialogue.

It is likely that a number of factors affect the impact of e-forums on students in relation to their increased capacity to reflect on practice, such as motivation, previous knowledge and skills, or levels of peer support. We believe we can improve students' ability to engage in critical reflective debate by structuring the activities carefully. Below is an example of activities in a series of forums.

- **Critiquing a journal article.**
- **Relating the conceptual content to practical contexts.**
- **Focusing on one specific aspect of the original article.**
- **Refocusing on the relationship between theory and practice.**

Through careful structuring, focusing and refocusing on specific content, deeper thought is encouraged.

Online formative and summative assessments

We believe that online formative and summative assessment offers greater efficiency for tutors and students as part of the learning process. However, tutors and students require different skills to engage successfully in online learning and to participate in the online assessment environment. From our experience, we have found that the students' e-learning skills improve over time as online tasks become more diverse and active engagement encourages greater independence of thought. Some advantages for students and tutors are as set out below.

- **Tutors may access student submissions online to provide formative comment, either to the whole group or to individuals.**
- **Tutors have opportunities to mark students' summative submissions in different ways.**
- **Assessments might be set that the virtual learning environment (VLE) will mark for tutors.**
- **A secure archive and record of student submissions is produced.**
- **Students and tutors may access different archives after assessments are completed, offering opportunities for further reflection and development.**

Utilising a web-based university VLE for assessment purposes presents challenges for both students and staff. The learning curve may be steep for all concerned. However, learning along with the students is not problematic and we think generates greater interest and co-operation from students as we collectively share in developing the programme.

For example, with our first-year cohorts, a variety of strategies are employed.

- **Blended learning and teaching from the start of the course.**
- **The learning objectives, content and assessed learning outcomes for developing ICT capability are embedded within other modules rather than teaching the skills in isolation.**
- **The different skills needed to submit assignments electronically are incorporated and practised in taught sessions using the VLE.**
- **Teaching rooms with individual PCs are booked for students as required.**
- **Timetabled, quality time is allocated for tutors to establish the new procedures for assessment, to teach online and engage in online support for students.**

It is recommended that a pre-course audit be undertaken for ICT skills to identify student competencies. This information allows tutors to offer tasks and activities that ensure students are able to communicate online with tutors and peers and to save, retrieve and forward work electronically. Developing confidence in such skills is necessary before engaging in web-based learning. Competent and confident students may support their peers during the early part of a course. In our initial sessions, we taught students basic procedures in online communication, such as:

- **to use email effectively to contact tutors and peers via different systems;**
- **to create and open an attachment to an email or a forum posting;**
- **to save their work in an online secure folder for a tutor to view;**
- **to retrieve and revise documents from their folder;**
- **to use synchronous communication features in 'chat' rooms.**

During taught sessions, tutors may offer support and formatively assess students with a range of tasks by monitoring:

- **samples of work in their folder;**
- **written directed tasks;**
- **engagement in e-sources via online reading;**
- **online feedback comments to the student by the tutor;**
- **students' levels of ICT competency.**

When working with students on individual PCs or using an interactive whiteboard there are opportunities for students to share their work 'on screen' with the tutor and other students. For example, we asked students to prepare six slides using PowerPoint for a future presentation, to access three of these slides in session and to share ideas in peer groups and with the tutor. This allowed the tutor to advise and guide students with their first attempts and to note competency levels for individuals. Students also enjoyed the opportunity to share and exchange ideas in the session. Paired peer assessment was helpful and supportive for students.

One of the benefits of online communication is the opportunity to provide formative feedback, especially to part-time students living off-campus. Our experience highlights a need to organise clear arrangements for online feedback and for students to be aware that it was not always possible for tutor responses to be immediate. Experience has taught us to insist on specific and constructive requests to be posed by the students, e.g. 'Have I cited author A correctly?', and we emphasise that requests such as, 'Is my essay OK?' or 'Am I on the right lines?' would neither be productive or ethically appropriate.

Online summative assessments require careful structuring to suit the programme at a given point, and as appropriate, for a particular module. A well-structured VLE usually records the date and time of submission, providing students with an email receipt and the tutor a notification. Opportunity for tutors to provide electronic feedback reduces delay in returning of scripts to students off-site, and utilising a PC tablet computer that enables handwritten electronic comments offers a more 'personalised' style of written feedback comments in preference to typed format. Overall, we believe that the virtual learning environment has much to offer in strengthening the students' capacities to reflect on their development through formative and summative assessment processes.

Conclusion

From our experience, not all students are consistent in their approach to learning and a range of factors influences engagement, such as maturity, previous learning experiences, academic qualifications, workplace experience and commitment. Each factor has the potential to impact on successful engagement and retention. Through reflective activities within the programme, we have aimed to enhance the quality of learning and teaching for students via increased levels of peer and tutor support and providing varied contexts for learning. We believe that developing student capability to reflect on practice within their work-based degree programmes is a fundamental requirement before focusing their thoughts on the contributions of other practical and theoretical perspectives. In our experience, becoming strongly reflective enables students to accept differing points of view with a higher level of criticality. If first-year students have their self-reflective skills developed, through a broad range of blended learning activities, we have a greater chance of engaging them in deeper learning and becoming worthy of honours-level graduate status in the future, in addition to becoming confident practitioners in their chosen field of work and employment.

References

Allen, K. (2005) Online learning: constructivism and conversation as an approach to learning, *Innovations in Education and Teaching International*, 42 (3), 247–256.

Ambrose, L. (2001) Learning online facilitation online, in Wallace, M., Ellis, A. and Newton, D. (eds) *Proceedings of the Moving Online 11 Conference 2nd – 4th September 2001*, Conrad Jupiters, Gold Coast Australia. Available online at **www.scu.edu.au/moconf** (accessed 25 May 2006).

Ashwin, P. (2003) Peer facilitation and how it contributes to the development of a more social view of learning. *Research in Post-Compulsory Education*, 8 (1), 5–17.

Bird, C.M. (2004) Sinking in a C-M sea: a graduate student's experience of learning through asynchronous computer-mediated communication. *Reflective Practice*, 5 (2), 253–263.

Bold, C. (2006) Peer support groups: Reflection-on-practice in *Pedagogical Action Research in Maximising Education* [PRIME] (to be published).

Bold, C., Hutton, P., Norton, B. and Stevenson, R. (2006) Developing confidence and competence in academic writing – An evaluative project, in *Pedagogical Action Research in Maximising Education* [PRIME] 1 (2).

Bolton, G. (2001) *Reflective practice – Writing and professional development*. London: Paul Chapman.

Bristol Business School (BBS) (2005) *Briefing Paper No 1 – Ways of knowing and the development of reflective capacity*. **www.uwe.ac.uk/bbs/research/drc/papers.shtml**, (accessed 20 June 2006).

Crème, P. and Lea, P. (1998) Student writing: challenging the myths, in *Proceedings of the 5th Annual Writing Development in Higher Education Conference Centre for Applied Language Studies*, University of Reading.

Chapman, C. Ramondt, L. and Smiley, G. (2005) Strong community, deep learning: exploring the link. *Innovations in Education and teaching International*, 42 (3), 217–230.

Department for Education and Skills (DfES) (2004) *Every Child Matters: Change for children*. Nottingham: DfES.

Ghaye, A. and Ghaye, K. (1998) *Teaching and learning through critical reflective practice*. London: Routledge.

Gilbert, P.K. and Dabbagh, N. (2005) How to structure online discussions for meaningful discourse. *British Journal of Educational Technology*, 36 (1), 5–18.

Higher Education Academy (2006) National Professional Standards Framework for Teaching and Supporting Learning in Higher Education. Avaiable online at **www.heacademy.ac.uk/reganaccr/StandardsFramework(1).pdf** (accessed October 2006).

Hurley, U. (2005) 'So wotz ring wiv dat?' The importance of context and creativity in developing students' writing skills. *Pedagogical Research in Maximising Education*, 1 (1), 61–69.

Joinson, A. (2006) Does your VLE virtually undress its users?. *Times Higher Education Supplement,* (15 September).

Leung, D.Y.P. and Kember, D. (2003) The relationship between approaches to learning and reflection upon practice. *Educational Psychology*, 23 (1), 62–71.

Moon, J.A. (1999) *Reflection in learning and professional development – Theory and practice*. London: Kogan Page.

Nightingale, P. (1988) Understanding processes and problems in student writing. *Studies in Higher Education*, 13 (3), 263–283.

Schön, D.A. (1991) *The reflective practitioner – How professionals think in action*. Aldershot: Arena.

Strong-Wilson, T. (2006) Bringing memory forward: a method for engaging teachers in reflective practice on narrative and memory. *Reflective Practice*, 7 (1), 101–113.

Topping, K. J. (2005) Trends in peer learning. *Educational Psychology*, 25 (6), 631–645.

van Aalst, J. (2006) Rethinking the nature of online work in asynchronous learning networks. *British Journal of Educational Technology*, 37 (2), 279–288.

Chapter *4*

Problem-based learning in higher education

Tessa Owens

Introduction

This chapter will consider the introduction of problem-based learning (PBL) as an increasingly popular learning and teaching pedagogy in UK universities today. Many claims are made for its inclusiveness, immediacy, and its development of transferable skills, in addition to the development of 'deep' learning in diverse curriculum areas. It has become established in a number of key discipline areas, particularly vocational programmes, and the author will consider its impact and validity as a mainstream teaching method.

A case study will be provided of its use within a university business school and its strengths and weaknesses are illustrated by use of this example.

Philosophical rationale for problem-based learning

Much traditional teaching depends on a positivistic philosophical stance which perceives knowledge to be 'out there' and existing independently of the learner. When knowledge is viewed in this way, people perceive that understanding can be transmitted from one person to another. Knowledgeable experts are expected to transmit their knowledge to their students, who, in such scenarios, are seen as empty vessels waiting to be filled by the teacher.

PBL is consistent with instructional principles derived from constructivism. Schmidt (1995) claims that *learning … (as) essentially an act of cognitive construction on the part of the learner is well implemented in problem-based learning* (p248). In constructivist learning theory, knowledge is conceived as a social construction, created by the individual learners as they attempt to make sense of their world. Accepting a socially constructed view of knowledge requires students to be active in their learning: they are not passive vessels waiting to be filled with facts but instead engaged in and structuring their own learning. This is the foundation on which PBL is built – that students will create their own learning and knowledge by actively engaging in real-life problems and handling the complexities of these problems and their solutions. Constructivist learning theory stresses the development of learning by an assimilation of new knowledge with existing knowledge and consequently a changed perception and understanding of the world by the learner. This construction is aided by collaboration with others. Enthusiasts of PBL would argue that this approach provides the perfect environment for construction of knowledge because at its essence is the group approach that encourages self-directed and independent learning. It encourages sense-making over content-accumulation. As the name suggests, the approach is based on providing students with a problem or issue that they may encounter in their everyday professional life and they are expected to explore the nature of the problem, analyse the issues, and use relevant theoretical frameworks to research possible solutions, dilemmas and conflicts. In this way, they are encouraged to become more responsible for the learning achieved and their tutor becomes a facilitator in that learning. Instead of providing answers, the tutor encourages useful lines of questioning and, only where considered absolutely necessary, provides some problem-solving structure.

PBL relies heavily upon group work. Johnson and Johnson (1993) believe that co-operation should be the preferred *modus operandi* within the classroom. Their analysis of 120 studies, carried out between 1924 and 1981, illustrated that co-operative learning experiences encourage higher achievement than their competitive or individualistic counterparts. This work also indicates that co-operative activities also tend to promote the development of higher-order levels of thinking, essential communication skills, improved motivation, positive self-esteem, social awareness and tolerance for individual differences. Tribe (1996) also found that students who only observe others working, or listen to conversations in which others explain things, are still not able to learn new knowledge. Students must be actively involved in the whole process for learning to take place.

Learning in university is seen by some to be detached from real life. Knowledge can appear to be without context and the student may perceive its only use and applicability to be in passing exams or completing prescribed assignment tasks (Entwistle and Entwistle, 1997). PBL allows a student to practise with 'real life' scenarios, behaving as a traditional apprentice in learning a craft before being allowed to act independently. Such learning allows the application of knowledge to the problem and the student to understand the complexity of the problem through that application.

The Professional Standards Framework

The Professional Standards Framework **(www.heacademy.ac.uk/regandaccr/Standards Framework(1).pdf)** sets out the activities, core knowledge and values which are considered desirable when teaching in higher education. There is a strong emphasis on supporting students' learning. This indicates a sector-wide appreciation of the need for a more student-focused approach to learning and teaching, which promotes student activity and the application of knowledge. The standards describe a *commitment to development of learning communities,* which implies a collaborative and supportive means of learning between individuals for mutual understanding. When reflecting upon many traditional teacher-centred and didactic methods, it is clear that much, therefore, needs to change in many higher education institutions. PBL with its emphasis on group work and its student-led approach could provide a learning and teaching approach which may satisfy these needs.

Considerations for the adoption of a PBL approach however, may depend upon an individual's conception of the purpose of higher education.

Ramsden (2004) considers that the purpose of higher education is to encourage 'deep' learning and that through this it is anticipated that students will change the way they view the world. There is

Discussion point |

What do you consider is the purpose of a university education in the twenty-first century?

increasing political pressure on universities to collaborate in the competitiveness of their home countries, to produce a competent and highly skilled workforce, thereby ensuring domestic economic success and competitive advantage. Yeo (2005a) identifies that the shift towards PBL in tertiary education has been triggered by the changing external environment and the needs of a global workplace. The use of PBL could therefore be considered as politically expedient as it requires students to constantly apply theory to practice, thereby focusing on their future employability.

The debate on the development of transferable skills is ongoing (see Hyland and Johnson, 1998). Nevertheless, the emphasis on skills has grown at all levels in UK education with a particular stress upon employability skills and lifelong learning. Whilst many would argue that the purpose of higher education is not to train people for work, it can be seen that adopting PBL approaches could naturally develop skills which may be used in work and other contexts of an individual's life.

Theoretical rationale for problem-based learning

Problem-based learning began in the 1960s in the Medical School in McMaster University, Canada. It arose out of dissatisfaction with the outcomes of traditional medical training and took, instead, a fresh approach which used sick patients and the symptoms they presented as the catalyst for learning. Trainee medics had to be able to diagnose the problem by filling in the gaps in their knowledge through a problem-solving/analysis approach, similar to the approach they would take once practising in the field. The approach was found to be highly successful because of this development of thinking and research skills and has consequently become popular throughout the world, particularly in the field of medicine. It has also become popular in other professional/vocational areas such as engineering, agriculture, law, business and computing. However, this popularity is spreading and there are now some examples of its use in more traditional academic subjects (see Schwartz et al., 2001).

Biggs (2003) encourages university teachers to consider all the component parts of the learning process when we seek to understand what occurs there. This systemic approach requires us to avoid a deficit model in which the teachers or students can be manipulated in isolation to change their behaviour and thereby achieve an improved outcome. What Biggs argues is that for any radical change to take place, there must be a concomitant change in all parts of the system. The implications of taking a systemic approach to PBL are discussed by, among others, Savin-Baden (2003), who suggests that a number of factors need to be considered before a move towards the adoption of PBL. These include the role of higher education; lecturers' conceptions of their role; resistance to change; administrative systems; physical infrastructure/environment (learning spaces); and stakeholder (e.g. student, parent, employer) expectations.

Yeo (2005b, p549) believes that flexibility in all parts of the organisation is required if a student-centred approach is to be adopted:

> A central finding ... indicates that PBL as an emerging teaching approach is not merely the responsibility of teachers and students. It requires close partnership with administrators of the institution to plan, implement, support and evaluate the variety of needs in ensuring optimum outcomes.

Ramsden (2004, p59) discusses three theories of teaching in higher education (HE). He describes them as Theory 1 – Teaching as telling or transmitting; Theory 2 – Teaching as organising student activity; Theory 3 – Teaching as making learning possible. He advocates Theory 3, believing that we need to move towards student-centred approaches if we are to prepare students for a complex and rapidly changing world. He believes that we need to move away from traditional transmission modes of education which encourage surface approaches:

> Surface approaches ... belong to an artificial world of learning, where faithfully reproducing fragments of torpid knowledge to please teachers and pass examinations has replaced understanding.

The lecturers' intentions for student learning are therefore pivotal in the learning and teaching approaches taken. If their conception of their role is that they need to increase the amount of knowledge their students have, then they may adopt a transmission mode of teaching and assess student learning through examinations and other methods which test recall. If, however, they conceive of their role as developing individuals who need to be able to deal with complex problems now and in the future, then they are more likely to adopt student-centred approaches, such as PBL. Both the lecturers' understanding and commitment to the reasons for using PBL are, therefore, significant factors in its potential success.

Summary

Since PBL is directed by the students, it is argued that it both taps into their existing knowledge and allows them to identify and explore gaps in their knowledge (Kingsland, 1995). This, in turn, leads to a greater self-awareness and provides students with new knowledge in the area being explored. It is also claimed that it develops general skills such as problem-solving, communication, research, application of knowledge, time management, group working, conflict management, assertiveness and creativity, along with reflection-in-action (Norman and Schmidt, 1992; Vernon and Blake, 1993; Schön, 1983). Albanese and Mitchell's (1993, p64) work at McMaster University reported that medical students found themselves:

> *better prepared (than their peers) in independent learning skills, problem solving, self-evaluation techniques, data-gathering skills, behavioural science information, and dealing with the social and emotional problems of patients.*

This approach is therefore considered by many to cultivate a deeper approach to learning which can stay with these individuals for the rest of their lives.

The PBL approach is not without its critics, however. Many students brought up on traditional teaching find the transition to such new methods difficult to deal with at first and early experiences are often fraught and anxious times. Students who are successful in traditionally taught scenarios may find the transition particularly painful. They are frequently excellent cue seekers (Miller and Parlett, 1974) and owe much of their success to their ability to seek out important information related to assessment. There is much anecdotal evidence of students' hostility and frustration to such new methods as they fear their ability to be as successful in these new scenarios.

Students' skills also need to be carefully nurtured and developed with their facilitators (see for example Woods, 1996). A frequent stumbling block for many PBL activities is group work. Students need help in handling group formation and conflict if they are to be successful. Learning to work co-operatively, sensitively and assertively in a team is a challenge not to be understated, and where students are given insufficient preparation and support this can be the cause of much distress to all concerned in the process. Incidents of 'social loafing' (Ringelmann, 1913) are frequently reported (and examples are provided later in the chapter) where some students do not pull their weight and the task burden falls to others in the group to complete the work. Frustrations can be expressed on both sides, by the 'workers' who feel let down and put upon, and by the 'shirkers' who can feel unable to express their views or challenge the dominant group members. Considerations of moving towards a PBL approach should seriously consider these potential problems before the outset.

No one approach to learning and teaching in HE can be considered ideal, however, and, these caveats apart, the case for PBL appears to be a powerful one and the author's own experience (found later in the chapter) confirms this.

The PBL process

As stated, the PBL process can initially seem frustrating to those who have only worked in traditionally orientated teaching environments. At the outset student groups will, of course, have differing views about the problem and what it means. This needs to be explored to unpack a shared understanding and conception of the problem under discussion. This is a difficult phase for students new to this approach as they may be unused to stating their views and may be reluctant to disagree with other more dominant members of the group. However, if students are not encouraged to clarify their understanding from the outset they will suffer the consequences at a later stage.

A typical PBL process is where student groups begin by identifying the nature of the problem; they must develop knowledge of the problem and then move toward providing a workable solution to the problem. This requires a structured and thorough approach and students are therefore encouraged to address the problem in a fairly systematic way. Figure 4.1 illustrates a typical process.

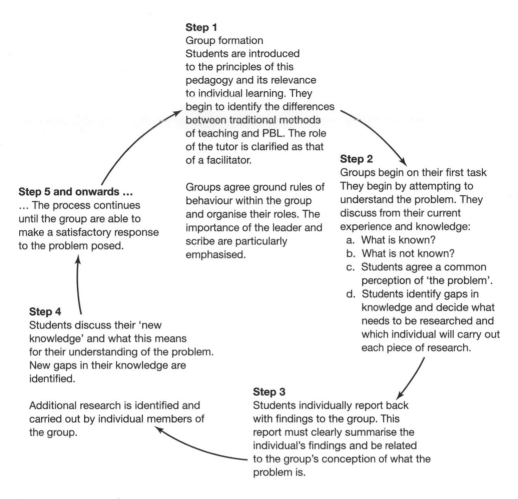

Step 1
Group formation
Students are introduced
to the principles of this
pedagogy and its relevance
to individual learning. They
begin to identify the differences
between traditional methods
of teaching and PBL. The role
of the tutor is clarified as that
of a facilitator.

Groups agree ground rules of
behaviour within the group
and organise their roles. The
importance of the leader and
scribe are particularly
emphasised.

Step 2
Groups begin on their first task
They begin by attempting to
understand the problem. They
discuss from their current
experience and knowledge:
  a. What is known?
  b. What is not known?
  c. Students agree a common
     perception of 'the problem'.
  d. Students identify gaps in
     knowledge and decide what
     needs to be researched and
     which individual will carry out
     each piece of research.

Step 5 and onwards …
… The process continues
until the group are able to
make a satisfactory response
to the problem posed.

Step 4
Students discuss their 'new
knowledge' and what this means
for their understanding of the problem.
New gaps in their knowledge are
identified.

Additional research is identified and
carried out by individual members of
the group.

Step 3
Students individually report back
with findings to the group. This
report must clearly summarise the
individual's findings and be related
to the group's conception of what the
problem is.

Figure 4.1 A typical PBL process

Roles

Before the PBL process can begin, time should be allocated to establishing the roles and processes within the group, setting up ground rules that are agreed by all and explaining to the students the role of the tutor. The students' roles can be rotated to ensure a fair distribution of the work and to allow for skills development within each individual team member. Two prominent roles at the outset are those of the 'task leader' and of the 'task recorder' or 'scribe'. The leader's role is to keep the group on task and ensure contributions from all members. The scribe's role is to record all the decisions made and tasks delegated within the group. This information can then act as the starting point for discussions at each meeting.

The tutor's role is to facilitate learning in each of the groups. The tutor will typically ask the task leader to summarise the group's position and detail what has been discussed to date, along with identified gaps in knowledge. The tutor will help them to discuss any outstanding problems, and help them tease out their understanding and decision-making processes.

A research study in business

Business studies is a largely vocational subject which does frequently adopt PBL amongst its learning and teaching approaches. It is commonly used in vocational programmes because of its immediacy and practical applicability to students' workplaces and professional experiences.

A recent research study conducted by Owens and Norton (2006) in a HE business school was carried out to compare students' perceptions and performance on a PBL module with that of a traditionally delivered module. The students concerned encountered PBL for the first time in their undergraduate programme on the module 'Developing management skills' (DMS) which ran in their first semester alongside a traditionally taught module, 'Marketing fundamentals' (MF). The students then undertook a second module with a PBL approach in the following semester, 'Human resource management' (HRM). Owens and Norton followed the students' development across one academic year in which they evaluated their experiences of PBL (using an evaluation tool reported by Martin, 2000, p160) and a written reflection along with an appraisal of student grades. Students were asked to record their experiences, of DMS against MF modules, i.e. PBL versus traditionally taught. In addition, the students also completed a written reflection of their experiences and a content analysis of these reflections determined the key themes identified by students in their learning. Subsequently the students' achievements were measured in both modules by a comparison of their grades. This process was repeated the following semester when students studied on the HRM module using PBL alongside another traditionally taught module.

The main findings from this study showed that although PBL was initially an unpopular learning and teaching approach, student evaluations ultimately revealed that they enjoyed their experiences and found the curriculum more relevant to real-life business issues (see Table 4.1). Their assessed results following the first module, however, were no better (or worse) than in their traditionally taught modules. However, this research reveals that there was a statistically significant improvement in student grades in their next PBL module, which took place in the following semester.

Questionnaire analysis

Table 4.1 shows student responses to given questions from the questionnaire. Scoring is from 0 (Totally disagree) to 9 (Totally agree). There were 126 students taking the PBL module, of which 42 questionnaire responses were received.

Table 4.1 Student responses

Percentage of students scoring 5 to 9 'agreed' up to 'strongly agreed' with these statements

	DMS (PBL module)	MF (Traditionally taught module)
Requires a lot of study time	83	81
Required me to be organised	88	86
Developed a deep understanding of the subject	79	67
Developed a wide range of knowledge	76	67
It was related to real-life issues	81	79
It was enjoyable	74	64

As can be seen, more students 'agreed' or 'strongly agreed' that the PBL module helped them to develop a deep understanding of the subject and develop a wide range of knowledge. In addition to this, students reported that the module was more enjoyable. However, these results were not found to be statistically significant.

Comparison of results for students taking PBL modules in semesters 1 and 2

Students who had already taken the PBL module (DMS) in Semester 1 performed significantly better in the Semester 2 PBL module (HRM) in both group work assignments and in their overall grades, but there was no difference in performance between modules on their individual piece of work, which was a report.

Table 4.2 Comparison of student performance on PBL modules

	Better	**Worse**	**The same**
Group work assignment 1 *	89	9	2
Group work assignment 2 *	58	35	7
Individual report	43	48	9
Overall grade*	49	21	30

(N=115)

Figures in percentages

* $p<0.05$ (Wilcoxon signed ranks test)

A similar pattern was shown in a comparison of results between the 13 students in Semester 2 who had not previously taken the PBL module in their first Semester and the 115 who had (Table 4.2). These students fared significantly worse in the Semester 2 PBL module (HRM) on both group work assignments and in their overall grades ($p<0.05$, Mann Whitney U test) although there was no difference in performance on their individual reports.

With such small numbers, it is difficult to draw firm conclusions about the long-term impact of PBL study. However, it would seem to be the case that performance improves over time in group work assignments, which suggests that once students understand the PBL process, they can become increasingly successful in it. These improvements appear to be sufficient to improve the students' final overall module grades, despite the fact that individual report marks (which have a high weighting) stay essentially the same. At worst, therefore, there appears to be no disadvantage to students in adopting the PBL approach and, at best, there may be an increase in attainment levels.

Analysis of students' written reflections

Students were asked to submit a written reflection at the end of their DMS module to discuss their learning on the module. An initial content analysis of this reveals that students believed the process of the PBL module helped their learning.

Of the sample taken, students identified group work as an important feature in their learning during the module. For example, they identified the experiences of playing different roles within the team, such as 'leader', as significant. The experience of dealing with conflict was also discussed in the majority of the students' submissions. Some students reported initial difficulties with the PBL process which were overcome or mediated by the end of the experience. This experience was not completely uniform, however, as there were varying degrees of positive/negative views.

Students' comments on group work and handling conflict include the following.

> I think that our inability to keep to our scheduled timetable was partly due to motivational issues. To a certain extent we have been 'thrown in at the deep end' with PBL, and so we struggled to come to terms with the 'vagueness' of the questioning and seminar set-up. Our uncertainty meant that we weren't as involved as we should have been, which led to us being unmotivated. In contrast there was a dramatic change in our progress in the second assignment. This time we constantly read and re-read the question; which not only concentrated our efforts entirely on the question, but also increased our confidence in the module. We seemed far more motivated and managed to complete our primary research in time, leading to a better report and better grade.

> You learn from each other and this makes working in a team more enjoyable than doing the work on your own. However it was not all positive when I was working in a group ... there was always one person who was not pulling their weight and the meeting times were sometimes a problem as we all had other priorities outside the university, e.g. work and family.

> *Finally we did the assignment on time but all in haste. It aroused quite a resentment in me because all my hard work and effort was in vain because other team members did not put in the effort and simply wanted a pass and did not aim for a higher grade.*

Some students' reflections also highlighted their interest in and appreciation of studying *real* tasks; although this was not a totally consistent experience either, with some students questioning the degree to which the process was related to real life/future work. The students did however report that the process of the PBL module did encourage reflection, which enabled them to recognise the reasons for a shortfall in grade, for example:

> *PBL required students to act on their own initiative and think for themselves rather than being told exactly what is required of them. I feel this is a better way to learn … as the student is solving problems rather than just giving back information.*

> *I learnt not only theory in this module, but also I practised the management skills … as the reports were done within a team, the process of doing the reports supplied the chances to use the management skills.*

> *When I moved into a new group initially it was hard to put my views across as I did not know some of the members. However I learned that if I were to be heard I would have to be fairly forceful. I did not have the confidence prior to this and it made me feel more comfortable about putting my views across in other lectures and seminars.*

> *If the subject had been taught students would have had a much better background and understanding for tackling the problems.*

> *I feel that because I was friends with a number of my group, I could not motivate them to work and did not force the issues I felt needed to be heard because of this.*

This small study appears to largely corroborate the findings of other studies in that it implies that PBL is a learning and teaching method which can encourage students to take a deep approach to their learning and is one which they enjoy. This is supported by Ramsden (2004, p56): *deep approaches are related to higher quality outcomes and better grades. They are also more enjoyable.*

For the remainder of this chapter a PBL activity is provided that was recently used with students. It is the writer's intention that this will provide a flavour of how PBL works and allow readers to consider similar activities and how these could be incorporated into their own teaching.

PBL need not form the entirety of a programme of study, even though the small research study quoted above indicates that there may be long-term benefits to student attainment where they are given long-term exposure to this method. Many academic tutors have found it to be a useful and enjoyable alternative in a more blended approach within the whole palette of approaches they use.

An example of a problem-based learning activity

(A comprehensive range of activities in other discipline areas can be found in Uden and Beaumont, 2006.)

Students were given the following question:

> *You have taken over as the new manager of* The Business, *a recruitment agency, with 86 members of staff. After your first month in post, you are trying to review* The Business's *mission statement and operational procedures. You are facing opposition from the Deputy Manager, who was the Acting Manager before you were appointed, and some other members of the staff team.*

In this activity, students would need to begin (once the group had formed and roles had been appointed) by identifying what the problems were and how they could be overcome.

In a general discussion at the outset, students would probably identify that the new manager had only been in post for one month and that there was opposition stemming from another member of staff who previously held that role in an acting capacity. They might hypothesise the reasons for this opposition and identify that seeking out theoretical frameworks in the study of conflict management might help them understand these issues further. This research would grow as the students developed their understanding to include questions such as 'What needs to be done to resolve this conflict?' and 'What would happen if nothing was done?' and so on.

Students might also begin to address the apparent catalyst for this problem, i.e. that the new manager had been reviewing the mission statement and operational procedures. Early student conversations might revolve around 'So what?' questions and the rights of the manager to change such things. Research of mission statements and communications theoretical frameworks would lead them towards understanding the need for sharing and consensus in such change-management situations.

In all these sorts of problems, every student can say something in early contributions. They all have a lay person's knowledge or experience of these matters. The discussion is open and free and no one need fear at this stage knowing very little because most students will be in this position. The best thing that students can do at this stage is ask simple questions (who, what, why, where, when, how) and this pure approach encourages engagement from the outset and consensual decision-making.

Plagiarism issues

Plagiarism is an ongoing and increasingly worrying phenomenon in higher education today. Problem-based learning is viewed as one of the potential antidotes to these issues as this method of learning and teaching requires close contact between the students and their tutor who work through the given problem in an incremental way on a weekly basis. This evolving process allows the tutor to closely monitor student understanding as it is the student who is central in all their meetings.

In traditional lectures and seminars, it is the teacher who is central to the structure and process. This invariably means that the teacher teaches for most of the time in meetings and these teachers consequently have little knowledge of their students' (mis)understanding until they reach summative assessment – usually at the end of the course – which some may argue is too late.

The PBL approach works particularly well in online environments where students contribute in a written format to weekly asynchronous forums. When the tutor follows the student through their learning journey in this way, it is not possible for the student to hide. Their weekly contributions to the written forums are viewed as their attendance record and in attending they must begin to visibly engage with the problem at hand and express their existing knowledge, about gaps in knowledge or similar issues. By the end of such programmes the tutor will have a good idea of each student's understanding and problem-solving abilities before summative assessments are submitted (see Owens and Luck, 2003).

Discussion point

Discussion points will of course depend upon the given problem. It is the questioning process which will begin the necessary discussion for determining areas of investigation. So the use of who, where, what, why, when and how, about any of the specific details is relevant.

- Why is any of this important?
- What are the consequences of doing nothing?
- What should be done and, on balance, why is that better than doing something else?
- Who should act and by when?

Reflective practice for HE teachers: What is it you are trying to achieve?

At the end of each problem event students are asked to reflect on their experiences of learning. At this stage the facilitator's role is essential in helping students complete their learning journey. The whole group discuss what worked and what didn't work in their attempt to solve the problem. They discuss where problems were experienced and identify the barriers to their learning. The ultimate aim here is that students understand themselves as learners and identify future action plans.

Useful pro-formas/record sheets/handouts

Appendix 1: assessment sheet

This example illustrates a grid format which the students are given before the assessment so that they can understand how they will be assessed. It illustrates to them that there are no right or wrong answers and that what matters is their ability to interrogate the problem and gain a critical understanding of the issues.

This assessment matrix also makes it clear that some of the marks available are given for a reflection of their learning journey, 'Organisation and management of own learning', which describes for the student and the tutor how the problem has been tackled and what this tells us about their approach and reflection on future actions.

Appendix 2: group contribution sheet

Ameliorating problems of 'social loafing' or 'freeloading' need to be considered. The appendix is an example which allows the tutor to assess who has done what and where there has been any imbalance in the work load/effort. Students can also be asked to award each other marks on this effort and attainment.

References

Biggs, J. (2003) *Teaching for quality learning at university*. (2nd edition). Buckingham: Open University Press / SRHE.

Entwistle, N. and Entwistle, A. (1997) Revision and the experience of understanding, in N.F. Marton, D. Hounsell and N. Entwistle (eds) *The experience of learning*. Edinburgh: Scottish University Press.

Hyland, T. and Johnson, S. (1998) Of cabbages and key skills: exploding the mythology of core transferable skills in post school education. *Journal of Further and Higher Education*, 22 (2), 163–172.

Johnson, D.W. and Johnson, R.T. (1993) *Cooperative, competitive, and individualistic procedures for educating adults: a comparative analysis*. Duluth: University of Minnesota Cooperative Learning Centre.

Kingsland, A. (1995) Integrated assessment: the rhetoric and students' view, in P. Little, M. Ostwald and G. Ryan (eds) *Research and development in problem-based learning*. Vol 3: *Assessment and evaluation*. Newcastle: Australian Problem Based Learning Network.

Martin, M. (2000) Preparing students for professional practice in occupational therapy using problem-based learning, in Bourner, T., Katz, T. and Watson, D. *New directions in professional higher education*. Buckingham: SRHE and Open University Press.

Miller, C.M.L. and Parlett, M. (1974) *Up to the mark. A Study of the examination game*. London: Society for Research into Higher Education.

Norman, G.R. and Schmidt, H.G. (1992) The psychological basis of problem-based learning: a review of the evidence. *The American Journal of Medicine*, 67, 557–565.

Owens, T. and Norton, B. (2006) Learning about learning: from student learning to the learning organisation. *HERDSA International Conference: Critical Visions Conference*, 9–12 July July, Perth, Australia.

Owens, T. and Luck, P. (2003) Problem-based learning on-line. *Journal of Problem Based Learning*, 1 (1). **www.ejum.fsktm.um.edu.my/VolumeListing.aspx?JournalID=9**.

Ramsden, P. (2004) *Learning to Teach in Higher Education*. (2nd edition). London: Routledge Falmer.

Ringelmann, M. (1913) Recherches sur les moteurs animés: travail de l'homme. *Annales de l'Institut National Agronomique*, 12 (1), 1–40.

Savin-Baden, M. (2003) *Facilitating problem-based learning. Illuminating perspectives*. Berkshire: SRHE Open University Press McGraw-Hill.

Schmidt, H.G. (1995) Problem-based learning: an introduction. *Instructional Science*, 22, 247–250.

Schön, D.A. (1983) *How professionals think in action*. New York: Basic Books.

Schwartz, P., Mennin, S. and Webb, G. (2001) (eds) *Problem-based learning: Case studies, experience and practice*. London: Kogan Page.

Tribe, D. (1996) DIY learning: self and peer assessment, in J. Webb and C. Maughan (eds) *Teaching lawyers' skills*. London: Butterworths.

Uden, L. and Beaumont, C. (2006) *Technology and problem-based learning*. London: Information Science Publishing.

Vernon, D.T.A. and Blake, R.L. (1993) Does problem-based learning work? A meta-analysis of evaluative research. *Academic Medicine*, 68 (1), 550–563.

Woods, D.R. (1996) *Problem-based learning: Helping your students gain the most from PBL* (3rd edition). Hamilton, Ontario: Donald R Woods.

Yeo, R.K. (2005a) Problem-based learning in tertiary education: teaching old 'dogs' new tricks?. *Education & Training*, 47 (7), 506–518.

Yeo, R.K. (2005b) Problem-based learning: lessons for administrators, educators and learners. *International Journal of Educational Management*, 19 (7), 541–551.

Further reading

Jarvis, P. (2001) *Universities and corporate universities: The higher learning industry in global society*. London: Kogan Page.

Norman, G.R. and Schmidt, A.G. (1992) The psychological basis of problem-based learning: A review of the evidence. *Academic Medicine*, 67, 557–565.

Sinnott, J. and Johnson, L. (1996) *Reinventing the university*. Norwood, NJ: Ablex.

Wilkerson, L. and Hundert, E. (1991) Becoming a problem-based tutor: increasing self-awareness through faculty development, in D. Boud and G. Feletti (eds) *The challenge of problem based learning*. London: Kogan Page.

Websites

www.heacademy.ac.uk/4304.htm (accessed February 2007)

www.economicsnetwork.ac.uk/handbook/pbl/ (accessed February 2007)

www.swap.ac.uk/learning/pblearning1.asp (accessed February 2007)

www.udel.edu/pbl/ (accessed February 2007)

www.materials.ac.uk/guides/pbl.asp (accessed February 2007)

www.interact.bton.ac.uk/pbl/index.php (accessed February 2007)

www.jiscmail.ac.uk/lists/pbl.html (accessed February 2007)

www.ukcle.ac.uk/resources/pbl/resources.html (accessed February 2007)

www.physsci.ltsn.ac.uk/Resources/PBL.aspx (accessed February 2007).

Appendix 1

Assessment sheet

Mark Scheme	A	B	C	D	E	F
Understanding of question set						
Clarity of written report						
Background research						
Critical understanding of conflict management issues and skills						
Organisation and management of own learning						
Overall grade and comments						

Appendix 2

Group contribution sheet

In the grid below students are required to:

- **record their names**
- **identify the contribution they have made to the assignment**

Name	Student number	Contributions	Percentage awarded

Chapter 5

Action learning and research and inquiry methods on postgraduate courses for professional practitioners

Anne Campbell and Moira Sykes

Introduction

This chapter will draw on approaches to teaching and learning which combine workplace and university learning contexts, together with relevant materials. It will discuss how higher education (HE) staff can support experienced professionals, engaged on part-time postgraduate programmes to use work-based learning to investigate and develop their professional practice. The development of action learning through critical friendship groups, peer coaching and critical evaluation and analysis will be illustrated in examples of activities for professionals working at postgraduate level.

The promotion of action learning and inquiry techniques will also be illustrated and developed with examples of practitioners' writing in log, diary and reflective writing formats. Techniques such as critical incident analysis, strengths, weaknesses, opportunities and threats (SWOT) analysis and force-field analysis will be explained and developed. Innovative assessment approaches will be exemplified and discussed, and peer and self-assessment approaches outlined.

This chapter will draw mainly upon the fields of education and health in linking action inquiry and professional development, although it is hoped that these will have wider application in other fields of professional practice such as social work and socio-legal practice, for example, probation officers. It may have some relevance for business studies students, as many of the practices in action learning evolved from early work in that field. The chapter will also encourage HE staff to reflect upon their own professional learning by using the above approaches with the aim of promoting pedagogical action research and inquiry in HE contexts (Kember, 2000).

Meeting the Standards

The UK Professional Standards Framework for teaching and supporting learning in higher education recognises the scholarly nature of subject inquiry and knowledge creation and a scholarly approach to pedagogy in HE. This chapter promotes the following activities for staff in HE, as described in Standard 1.

- **Integration of scholarship, research and professional activities with teaching and supporting learning by using research about inquiry-based learning in the workplace.**
- **Evaluation of practice and continuing professional development by encouraging reflection and evaluation by HE staff.**

Standard 2 promotes 'core knowledge' in HE and this chapter addresses key aspects.

- **Knowledge and understanding of appropriate methods of teaching and learning at postgraduate level by utilizing the professional contexts of experienced professionals who have returned to study.**
- **Methods for evaluating the effectiveness of teaching by looking at how work done on courses impacts on professionals and their contexts.**

Standard 3 is about professional values and this chapter endorses those below.

- **Commitment to incorporating the process and outcomes of relevant research and professional practice by linking these in the activities designed to support inquiry into practice.**
- **Commitment to development of learning communities by encouraging critical friendships and critical communities of learners and teachers.**

Why promote action learning and inquiry approaches?

Many part-time postgraduate courses for practitioners in the caring professions, education, social care and health fields aim to mesh the academic with the professional aspects of their students' lives. One of the main reasons for promoting action learning and inquiry approaches is that they can facilitate a much better interaction between theory and practice, i.e. praxis in professional learning, and can support learning from experience in the workplace. Due to the practical and individual focus of these workplace approaches, it could be said they increase learner autonomy and help solve practical problems in real situations, avoiding prescription and 'one size fits all' approaches on courses. Learning in the professions has been extensively explored by Eraut (1985, 1994) and Eraut *et al.* (1998), and they advocate learning both in and out of the workplace, with a 'learner-focused perspective' being a key element. Action learning in the workplace, initially in industry, has been researched and promoted by Pedlar (1997), Mumford (1997) and Rothwell (1999) and has emerged as a successful approach in a much wider group of professionals in health, education and other public and private-sector organisations (Stark, 2006).

Action inquiry and research-based approaches are not new as the extensive literature in education, health and management demonstrates: Kinchloe (2003), Elliott (1991), Frost *et al.* (2000), Day (1999), Campbell *et al.* (2004) in education; Bolton (2005, 2006), Reason and Bradbury (2002) and Boutall and Pedlar (1992) in management. These approaches demonstrate how practitioner professionals can inquire into their practice to improve and develop it while using previous research to support their theorising about their work.

Discussion point

What do you think of action learning and inquiry? Can these approaches be justified as valuable methods of bringing together theory and practice?

What is action learning and what is action inquiry?

It may be useful to start with some definitions. Action learning:

is a process of learning and reflection that happens with the support of a group or set of colleagues working on real problems with the intention of getting things done.

(Dewar and Sharp, 2006, p220)

Action learning has a framework and principles based on questioning and challenging practice and thinking and taking responsibility for one's own learning. Often there is an external facilitator who helps to foster professional development and learning. Action learning began in the UK (Revans, 1971) in industry, but now it has a much wider application in professional learning.

Action inquiry or research is similar to action learning in that it is based on learning from experience. Carr and Kemmis (1986, p162) offer the following as a starting place for discussions:

> Action research is a form of self-reflective inquiry undertaken by participants in social situations in order to improve the rationality and justice of their own practices, their understanding of these practices, and the situations in which the practices are carried out.

Action learning and action inquiry and research have much in common but they are different, and Dewar and Sharp (2006) use Kember's (2000, p35) work which characterises action research as a methodological and rigorous form of action learning in which results are published, and argues that:

> All action research (inquiry) projects are therefore action learning projects, but the converse is not true.

Dewar and Sharp conclude that action learning focuses on the specific processes of learning taking place and that action research is the publication and dissemination of that learning.

For the purposes of this chapter, and to avoid unnecessary complication, action inquiry and action research are taken to mean the same thing and the term 'action inquiry' will normally be used. Quite simply, action learning is a process of investigating problems or concerns within a group or set (a small group of people who meet together on a regular basis) which results in new knowledge, insights and practices. Action inquiry can be undertaken either by individuals or collaborative groups, and is generally more rigorous in design and conduct than action learning and results in a form of publication or dissemination.

Discussion point |

What use could be made of either action learning sets or action inquiry approaches in your field? How could you use these approaches in the development of your own practice? What would an action learning set focus on for an HE tutor?

What follows are practical examples of activities that promote action learning and action inquiry in a variety of professional contexts.

Action learning sets

Action learning sets are common in management education and business contexts. They enable those with a common place of work and research interest to gain the benefits of collaboration. Such collaboration encourages the reflection through discussion and questioning which is so necessary to any practitioner research.

The following draws on examples from Stark (2006) and Dewar and Sharp (2006) to illustrate the processes involved in action learning sets with nurse practitioners. The focus is on developing clinical practice.

Developing nurse leaders: action learning sets to implement organisational change (four to six participants in the set)

A facilitator is appointed, usually someone external to the group of practitioners, who undertakes several roles.

- **Modelling good communication skills and questioning.**
- **Support for change.**
- **Ensuring the group functions well.**

The facilitator may withdraw when the group feels it can take over that role. It is the group's decision.

Action learning sets need to meet regularly (monthly or fortnightly) and undertake the following activities:

- **get to know each other and the contexts in which they work;**
- **identify and discuss the organisational change to be implemented in all practitioners' contexts (improve clinical supervision);**
- **discuss issues or problems relating to the change (taking turns over the series of meetings);**
- **share ideas and practices (members had different experiences of clinical supervision depending on specialist area);**
- **ask questions to probe the issue or problem and to support learning;**
- **gather data about the different models of clinical supervision and how they work;**
- **reflect on the potential effectiveness of the models if applied to their context;**
- **discuss and critique their own model in the light of knowledge of other models;**
- **implement an individual action plan based on new learning.**

Many members of action learning sets are encouraged to keep a journal of the discussions and actions arising from the set, especially if members are engaged in an award-bearing programme where it may form part of the assessed work.

> *Discussion point*
>
> How might these action learning sets become action research? What would be the benefits to practitioners and tutors?

Action inquiry and research projects

Small-scale inquiries and research projects abound in both undergraduate and postgraduate programmes for professional degrees. The action inquiry or research project is particularly suitable for the development of practice in the workplace and for evidencing professional learning and growth. It allows the course to be taken to the workplace, and vice versa, and facilitates theory–practice dialogue. Further examples of action inquiry approaches can be found in Dewar and Sharp (2006), Winter and Munn-Giddings (2001), Campbell et al. (2004) and McNamara (2002). In all cases, some preparatory work on the nature of practitioner inquiry and research and appropriate methodologies and methods is essential to ground concepts and develop knowledge and understanding of the processes involved.

Stage 1: first steps

1. Is this a collaborative or individual inquiry? All practitioners should have a group with whom they can discuss their inquiry – the course group, colleagues at work or in similar institutions. These can be the critical friends (see later) who act as a sounding board. If it is to be collaborative, for the purposes of assessment, there must be clarity about individual contributions and foci.
2. What is the interest area or topic? What is the context of the topic? This should be a statement of broad interest at this stage, though it will have to be refined later. Two things matter about the topic. How keen is the practitioner to find out about it? How integral is it to professional practice? These questions will help maintain an interest in the context of a busy professional life. Practitioners should write a draft of some ideas and discuss these with the group.
3. Choose a topic. What is already known about this topic? What previous research or knowledge is there about it? What questions does the practitioner want to answer about the topic? These should be discussed with the tutor and critical friends. Are the questions feasible? Are they ethical? Focused reading should be undertaken.

4. How will this inquiry be done? What methods are available to the practitioner? What methods will be used to collect data? Why are they suitable for the inquiry? How will the data be analysed when it has been collected ? Some reading about data analysis is necessary.
5. In order to undertake the inquiry, from whom is permission needed? When will the project start and how long will it take? There will need to be comments on the ethics of the proposal.

Stage 2: further steps

6. A first draft proposal should be drawn up covering the following:
- **background to the proposal (context, interest, area of practice);**
- **questions for the inquiry focus;**
- **key concepts of ideas informing the inquiry methodology and cycles of inquiry;**
- **ethical issues;**
- **timescale for a project.**

7. The draft proposal should be discussed with critical friends and the tutor and then modified in the light of points raised. Some extended reading would be useful to further focus the topic.
8. The proposal can be started when it has been approved by the tutor.

Stage 3: final steps

9. Regular contact with critical friends and the tutor should be maintained. A diary of the way the inquiry is being conducted should be kept. The cycles of planning, implementing and reviewing should be adhered to during the life of the project. Follow the action cycles of:
- **document actions taken;**
- **undertake relevant reading;**
- **analyse the data;**
- **speculate about what is happening.**

10. The appropriate writing-up guidelines and the assessment criteria should be consulted before writing up. A draft should be discussed with the tutor before submission.

> *Discussion point*
>
> What would you need to do to develop your practice as a tutor supporting a practitioner undertaking an inquiry? What learning would you be involved in? What do you see as the value in action inquiry projects? Can you think of an action inquiry you could undertake to improve your own practice?

Critical friendship groups

Critical friendship groups, as in action learning sets, provide researchers with the means by which to reflect on their actions within a supportive environment. However, unlike the sets, the critical friends will not be involved in the research. They will provide challenge, scrutiny of work and feedback but may not be an 'expert' in the field that is being researched. The ability to reflect is provided by the questioning of the critical friend, not the directives of a 'supervisor'.

Critical friendship groups are closely related to action learning sets.

Day (1999, p144) describes them as being:

> *based upon practical partnerships entered into voluntarily, which presuppose a relationship between equals and are rooted in a common task of shared concern.*

While there is a notion of friendship about these groups, there also is a need to both support and challenge to facilitate learning. The role of critical friends in an inquiry project can be beneficial to both the inquirer and the critical friends. The role of a critical friend is to provide support and challenge within a trusting relationship. It is different from the 'mentor' relationship in which one person (the mentor) holds a superior relationship by virtue of his/her experience, knowledge and skills. The critical friend is recognised as having knowledge, experience and skills which are complementary.

An example of critical friendship working within a group of practitioners undertaking small-scale inquiry projects as part of their course might involve them in the following activities:

- **discussing ideas put forward by the researcher;**
- **commenting on the writing draft (not editing);**
- **trying out and commenting on materials;**
- **providing knowledge and expertise in the research area and offering an 'informed' opinion;**
- **providing a different perspective from that of the inquirer;**
- **asking 'difficult' questions and challenging assumptions;**
- **supporting inquirers in their development of ideas;**
- **confirming the validity of the inquiry;**
- **commenting on the inquiry design and project aims;**
- **providing a critical perspective on the inquiry.**

Both action learning and critical friendship require commitment from members and a set of qualities that promote collegial and collaborative behaviour for change and development. Some qualities that critical friends and action learning set members may need to develop are as follows:

- **an ability to listen carefully;**
- **interest in and knowledge about the learning process;**
- **empathy with adult learners;**
- **an ability to provide support in a variety of ways, e.g. experience in giving constructive feedback;**
- **skill in asking probing and challenging questions;**
- **an ability to articulate ideas and beliefs, but also to be sensitive to others' opinions;**
- **a willingness to share expertise and knowledge.**

> *Discussion point*
>
> What would be the ethical issues for HE tutors involved in facilitating an action learning set or critical friendship group? Consider confidentiality, professional codes of behaviour and trust as some issues to reflect upon.

Peer coaching collaborations

Mentoring and coaching activities are arguably undergoing a current revival in educational contexts, building on the work done by Joyce and Showers (1982) in the USA. A new framework, DfES and CUREE (2005), has been produced to support peer coaching as an integral part of teachers' school-based professional learning and the UK Professional Standards Framework for teaching and supporting learning in higher education also supports these peer processes. What do we mean by peer coaching and how is it related to action learning and inquiry? Peer coaching involves colleagues working together and learning to do something new or something better. This may involve some anxiety, assistance of different types, incremental skill development and eventually ownership. Coaching is about practitioners supporting others in craft learning. We would argue that it diminishes in worth if there is not also a critical evaluation of practice, which would also give the activity an academic dimension as professional learning involves more than craft learning. It involves thinking and theorising about practice. This could also serve the purpose of relating it to postgraduate course assessment criteria.

The aims of coaching are to build communities of practitioners who continuously engage in the study of their craft and develop a shared language and a set of common understandings for collegial study and investigation of practice (Joyce and Showers, 1982). This involves similar skills and qualities to action learning and inquiry but the main difference is that peer coaching is undertaken in the actual workplace, requiring there to be two members of the course in each workplace, or able to visit each other on a number of occasions. Many professional courses ask for two from each workplace for this reason and for capacity-building reasons. Participant coaches should have credibility in the workplace; have their colleagues' trust; encourage mutual respect and be self confident but not egocentric. Other key qualities and skills for coaching are:

- **analytical ability to critically appraise practice and look for effectiveness;**
- **creativity and ability to provide diverse opportunities;**
- **confidence to appraise own practice;**
- **good interpersonal skills;**
- **active listening skills;**
- **responsibility and commitment to collaborative and collegial work.**

What does a coach do? The following apply:

- **develops a joint, mutual action plan;**
- **agrees a way forward and commits to the plan;**
- **prods, stretches and challenges the partner;**
- **demonstrates;**
- **gives constructive feedback.**

The following are examples of coaching activities in education, social work and health.

Education

Focusing on the structure and pace of a lesson to improve pupil engagement, two teachers jointly plan a lesson and the coach team teaches, observes and evaluates a lesson and discusses professional learning. The roles are then reversed with the next lesson.

Social work

Focusing on the feedback to parents after a child's case conference, two social workers discuss how to give feedback to parents, then the coach models, observes and gives constructive feedback to partner. The roles are then reversed with the next case conference.

Health

Focusing on the development of the role of the nurse leader in the ward, two new ward leaders work together to explore an aspect of the role of ward leader, then one coaches the other after peer observation and feedback. The roles are then reversed for another aspect of practice.

Peer coaching aims to promote reciprocity, mutuality and collegiality between professional partners. There are, however, some risks and 'health warnings'. A climate that supports collaborative professional learning needs to be established where experimentation and change are accepted.

> *Discussion point*
>
> What aspect of work with the professions in your field would lend itself to peer coaching? What place does peer coaching have in the development of practice in HE teaching?

Critical evaluation of professional practice

Too much emphasis on the performance aspects of professional practice at the expense of the intellectual and emotional aspects could result in an overly technical approach to learning. Retaining the criticality can be done by addressing a variety of points exemplified below.

- **A written analysis of the components of the practice observed should be compiled. Examination of the details and a studied critique of the nature of the evaluation of practice should be presented.**
- **A discrimination of differences and similarities and differentiation between aspects of the practice should be undertaken and presented.**
- **An appraisal and evaluation of what was observed should be discussed between practitioners. Questions and judgements about the value of the information or argument should be the subject of a joint review. A consideration of the evidence available to support conclusions should be discussed.**
- **Reference should be made to other research or literature. There should be reflection on the pedagogical health or social theories or concepts underlying the practice.**
- **Practitioners should be encouraged to make their thinking explicit and open to discussion and challenge, and to engage in vigorous questioning.**
- **A healthy scepticism about what has been observed and read should be developed.**
- **Practitioners should look for evidence to support arguments and question the arguments of others.**
- **A comparison of ideas from reading and discussions should be made.**
- **'Recipes' for good practice should be avoided.**
- **Over-generalisation, e.g. the use of 'all', 'none', 'always' and 'never', should also be avoided.**

There are various techniques to support action learning and action inquiry and these are discussed below.

Critical incident analysis

The in-depth analysis of a specific incident, within the context of a wider inquiry, enhances the students' ability to think and respond critically. In their analysis, they are able to contextualise the theory they have studied and are using theory to develop their professional learning. Such analysis may involve critical friends as, in the early stages, students may find some difficulty in analysing their own practice rather than the simpler task of merely describing and critically evaluating the actions of others. Tripp (1993), Campbell et al. (2004), Somekh (2005) and Bolton (2005) provide detailed guidance for students embarking on critical incident analysis and usefully relate this to logs and diaries. Some of the key questions used are summarised below.

- **What led up to the event?**
- **What actually happened?**
- **What was the outcome?**
- **How would you take action from this critical incident?**
- **How can you make action judgements, diagnostic judgements, explanatory judgements, reflective judgements and critical judgements?**
- **How will you check your perceptions of the events with another observer or participant?**

(Adapted from Tripp, 1993, p64)

One case study example of a postgraduate in the field of education exemplifies the difficulties referred to above.

Case study

Mathew was a co-ordinating mentor for teacher training in a large secondary school. His role was to monitor the training of beginning teachers by subject mentors. The critical incident involved a failing trainee. In the first draft of his writing, Mathew described the actions of three of the parties involved: the trainee, the mentor and the university tutor from the school's HE partner. There was brief reference only to his role in liaison. Whilst some of the issues and possible 'solutions' were identified, these were limited to the trainee and the role of the university.

His critical friendship group was able to provide different perspectives, and ask 'difficult' questions and challenge his assumptions, as described earlier in this chapter, and thereby encourage critical thinking. As a result, Mathew's final written assignment included an analysis of his own relationship with the other parties and an action plan for the school aimed at improving its work with failing trainees. These included actions for the mentor and himself and involved reading literature on teacher training. By critically analysing an incident, Mathew was able to learn about his own professional actions, which would not have been possible with reference to the literature alone. Being grounded in his own professional context enabled him to take steps to develop intellectually and also to improve his own practice. Subsequently, the benefits of postgraduate study became more pertinent.

Discussion point

How might you use critical incident analysis in your teaching to enhance learning? Are there ways in which you could use this in your own learning? Consider some critical incidents in your own professional life.

SWOT and force-field analysis

Analysing strengths, weaknesses, opportunities and threats (SWOT) has been a feature of business practice since the 1970s. Increasing use was made of this method in other settings in the 1980s to analyse institutions and support development planning. Such a method can equally profitably be applied to the practice of small groups or even individuals, to provide them with a means to critically evaluate actions and projects within the context of academic study. As with critical incident analysis, however, there is a danger of individuals analysing all but themselves, although this can be overcome through the use of critical friends.

One such case study was action research by a teacher implementing increased use of group work into her teaching. The SWOT analysis was her starting point. In examining strengths, she considered literature on how children learn and, amongst other issues, the social interactions of the pupils she was teaching. However, such interaction she also identified as a weakness. In order to identify other weaknesses she referred to critical friends, who elicited from her an evaluation of her own teaching overall. Examining opportunities caused her to observe the practice of other teachers. The threats again referred back to literature on learning but also on classroom management. As a starting point, then, for action research she had already learnt much through literature and critical analysis about teaching, regardless of the particular actions she was about to implement.

Similarly, force-field analysis, first devised for organisational change by Kurt Lewin (1948), the American social psychologist, can usefully be employed as a framework to support critical analysis, especially in action inquiry. Lewin (1948), claimed that *an issue is held in balance by the interaction of opposing sets of forces*, i.e. those seeking to promote change (driving forces) and those attempting to maintain the status quo (restraining forces), the field being the organisation or other social context. The forces may include a wide range such as people, attitudes, finances, customs. At its very simplest level, it appears to some, erroneously, as a mere matter of 'pros' and 'cons'. In a more sophisticated model, whereby driving and restraining forces are analysed and graded in relation to each other, it provides a useful framework for developing an ability to analyse critically.

Assessment for action learning and action inquiry approaches

The means of assessing action learning and inquiry, whilst remaining related to the academic level at which the student is studying, can integrate with data collection, analysis and communication in a way which transcends the possibilities available through the traditional assignment.

An inquiry into the benefits of peer coaching may be presented as a video of the discussion which took place after the action upon which the coaching was centred. Alongside the video would be a written commentary which allows for the analysis of the data. For the assessor, there is the added benefit of being able to access the data directly rather than through transcription, also saving time for the student on such a laborious task. It enables the assessor to judge the accuracy of the student's analysis, which would not be done were this presented as a written assignment alone. A further way in which data and analysis can be integrated and therefore directly related to the professional activities of the student is through diaries, logs and journals (Campbell et al., 2004). Such an example is that used by practising professionals to evaluate their professional learning over a period of time and judge its impact on their activities through a journal. The potential dangers are that the journal becomes merely descriptive or a collection of evidence which has implicit meaning for the student but does not allow for the assessment of academic learning, as there is no explicit critical evaluation or reference to literature. This also presents the practitioner with a dichotomy – how much guidance should be given in constructing journals to those embarking on academic study, whereby a degree of independent interpretation is expected, against giving no guidance in a method with which the individual is not familiar? Problems of assessing sensitive, reflective writing are perennial and some tutors prefer not to assess this kind of writing. Winter's (2003, p121) solution to this problem is to engage in 'Patchwork Text' assessment, which requires students to present a series of fragments from their learning experience and synthesise these into a final submission. This is *an essentially creative process of discovering and presenting links between matters that may seem to be separate*. Another solution is the combination of self, peer and tutor assessment, in an exercise which provides a real stimulus for triadic assessment. We would argue that building a culture of trust and openness with a group is important where this type of assessment is used. See Winter et al. (1999) for a useful set of criteria for reflective writing assessment.

The presentation of critical friendship groups' discussion provides some areas of difficulty, as does all assessment of collaborative work in identifying the contribution of individuals. Providing individuals with the means to privately evaluate their own contribution, and comparing and contrasting these, is one way forward.

Assessing group presentations can be a challenge for tutors. The following criteria have been tried and tested with a number of groups over recent years.

- **Exploration of appropriate professional practice: is there evidence of approaching the study in a professional way?**
- **Presentation of information: is information presented in a logical and sequential way?**
- **Powers of reflection: are the strengths and weaknesses of the topic identified and reflected upon?**
- **Literature: has a range of appropriate literature been used?**
- **Data: has the data been used to inform analysis and support recommendations?**

This chapter has aimed to provide an introduction to teaching, learning and assessment approaches for use in supporting professional practitioners in action learning, research and inquiry activities. For further reading and development of practice, the following texts and resources are recommended.

References

Bolton, G. (2005) *Reflective practice writing and professional development*. London: Sage.

Bolton, G. (2006) Narrative writing: reflective enquiry into professional practice. *Educational Action Research*, 14 (2), 203–218.

Boutall, J. and Pedlar, M. (1992) *Action learning for change. A resource book for managers and other professionals*. London: NHS Training Directorate.

Campbell, A., McNamara, O. and Gilroy, P. (2004) *Practitioner research and professional development in education*. London: Paul Chapman.

Carr, W. and Kemmis, S. (1986) *Becoming critical: education, knowledge and action research*. London: Falmer.

Day, C. (1999) Teachers as inquirers, in C. Day *Developing teachers: The challenges of lifelong learning*. London: Falmer.

Dewar, B. and Sharp, C. (2006) Using evidence: how action learning can support individual and organizational learning through action research. *Educational Action Research*, 14 (2), 219–237.

DfES and CUREE (2005) *Mentoring and coaching CPD capacity building project*. London:DfES.

Elliott, J. (1991) *Action research for educational change*. Buckingham: Open University Press.

Eraut, M. (1985) Knowledge creation and knowledge use in professional contexts. *Studies in Higher Education*, 10 (2), 117–133.

Eraut, M. (1994) *Developing professional knowledge and competence*. London: Falmer.

Eraut, M., Alderton, J., Cole, G. and Senker, P. (1998) *Development of knowledge and skills in employment*. Research Report No. 5, University of Sussex, Institute of Education.

Frost, D., Durrant, J., Head, M. and Holden, G. (2000) *Teacher-led school improvement*. London: Routledge Falmer.

Joyce, B. and Showers, B. (1982) The coaching of teaching. *Educational Leadership*, 40 (2), 4–10.

Kember, D. (2000) *Action learning and action research: improving the quality of teaching and learning*. London: Kogan Page.

Kinchloe, J.L. (2003) *Teachers as researchers: Qualitative inquiry as a path to empowerment*. London: Routledge Falmer.

Lewin, K. (1948) *Resolving social conflicts*. London: Harper Row.

McNamara, O. (ed.) (2002) *Becoming an evidenced-based practitioner*. London: Falmer.

Mumford, A. (ed) (1997) *Action learning at work*. Aldershot: Gower.

Pedlar, M. (1997) *Action learning in practice*. Brookfield, VT: Gower.

Reason, P. and Bradbury, H. (eds) (2002) *Handbook of action research. Participative inquiry and practice*. London: Sage.

Revans, R.W. (1971) *Developing effective managers: a new approach to business education*. London: Longman.

Rothwell, W.J. (1999) *The action learning guidebook*. San Francisco, CA: Jossey Bass.

Somekh, B. (2005) *Action research: a methodology for change and development*. Maidenhead: Open University Press.

Stark, S. (2006) Using action learning for professional development. *Educational Action Research*, 14 (1), 23–43.

Tripp, D. (1993) *Critical incidents in teaching: Developing professional judgement*. London: Routledge.

Winter, R. (2003) Contextualising the patchwork text: problems of coursework assignment in higher education. *Innovations in Education and Teaching International*, 40 (2), 112–122.

Winter, R. and Munn-Giddings, C. (2001) *A handbook for action research in health and social care*. London: Routledge.

Winter, R., Buck, A. and Sobiechowska, P. (1999) *Professional experience and the investigative imagination: The art of reflective writing*. London: Routledge.

Further reading

Developing the skills of support

Egan, G. (1990) *The skilled helper: a systematic approach to effective helping*. Pacific Grove, CA: Brooks/Cole.

Critical friendship

Campbell, A., McNamara, O. and Gilroy, P. (2004) *Practitioner research and professional development in education*. London: Paul Chapman.

McNiff, J., Lomax, P. and Whitehead, J. (1996) *You and your action research project*. London: Routledge.

Action research

Reason, P. and Bradbury, H. (2006) *Handbook of action research*. London: Sage.

Somekh, B. (2005) *Action research: a methodology for change and development*. Maidenhead: Open University Press.

Somekh, B. and Lewin, C. (2005) *Research methods in the social sciences*. London: Sage.

Chapter 6

Who do they think they are? Students' perceptions of themselves as learners

David Walters

Introduction

This chapter explores students' perceptions of themselves as learners in higher education (HE) and makes reference to a study of a group of first-year students in music, looking at their perceptions of themselves as learners in order to better understand their attitudes and approaches to study. The research studied student responses to a constructivist questionnaire, a version of the Ideal***Inventory (Norton et al.) (1995), applied at the beginning and end of the first year.

'Who do they think they are?' Is this a question you've found yourself asking about your students after a teaching session or when marking assignments? Perhaps you have asked this question out of sheer frustration or you were simply perplexed by the unexpected nature of your students' response to a carefully prepared learning or teaching activity. Maybe things have not gone the way you had planned or your students seem to 'run off with the ball' in a totally unexpected direction, either in class or in addressing coursework tasks or examination questions. What has gone wrong? Is it the students who have got it wrong or is it the way you have been teaching?

In the context of this chapter the emphasis in question is not on the rhetorical. Not 'Who do they think they are?' but rather a more reflective, 'Who do *they* think they are?' How do students see themselves in the context of HE? This chapter looks at how knowing the answer to this question, posed in this way, might help us to assist our students in becoming more effective learners in HE. It will explore why understanding the nature of our students' approaches to learning and their learning habits is important for us as learning facilitators.

Meeting the Standards

Understanding what motivates our students as learners and what they think is a good approach to learning in HE is crucial to our success as teachers. For, if a teacher misunderstands or misinterprets students' motivations, much of what that teacher does may well be irrelevant to the students and time wasted, both for them and for the teacher. Therefore, taking into account students' perceptions of what constitutes their learning process is vital.

Accounting for that which our students, as individuals, bring to their learning is always going to be helpful in the planning of learning activities or programmes of study. Supporting student learning (and for each student this can be considered as a personal learning journey) in ways which account for their individual starting point will obviously be more effective than our making assumptions about their prior experience. This goes beyond subject-based knowledge and skills, reaching into a more difficult to assess area which might be described as fitness, or readiness to learn. As teachers, we are expected to be knowledgeable about the subjects we teach. Indeed, this is core to what we do and often our students assume we know everything there is to know about everything they think we should know. But this emphasis on subject knowledge is not necessarily the most important part of our individual learning journeys. Certainly, in our subject studies, something would be very wrong if we did not gain more knowledge. But neither we, nor our students, can continue cramming more and more information into our brains indefinitely. We would be like ageing computers running out of hard disc storage space, functioning increasingly slower, working less and less efficiently. Therefore, the most important aspect of HE has to be learning about how to learn, how to use information we gather efficiently, and how to apply this skill to new and unpredictable situations.

There is, however, something of a problem. Whilst we must have regard for learners as individuals, whose knowledge and skills have been built upon a myriad of different experiences, it may not be possible for us as teachers to design learning environments which wholly account for such diversity, without driving ourselves to distraction.

The Higher Education Professional Standards descriptors (as enumerated in the framework document) to which this chapter relates include the following.

Areas of activity

- **Design and planning of learning activities and/or programmes of study.**
- **Teaching and/or support of learning.**
- **Assessment and giving feedback to learners.**
- **Developing effective environments and student support and guidance.**
- **Integration of scholarship, research and professional activities with teaching and supporting learning.**

Core knowledge

- **Appropriate methods for teaching and learning in the subject area and at the level of the academic programme.**
- **How students learn, both generally and in the subject.**
- **Methods for evaluating the effectiveness of teaching.**

Professional values

- **Respect for individual learners.**
- **Commitment to development of learning communities.**
- **Commitment to encouraging participation in HE, acknowledging diversity and promoting equality of opportunity.**
- **Commitment to continuing professional development and evaluation of practice.**

So, is it possible to build learning communities which promote equality of opportunity and acknowledge diversity? The remainder of this chapter, whilst not necessarily offering a complete solution to the problem, is devoted to discussion of one method of finding out more about our students' perceptions of themselves as learners in HE and, hopefully, as a result, this will provide some clues to possible solutions to the problem.

Background, concepts, theories and issues

What is it like to be a new student in HE? Marton et al. (1997) state:

In addition to gaining understanding of the course content there are personal and affective aspects of study:

- *gaining confidence;*

- *changing attitudes;*

- *increasing critical awareness;*

- *scepticism.*

Such aspects are, in the writer's view, central to the nature of higher-level study. No matter how much students may know about their subject they will never be able to fully engage and move towards cutting-edge study of their chosen topics if they have not acquired these personal and affective aspects. We should not only be aiming to teach subject skills and knowledge, as in the transmission model of teaching (Kember and Gow, 1994), but we should also be seeking to act as facilitators of learning in which the outcomes go beyond subject knowledge and reach into the promotion of deeper-level learning capacities, which are transferable to new and less predictable areas. Whilst subject skills and knowledge are indeed of great importance, they lose their significance if our students do not also develop the capacity to apply these to new problems and new situations. It may be helpful to think again of our students on their journey of learning and whether or not they are passengers on this journey, following directions and doing as they are told (as in the transmission model). It would be preferable that we enable them to become 'drivers' capable of making their own choices, determining their own learning direction and route. At this point we must consider what it is we are looking at here. What makes the difference between learners who are passengers, and learners who are in control of their learning? This idea has, relatively recently, been accepted as the concept of meta-learning.

The term 'meta-learning' was first suggested by John Biggs (1985), who defined it in terms of two properties: awareness of, and control over, self as learner in context: an empowering process of *developing skill in learning; the quality of an interaction* (Svennson, 1984). Meyer describes the concept as: *A deep level, holistic, and self-regulated skill* (Meyer, 2005).

Meta-learning goes beyond the more specific, and more frequently discussed, concept of metacognition, which encompasses what Flavell (1979) describes as the three types of knowing: knowing about one's own and other peoples' thinking; knowing that different types of thinking are required for specific tasks; and knowing that there are appropriate strategies for improving learning and success in achieving specific outcomes. An important feature of meta-learning is that it takes into account the learners' perception of the learning context as well as their perceptions of the expectations of the discipline being studied. In this chapter we are attempting to find a manageable method of investigating our learners' conceptions of learning (in context), their epistemological beliefs, their understanding of their personal learning processes as well as their understanding, or personal view of their practical and academic skills. The mixture of practical and academic is particularly important here as this discussion is based on a study of music students: music being a well-established academic subject as well as being thoroughly practical. It is important to note, however, that the practical and academic skills can exist separately but that both need to be present for study of this type of subject to be deemed academically successful, as demanded by subject benchmarks. Put more simply, it is perhaps this unified combination of the 'ability to do' together with the understanding of the 'what' and 'how to do' that best typifies meta-learning in this context.

At the risk of oversimplifying this fascinating, multi-faceted and complex area of the understanding of processes of learning, meta-learning might be described as the factor which most of us would recognise as existing in a good, promising student's approach. Therefore we should, in our teaching, or rather, facilitation of learning, be aiming to prompt, promote and assist our students in developing their meta-learning capacities.

So, what do students think of themselves as learners in context? We should ask ourselves why students have come to engage in a course of study and what are their aims for their studies and for what purpose. Indeed, what is their motivation for studying at this level? It may be possible to summarise these, at the risk of making some sweeping generalisations, as falling into one or more of the following five categories:

- **academic;**
- **vocational;**
- **self-development;**
- **peer pressure;**
- **family expectations.**

Academic motivation, at the top of this list, is the purest reason for wanting to study, but in reality, is probably the rarest. Vocational reasons for study can be quite a strong driver as, usually, people have made a conscious decision to prepare for a specific career and the nature of the study they are undertaking is a prerequisite for entry into the chosen field of employment. One might reasonably expect self-development to be present in most who choose to study at tertiary level, but we cannot assume that this desire is present in every case. Some who find their way into HE may have done so out of peer pressure, and perhaps even out of a lack of desire, imagination or, perhaps, guidance to do anything else. There can also exist quite strong expectations from family that higher-level study is 'the next thing to do' after school.

Motivation for study is clearly a key factor for student success and, therefore, we must consider this when designing courses and learning activities. However, how can we provide students with motivation and can it be taught?

In considering motivation I would like to borrow ideas from the world of music – after all, the study on which this chapter is based focused on work with music students. Therefore, it may be helpful to indulge in some thought about the process of learning a musical instrument – a process which may not be totally unfamiliar to many readers either through trying to learn an instrument themselves or, perhaps, through observing the efforts of others.

Such a process involves a commitment to practise regularly and many find it difficult to find the motivation to do this effectively. The factors involved include both extrinsic and intrinsic motivations. Chafin and Lemieux (2004) describe these motivations in the context of children learning an instrument and point out that the literature identifies *the initial motivation to practise comes largely from their parents*. They go on to suggest: *Internalisation of the motivation to practise represents the development of intrinsic motivation as students begin to undertake practice of their own volition*. This notion of the internalisation of motivation (in the context of this chapter) equates to the development of higher levels of meta-learning where the will to succeed in academic study becomes its own reward and incentive.

Paul Ramsden (2003) states that [*we*] *expect students to change their interpretations of the world in which they live through developing their understanding of the subjects they have studied*. However, whatever our expectations of students might be within our own area/s of teaching it is probably a good idea for us to take into account our learners' current views of their world in order that we might best enable and encourage the change of interpretation we seek to promote. Marton *et al.* (1997) account for these views, meaning students' interpretations of their learning experience, as 'learner orientation'. They describe this as *a quality of the relationship between the student and the course rather than an inherent quality in the student*, and point out that learner orientation may change over time. They also advise that in identifying aspects of learner orientation we should not simply label our students as being of a particular type but that we should be aware of the implications of our students' approaches to learning and adjust our teaching accordingly.

So, what is it that makes a good learner? Is a good learner one whose approach includes skill in learning suited to the subject being studied? According to Morgan and Beaty (in Marton et al., 1997), skill in learning involves:

- **confidence;**
- **competence (in undertaking learning tasks and activities);**
- **autonomy in learning.**

Most would not disagree with this view. The importance of this approach to learning is that it is directly linked to the content and quality of the learning outcomes as identified by Marton and Säljö (in Marton et al., 1997).

Therefore, what can we do to make the learning experience more effective?

> *Students study in a strategic way to maximise their achievement but within their own definition of what achievement means.*

> (Beaty, Gibbs and Morgan, in Marton et al., 1997)

This is the crux of the matter: students' personalisation of what learning and achievement means for them.

Perhaps we should consider extending the challenge of Biggs' (1985) (constructive alignment) to include, as well as aims and objectives for teaching aligned with teaching methods, our students' starting points (personal views of the subject world currently inhabited) in terms of their learning capacities. Taking learning capacities, starting points and learner orientation into account at the beginning of a course should help the tutor to build learning tasks more suited to the students, not just their learning needs in the subject context but also their learning orientation. It follows, therefore, that it would be helpful to seek some kind of meta-learning diagnostic to help the hard-pressed lecturer in understanding the nature and cognitive orientation of his/her students. The case study that follows shows how such a diagnostic has been used.

Case study

What do first-year students perceive to be the qualities of a good learner in music?

Approximately two weeks into the start of their course, first-year music students were asked the question: *What makes a really good learner in music at university?* They were given a questionnaire (see Figure 6.1) which required them to think of up to five qualities or abilities that they thought a really good learner in music would, or should, have. Against each of these 'really good learner' aspects they were encouraged to think of the opposite of each of these qualities or abilities; not necessarily the literal opposite but perhaps the things a 'not very good learner in music' might do instead. In this constructivist approach, it is these opposite or negative poles that help define and qualify the thinking behind each response. Having defined their own idea of a good student, set against the backdrop of their own description of a 'not good' student, they then were asked to estimate where they felt they currently were on a seven-point scale between these two points.

Figure 6.1 What makes a really good learner in music at university?

1. In the column headed 'the really good learner' write down up to five qualities or abilities that you think a really good learner in music at university has.
2. In the column headed 'the not very good learner' write down the opposite of these qualities or abilities. It does not necessarily have to be the literal opposite. It could be something that a not very good learner does, or is, instead of what a really good learner does or is.

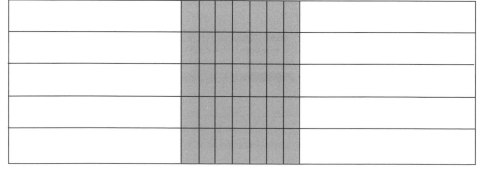

the really good learner: the not very good learner:

3. By placing an 'x' in one of the seven boxes between each of your two statements please show how close you feel you come to being a really good learner at this point in time. For example, if you feel you are very close to your idea of the really good learner's ability or quality, place the 'x' nearest that column. If you feel you are the complete opposite, place the 'x' nearest the not very good learner column. If you are somewhere in between, then place an 'x' in the box that best represents your position.

In analysing and reflecting upon the results, it is possible to build up a picture of individuals' approaches to learning, their learning needs and preferences whilst also giving the lecturer an overall impression of the student cohort. Most importantly, these impressions are based on the students' personal constructs, a most valuable source of information for the teacher to reflect on when dealing with an increasingly diverse student body.

This type of questionnaire presents many fascinating aspects of the topic that is under consideration and is rich in the information it provides. However, it is prudent to point out that the sheer amount of information contained within the responses can also be one of the drawbacks because of the time it could take to tease out the various aspects that are presented. Whilst much valuable research information can be gleaned from the questionnaire, research is not what we are aiming to do here. The *Good Learner Inventory* will be far more valuable to busy lecturers, and to their students, if it is used as the basis for discussion about the expected outcomes of the course, and the rather more difficult to define meta-learning aspects required for meaningful and successful study at HE level.

As previously mentioned, having two poles to each quality or aspect gives insight into the mind of the respondent: for example, the perceived range of difference between good and not good aspects.

Some more or less randomly selected examples of student-generated parameters for the really good/not very good learner are shown in Table 6.1 and have been roughly categorised into three areas – general attributes, meta-learning type responses and the more day-to-day aspects of being a student.

Table 6.1 General attributes

'Really good learner'	'Not very good learner'
enjoys	wasting time
enthusiastic	lethargic
motivation	not doing work lazy apathetic not motivated lack of motivation
motivated	bored
passionate	finds everything boring
wants to learn	lack of motivation
concentration	unfocused no attention span ADD
participates in lessons	not understanding/not asking [questions]
attentive/good listener	tired
participator	lazy person
dedicated	stressed
ambition to succeed	doesn't want to succeed
ambition	no interest lack of interest in subject
wants to use music in the future	doesn't care about music in the future
wants to do the best they can	doesn't want to learn/do well

Possible meta-learning aspects

open-minded	closed-minded narrow-minded tunnel vision set in ways small-minded
being able to ask questions and ask for help	struggling with work
extra-curricular learning	no extra research
individual learning outside	just lecture learning
good critically	doesn't want to develop skills
good analytically	not able to look at both sides
personal development	never asks questions or argues opinions
willing to try new things	rigid
open mind to new musical styles	fixed on one style
takes and implements new ideas well	takes time to embrace new ideas and theories
reads up on things that interests them even if not asked to do so	does no additional work
makes use of help and facilities offered	tries to do it all by themselves
takes note of advice	does their own thing

Day-to-day aspects of being a student

good at taking notes	not good at taking notes
meticulous note-taker	poor note-taker
organised	hung-over
planning	chaos
practises instrument well and regularly	doesn't practise
practises a lot (sensibly)	not practising regularly
time management	poor timekeeper
completes the work set in time for deadlines	hands work in late
has a lot of free time	has a busy life
does all work	not interested

Biggs (2003) gives guidelines for effective teaching and suggests we need to set the stage for our students and states: *Successful teaching is a construction site on which students build on what they already know.* He goes on to say: *The teacher's role varies, from highly directive, specifying procedures and correcting answers, to supervisory, to consultant, to group leader. The role adopted defines the nature of the different teaching/learning activities (TLAs), each of which is best suited to achieve different purposes* (p74). It follows that it is necessary to provide students with a clear structure and an explanation of procedures in order that the learning and the outcomes expected can be understood. However, there is also a necessity to ensure that the structures and instructions provided are presented in a way that students can relate them to what they already know. If students find a learning task difficult to relate to, they will not value it and hence will not expect to be successful in that task (as in expectancy value theory). The more cynical among us may think this is the beginning of an argument in support of dumbing-down the curriculum to meet the requirements of the widening participation agenda. However, this could not be further from the truth. Rather, it is a challenge to our own preconceptions of what our students should bring, in terms of prior knowledge and skills, to their studies at this level. It is pointless for us to provide them with a map (i.e. teaching for their learning journey) which is designed to take them from A to B if, in fact, the majority of them are starting from point C, or any other point in the spectrum of knowledge and skills of the chosen subject area.

As well as the quality of the relationship between student and course, it is arguable that learner orientation, as described above, is affected by the student's previous experience of learning. This can be described as learning capacities and learning skills and can be further broken down as below.

Learning capacities:

- **subject knowledge;**
- **subject ability;**
- **creative;**
- **cognitive;**
- **technical;**
- **meta-learning.**

Learning skills:

- **writing;**
- **listening;**
- **creative activity;**
- **questioning.**

Learning skills are clearly related to the more practical, day-to-day, aspects of being a (successful) student and are of great importance and should be developed through our teaching. However, in the context of wider participation, we cannot always assume that subject knowledge comes from traditional sources and so we may have to adapt what and how we teach to take this into account. However, this need not affect the final outcome of our overall teaching aims. Subject ability has to be taken as being inherent, or latent, and it is our role to ensure that we enable the student to find that ability within. Promotion of meta-learning capacities, through discussion of approaches and perceptions of learning, may well be the key to unlocking this potential and motivation for learning within our students. This does not necessarily mean we, as teachers, need to do more, or do what we do better. What is required of the teacher is a reflective approach to course design which takes account of our students' interests (as a starting point), their capacities and learning orientations. Sotto (2003) puts this neatly: *When a teacher sets out to motivate, the focus is on the teacher. But when a teacher sets out to create carefully structured and inherently interesting learning situations, the focus is on the learners* (p28).

Examples of student writing

This section reports on some of the findings from the questionnaire study, looking specifically at examples of student responses, from the beginning and the end of the year, in relation to their overall performance in their first year of music studies. In Tables 6.2–6.5, the scores which appear in the central column indicate the students' own assessment of how close they feel they come to being a 'good learner' for each, self-generated, aspect. A high score (maximum of 7) indicates that the student feels that he/she is close to his/her optimum for that particular quality or ability whilst a low score (minimum of 1) indicates the opposite: that they feel they are far from their ideal. Each of the cases has been given pseudonyms but the characteristics and the scores represented here are those of real first-year music students.

Table 6.2 John's responses

Start of year

The really good learner	Score	The not very good learner
turn up (preferably sober)	4	don't (because you're drunk)
practise	6	be a crazy b***rd [sic]
have a clever diet	2	eat whatever
listen and be involved	6	don't contribute or listen
planning	4	just getting down to work

End of year

The really good learner	Score	The not very good learner
listens to tutors, seminars, etc.	6	pays no attention
attends all things needed	5	very lazy
has good punctuality [sic]	6	is always late
takes notes of what happens during concerts (at least musically)	4	sits and pretends to be interested in music
gets work completed before deadlines	5	finishes last minute or not at all

It might not come as a surprise that John failed overall due to the non-submission of coursework and as a result of a poor record of attendance (Table 6.2). The positive pole of 'have a clever diet' is obviously something which should be explored, as might the reference to drinking habits. Other aspects which seem to cry out for further discussion in this instance include the somewhat passive approach to learning evident in statements such as 'listens to tutors' and 'attends all things needed'. There appears to be a lack of passion for the subject and motivation to study well.

A postscript to this is that this particular student, although unsuccessful in redeeming the failure, has restarted the year. It can be reported that, at the time of writing, this student's engagement with the course second time around has improved quite considerably.

Table 6.3 Carol's responses

Start of year

The really good learner	Score	The not very good learner
open minded	4	close minded
good listener	5	not willing to develop ideas
good critically	4	not willing to develop skills
good analytically	4	not able to look at both sides
personal development	7	never asks questions or argues opinions

End of year

The really good learner	Score	The not very good learner
organisation	7	messy, lazy
self-disciplined	5	lack of motivation
willing to try new things	6	rigid
people skills	6	cold, rude, etc.
literate – essays, notes	6	bad writer – doesn't do it or not well

The example of Carol shown in Table 6.3 is at the other end of the scale, both in terms of the student's overall result (a high 2:1 at the end of the first year) and in the content of the responses. It is particularly striking that Carol's start-of-year inventory contains so much that looks to be meta-learning aware. It is also interesting to note that the negative, or opposite, pole sometimes qualifies the thinking behind the good learner response. For example, instead of good listener being opposed by the more obvious bad listener, Carol has demonstrated a meta-learning awareness through choosing to define (or refine) this aspect with 'not willing to develop ideas'. The same is true of most of the responses in this first measure.

Carol's end-of-year response is perhaps a little disappointing in that there appear to be fewer meta-learning qualities displayed. However, if one looks more closely (in particular the self-rating scores) there is a sense of increasing confidence in evidence. This is a good sense of organisation and being in control: 'self-disciplined' vs. 'lack of motivation', whilst still offering an open-minded approach: 'willing to try new things'.

Table 6.4 Jenny's responses

Start of year

The really good learner	Score	The not very good learner
ability to work well in a group	3	unable to work in a group
be a good listener	5	not a good listener
accept new ways of working	6	unable to accept new ways
good time management	6	bad time management
ambition to succeed	6	don't want to succeed

End of year

The really good learner	Score	The not very good learner
being able to take effective notes during a lecture	4	not so good notes
being able to listen well during a lecture	6	not listen[ing] and have a conversation with your mates
being able to communicate well and participate in a more activity-based time	4	being extremely quiet and sitting in a corner
being able to ask questions and ask for help	4	struggling with work
wanting to learn about different areas of different types of music	6	just doing and learning what you are given

In Table 6.4, we can see a middle-of-the-road (lower 2:2) student, Jenny, who at the start of the year seems most concerned about her ability to work in a group. She seems to understand the need for good time management, has ambition and is willing to work in new ways. At the end of the year the picture changes a little. Now effective note-taking and the ability to ask questions when necessary seem to be more of a concern – perhaps a result of Jenny's experience so far. Her concern about group work appears in a slightly more clearly defined statement where the problem appears to be shyness.

Finally, one more case is presented in Table 6.5.

Table 6.5 Josh's responses

End of year only (did not complete the start-of-year inventory)

The really good learner	Score	The not very good learner
time management and good organisation	2	not as organised as should be
takes to, and implements new ideas well	5	takes time to embrace new ideas and theories
attends every/most days	3	misses lessons
generally shows a great interest in music	5	interest in music is not obvious
willing to practise to familiarise with new theory knowledge for their instrument	4	doesn't practise to understand new theories relevant to their instrument

Josh's response has been included here as it was one of the lowest scores in the self-rating. No start-of-year-inventory was available because the student was not in attendance – which takes care of at least one of the categories mentioned. This appears to be an honest reflection by the student of his situation. The low score on the time-management aspect is probably a predictor of impending doom. Josh failed Year One at the first attempt but did redeem the situation at resit.

Suggested assessment (diagnostic)/ research tool

The *Good Learner Inventory* is recommended here as a useful research tool for those wishing to investigate the effects of their teaching on student perceptions. This is largely what has been done in the preparation of this chapter. However, the next stage should be finding ways of using the inventory as the basis for discussion with our students, either in class or one-to-one, to promote awareness of the meta-learning requirements for truly successful study at this level. Such discussions should provide opportunities for students (and their teachers) to deal with their transition into the different levels of study. We often expect students to adapt to our ways of working. However, this is a dangerous assumption because the evidence suggests *that teachers with a student orientation [have] more effect on student outcomes than almost any other variable* (Astin, 1993, cited in Zepke and Leach, 1995). Zepke and Leach, in looking at the challenges of taking into account our students' backgrounds and perceptions, conclude that *students should maintain their identity in their culture of origin, retain their social networks outside the institution, have their cultural capital valued...and experience learning that fits with their preferences.* A tall order, perhaps, but using the *Good Learner Inventory* is one tried-and-tested way of gaining an insight into our students' perceptions of themselves as learners in their own context.

Discussion point

Trigwell & Prosser's (1991) article supports previous research in identifying relationships between perceptions/evaluations of the learning environment and approach to study and the quality of learning outcomes. In their article they identify a relationship between perceptions, approaches to study and the quality of the outcomes. In the light of this, the following questions may provide useful prompts for the interested reader.

● How might the *Good Learner Inventory* be used as a tool for the personal support of your students?

● How might the *Good Learner Inventory* be used as a tool for the academic support of your students?

● In what ways can the understanding of students' perceptions of themselves as learners help us create more effective learning environments?

● Is it helpful to extend Biggs' (1985) challenge of constructive alignment to include, as well as aims and objectives for teaching aligned with teaching methods, consideration of our students' starting points? This means not only their prior knowledge but also their cultural approach to study of the subject, their learning capacities (including meta-learning), and their motivation.

References

Astin, A. (1993) *What matters in college? Four critical years revisited*. San Francisco, CA: Josey-Bass.

Biggs, J.B. (1985) The role of meta-learning in study processes. *British Journal of Educational Psychology*, 55, 185–212.

Biggs, J.B. (2003) Teaching for quality learning at university (2nd edition). Buckingham: Open University Press.

Chafin, R. and Lemieux, A., cited in A. Willamon (ed.) (2004) *Musical excellence. Strategies and techniques to enhance performance*. Oxford: Oxford University Press.

Flavell, J.H. (1979) Metacognition and cognitive monitoring: A new area of cognitive-developmental inquiry. *American Psychologist*, 34, 906–911.

Kember, D. and Gow, L. (1994) Orientations to teaching and their effect on the quality of student learning. *Journal of Higher Education*, 65 (1), 58–74.

Marton, F. Hounsell, D. and Entwistle, N. (1997) *The experience of learning: implications for teaching and studying in HE*. Edinburgh: Scottish Academic Press.

Meyer, J.H.F. (2005) *Developing students' meta-learning capacity: a grounded assessment framework*. Paper presented at the 13th Improving Student Learning Symposium, Imperial College, London, 5–7 September.

Norton, L.S., Morgan, K. and Thomas, S. (1995) The Ideal Self Inventory: A new measure of self-esteem. *Counselling Psychology Quarterly*, 8 (4), 305–310.

Ramsden, P. (2003) *Learning to teach in higher education* (2nd edition). London: RoutledgeFalmer.

Sotto, E. (2003) *When teaching becomes learning*. London: Continuum Education.

Svensson, L. cited in Marton, F., Hounsell, D and Entwistle, N. (eds) (1984) *The experience of learning: Implications for teaching and studying in higher education*. Edinburgh: Scottish Academic Press.

Trigwell, K. and Prosser, M. (1991) Improving the quality of student learning: the influence of context and student approaches to learning outcomes. *Higher Education*, 22, 251–266.

Zepke, N. and Leach, L (2005) Integration and adaptation. Approaches to the student retention and achievement puzzle. *Active Learning in Higher Education*, 6 (1), 46–59.

Further reading

Cross, K.P. (1986) A proposal to improve teaching, *AAHE Bulletin*, Sept. 9–15.

King, P.M. and Kitchener, K.S. (1994) *Developing reflective judgment: Understanding and promoting intellectual growth and critical thinking in adolescents and adults*. San Francisco, CA: Jossey Bass.

Lucas, U. and Meyer, J.H.F. (2004) Supporting student awareness; Understanding student preconceptions of their subject matter with introductory courses. *Innovations in Education and Teaching International*, 41 (4), 459–471.

Meyer, J.H.F. and Shanahan, M. (2004) Developing meta-learning capacity in students – actionable theory and practical lessons learned in first-year economics. *Innovations in Education and Teaching International*, 41 (4), 443–458.

Norton, L.S. (2001) The Ideal *** Inventory. The Higher Education Academy Resources Database: **www.heacademy.ac.uk/resources.asp?process=full_record&section=generic&id=495** (accessed January 2007).

Norton, L.S. (2004) Personal development planning: the role of meta-learning. Invited presentation to Teaching and Learning Committee, University of Durham, 27 September 2004 (available from the author).

Norton, L., Owens, T. and Clark, L. (2004) Encouraging meta-learning in first year undergraduates through reflective discussion and writing. *Innovations in Education and Teaching International*, 41 (4), 423–441.

Norton, L. and Walters, D. (2005) Encouraging meta-learning through personal development planning: first year students' perceptions of what makes a really good student. *PRIME (Pedagogical Research In Maximising Education)*, in-house journal, Liverpool Hope University, 1 (1), 109–124 – Available at: **www.hope.ac.uk/learningandteaching/downloads/learnwise/prime1.pdf** (accessed January 2007).

Yorke, M. (2004) Increasing the chances of student success, in *Improving Student learning: Diversity and inclusivity*. Rust, C. (ed.) 12th Improving Student Learning Symposium, Oxford Brookes.

Chapter 7

Moving from dependence to independence: the application of e-learning in higher education

Anthony Edwards and Stephen McKinnell

Introduction

The reach of those who have access to new technologies is extensive. In theory they can raid the catalogues of great museums and libraries, explore the planets, address injustice and see who is in the local park, all at the press of the same button. The immediacy of these events, to those who have grown up in slower times, is staggering, and yet to some this is normal. Our challenge as educators is to use the technologies that make these things possible effectively in our teaching.

The purpose of this chapter is to explore the vexed question of how these new technologies can be applied to teaching and learning in higher education. The notion that the creative application of e-learning readily facilitates the transition of students from dependence to independence will underpin it. The term 'e-learning' in this context will apply to activities that involve some form of interaction with information networks such as web-based and virtual learning environments (VLEs) (Tinio, 2003) but the conclusions reached will be applicable to information and communications technologies (ICTs) in general.

Meeting the Standards

The process of analysis and the design of new programmes using e-learning is an excellent means by which professional approaches to supporting student learning can be fostered through creativity and innovation. Standard 2 within the National Professional Standards Framework specifies knowledge of the student learning experience while incorporating research, scholarship and/or professional practice into teaching and learning. The standards can be readily met by this type of activity. The designer of effective e-learning packages has to have a clear understanding of how students learn and what motivates them. The caution issued in the section on web-dependent online learning about the pressures on student time is a clear indication of how well one must know one's target audience before engaging them in using these new technologies. It is essential to be informed about the different perspectives associated with the place of e-learning in the teaching and learning hierarchy. The development of new pedagogies or the application of those that already exist to e-learning will not happen otherwise.

Similarly, to fully engage in e-learning, the following five of the elements in areas of activity is crucial. Specifically covered in the national framework are:

1. design and planning of learning activities and/or programmes of study;
2. teaching and/or supporting student learning;
3. assessment and giving feedback to learners;

4. developing effective environments and student support and guidance;
5. integration of scholarship, research and professional activities with teaching and supporting learning.

Similarly, among the professional values, strict attention should be paid to the three below.

1. Respect for individual learners.
2. Commitment to development of learning communities.
3. Commitment to encouraging participation in higher education.

By having the Professional Standards Framework to the forefront of one's planning, a guarantee is offered that the students' e-experience, while significantly different from the forms of previous centuries, will nonetheless be seen to be perfectly valid and Socrates need not turn in his grave.

The chapter will seek to achieve the functions listed below:

- **Examine how education is being forced to change because of new technologies.**
- **Establish the benefits and threats.**
- **Identify the key factors that need to be addressed in the design of e-learning packages.**
- **Explore the pedagogy associated with these technologies.**
- **Identify best practice.**

A case study will be presented illustrating how e-learning can be used to accommodate individual need, support curriculum enrichment and offer a wide variety of opportunities to track student progress. Reference will also be made to the challenges that e-learning generates including the tendency to view it as a substitute for direct contact with students, the issues of technical infrastructure, getting the context in which e-learning is used right and, finally, what happens if the lights go out.

Trends in education

Teaching and learning are being forced to change partly because of the significant impact of new technologies on the way we relate to the world around us. Power is shifting from the teacher to the learner because knowledge no longer resides in exclusive locations. The internet in particular allows for the creation of learning communities that defy the constraints of time and distance and dependent relationships. Professor Stephen Heppell, one of the Europe's foremost thinkers on teaching and learning, has identified 13 features of education that are being transformed by new technologies (Learnometer, 2006) (see Figure 7.1).

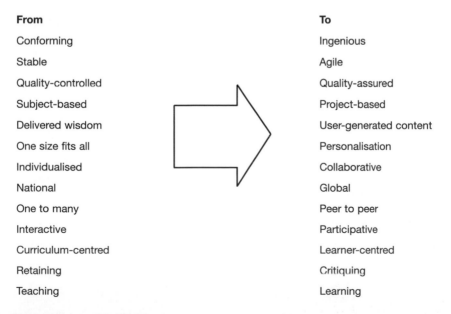

From	To
Conforming	Ingenious
Stable	Agile
Quality-controlled	Quality-assured
Subject-based	Project-based
Delivered wisdom	User-generated content
One size fits all	Personalisation
Individualised	Collaborative
National	Global
One to many	Peer to peer
Interactive	Participative
Curriculum-centred	Learner-centred
Retaining	Critiquing
Teaching	Learning

Figure 7.1 Heppell dashboard

Heppell (2006) suggests that in different countries the movement may be more or less pronounced and the rate of progress slight, or may be rather greater, but the trends are universal. Even if you do not agree that our future will inevitably be shaped by globalisation and technology, our students live in an age of instant access. (See Clegg *et al.*, 2003.)

Benefits

Victoria Tinio (2003, p3) cautions that the full realisation of educational benefits of new technologies is not automatic. It is *a complex multifaceted process that involves not just the technology … but also curriculum and pedagogy, institutional readiness and teacher competence*. Ehrmann and Chickering (2006) take the seven principles of good practice that underpin undergraduate education and explore how new technology can be used to advance each of them. They suggest that the typical communication and assessment tools found in a virtual learning environment (VLE) can support the seven principles in the ways outlined below.

1. Encourage student–staff contact. A VLE can help contact between tutors and their students through the communication tools in a VLE. Students can post messages at a time and place convenient for them. For example, tutors can set up a Q&A area in the discussion board (in some VLEs this could be anonymous), which tutors read and respond to on a regular basis.
2. Encourage co-operation among students. The discussion tools can be used to encourage student co-operation in small or large groups, face-to-face or online. Areas can also be created in a VLE for students to share work. For example, groups of students can have a private area where they develop their group presentation. They may choose to work together face-to-face and then load their work into the VLE for others, including the tutor, to review.
3. Encourage active learning. Through careful course design, focusing on student activities, one can encourage active learning. For example, before loading materials into the VLE, think about what you want the students to do and how these activities will help fulfil the learning outcomes. For example, if you want them to review a poem from the First World War, you would divide the class into groups and ask them to review the poem from different perspectives: from the reader, the poet, the narrator, the friend. These could all be housed in the VLE, with groups commenting on each other's work.
4. Give prompt feedback. The assessment tools including quizzes and the assessment dropbox will assist timely feedback. Quizzes can provide a wealth of feedback for students. Not only can they inform students if the answers are correct but they can provide pointers to further study, hints and tips and links to additional readings.
5. Emphasise time on task. By using a VLE, to link to library resources and online resources, students can spend time working through activities that have been specially developed rather than searching through shelves and surfing the web. This means they focus on the task rather than getting the materials for the task.
6. Communicate high expectations. As the tutor, you can use a VLE to show what you expect of your students. With agreement from students, you can use examples of previous students' work to show the level of work that you expect and why.
7. Respect diverse talents and ways of learning. The online discussion area can be used to build a community of learners which shows how the diverse talents of its learners can all contribute to everyone's learning. For example, a distance-learning programme in marketing can call upon its students from all over the world to provide examples of how they would market a product.

Tinio (2003) offers additional insights into how we should harness e-learning. She notes that properly designed and implemented e-learning packages can promote the acquisition of the knowledge and skills and empower students for lifelong learning. There is an interesting similarity between this position and that held by Heppell about the changing relationship between the teacher and the taught. Tinio also contends that a new pedagogy is being generated. She states that:

> *Computers and internet technologies enable new ways of teaching and learning rather than simply allow teachers and students to do what they have done before in a better way. These new ways of teaching and learning are underpinned by constructivist theories of learning and constitute a shift from a teacher-centered pedagogy – in its worst form characterized by memorisation and rote-learning – to one that is learner-centered.*

(*Tinio, 2003, p9*)

Tinio's view, however, is not universally held. There is an ongoing debate about new methods of teaching and learning emerging from the use of these information systems. Some claim that an e-pedagogy exists because more is happening than just converting a traditional course into an online version. New modes of teaching, learning and assessment activities are possible because they are supported by technology (University of Warwick, 2006). Some others, particularly those who view the use of technology in this context as an anti-intellectual force, contest this view. They call for a reaffirmation of the principles of liberal education founded on the Socratic method of discovering truth through questioning and debate and exemplary modelling which avoids narrow vocationalism. Motivation, presence, participation and open thinking can be achieved electronically, although careful selection of how the student engages with the material is paramount.

Regardless of this debate, e-learning offers a unique opportunity to provide a blend of learning opportunities. Caroline Gray (2006) refers to this as the 'mix-and-match format', which she suggests *represents an effective and proven learning model. It capitalises on the strengths and benefits of technology-based training as well as classic self-study, classroom, and on the job instruction.* Tinio agrees that it combines the best of traditional teaching and learning approaches with information. Oliver and Trigwell (2005) argue rather unflatteringly that the term 'blended learning' is confusing and hence does not lend itself readily to systematic enquiry. They ask what is new about it. Despite this controversy, what is clear is that e-learning has the potential to offer a very broad range of learning experiences.

Challenges

E-learning is a relatively new discipline, having been developed from computer and technology-based training. It raises many challenges for its designers and users.

Development costs, which can be high, have driven many involved in the creation of e-learning packages to use freely available materials (on the internet) instead of producing their own. These, however, need to be employed cautiously because some external packages have little capacity for modification and can be culturally inappropriate.

A poorly managed transition from limited to substantial use of e-learning can be also very damaging if done without due care and attention (Bates, 2005; Horton, 2001). It is essential to take realistic account of how much awareness-raising and training is required to make e-learning viable from both the student and tutor perspective. Some technophobes may recoil at the size of the challenge. If the technology does not lend itself to be used readily, students and staff will opt out rather than in. Reliability issues, ease of access, download times for resources, and security are also key factors. Students with special needs may face additional challenges if the technology is inappropriate.

Problems may also be generated because of lack of compatibility between different e-learning initiatives. Organisational structures may need to be adjusted. If the technical infrastructure is not robust enough to support the initiative or requires disproportionate financial input, it will fail. Any change needs to be properly costed and evaluated. It is not just a question of providing access to the technology but making sure that it is has a demonstrable impact on student attitudes, behaviour, knowledge and understanding. Finally, it must be based on sound pedagogy. It is important to remember that educational good practice is universal, whether it occurs in traditional face-to-face teaching or otherwise. Those skills that have been traditionally applied to teaching and learning to make it effective must be applied with equal vigour to the design of courses using e-learning. It is also important to have a fuller understanding of the evolutionary phases your use of e-learning can go through.

Modes of online learning

The University of Western Australia (see **www.staff.webct.uwa.edn.au/webct4/faqs/online_modes_definitions**) defines online learning as a subset of flexible teaching and learning that seeks to provide greater access to learning for all students (flexible teaching and learning itself being defined as below).

Flexible teaching, in the context of higher education, is concerned with the provision of a learning environment for students that incorporates a variety of access opportunities as well as a variety of learning modes...Flexible teaching includes conventional teaching practices and learning modes as well as alternatives and options provided by various media including, but not exclusive to, the recent developments in communications and information technology.

(www.catl.uwa.edu.au/elearning/online/definition)

The three modes of online learning, identified by the University of Western Australia, include web-supplemented, web-dependent and fully online. To these can be added a fourth mode of online learning in which the amount of face-to-face teaching is significantly reduced but not to a level found in the fully online mode. This mode will be referred to as the mixed mode of online learning. These four modes can be regarded as an evolutionary progression in terms of the skill sets needed by staff and students, the pedagogical models employed and the degree of reliance on technology. If it is accepted, however, that teaching in the context of higher education will always involve some face-to-face interaction between students and lecturers, then the fully online mode is likely to be an evolutionary step too far and will only be mentioned briefly in this chapter. The mixed mode of online learning is more likely to be the endpoint and is explained in detail through a case study.

Mode 1: web-supplemented online learning (WSOL)

The web-supplemented mode of online learning is, at its most simplistic, nothing more than what might be described as paper behind glass. This is what Sigala (2002), in her overview of internet pedagogy, describes as the first stage in the use of e-learning, through which tutors provide web versions of their classroom activities. Teaching materials that would normally be made available to students on paper are also made available digitally through the web. There is no compulsion for students to access these materials but they are on hand if needed, usually after the loss of the original paper-based products. At first glance there seems to be little if any benefit to this mode of online learning, but even at this basic level there are clear advantages to both staff and students. The information on paper-based handouts can just as easily be accessed by students in digital format through the web. They can make the decision about whether they want a paper copy or not. Furthermore, for certain groups within society, digitally distributed information can be more accessible. For example, visually impaired individuals might use a text-reading application to convert digital text into audible narrative or adjust the font size and colour before printing in order to aid their ability to read it.

Another advantage of digital distribution is the ability to make the information readily available. It can also be amended or edited without having to reproduce another set of handouts for reissue. In many subjects, topical questions can be readily blended into the teaching mix through WSOL. There are no restrictions imposed by the need to send material for copying.

The web-supplemented mode of online learning can be more than just a digital file repository duplicating what has already been provided as paper-based handouts. Additional materials can be made available through the web which individualise learning. For example, formative diagnostic tests could direct students to supplementary materials which help them address identified weaknesses. Access to these materials can still be optional.

Mode 2: web-dependent online learning (WDOL)

The web-dependent mode of online learning differs from WSOL because student participation is now compulsory. There is a blend of traditional face-to-face teaching with online delivery and if students fail to actively engage with the online component, they run the risk of underachieving or even failing the unit of study.

At a basic level, a very simple example of WDOL might involve an extension to the web-supplemented mode whereby no paper-based handouts are made available to students and they are directed to online copies instead. This might at first glance appear to be a significant cost transference to students, i.e. they now have to pay for the print costs of all the handouts, but in reality not all online provided materials have to be printed out. It is access to the information which is important, not the paper it comes on.

One of the main advantages of adopting the use of WDOL, blended with traditional face-to-face strategies, is that online learning opportunities exist outside the constraints of a normal timetable. Students can start to study at times and places that best meet their needs. However, this needs to be managed carefully because too much reliance on this type of engagement with the material can lead to overwork and stress, particular amongst those students who need to work to support themselves.

Web-dependent online learning can make significant use of the many tools that are routinely associated with VLEs. Many VLEs have a range of assessment facilities and text-based communication tools such as discussion forums and chat rooms. Use of these tools starts to take online learning beyond content delivery, i.e. it is no longer simply 'paper behind glass'. For example, a video made available (streamed) over the web can be discussed through text-based forums or chat rooms. Students can decide for themselves (or be directed) when to watch the video, thus relieving pressure on an already crowded timetable. The subsequent review could take place during a contact session. A possible development might involve the post-viewing discussion running for a set period of time in a discussion forum. This has a number of advantages including these that follow.

- **Allowing the asynchronous contribution of items: the inability to attend a particular timetabled session no longer excludes students from contributing to a particular discussion.**
- **Analysis at a later stage to determine what contribution students have made. This might be a measure of both quality and quantity and contribute towards some form of summative assessment.**
- **Facilitating student input in discussions. Many students who are often reluctant to contribute to a live discussion in the real world find virtual discussions less intimidating; this is particularly true with asynchronous discussions where time can be spent composing one's thought before replying.**

The role of the educator also starts to change with the development of web-dependent units of learning. This issue has been concisely summarised by Salmon (2004), who describes how the tutor moves from being the *sage on the stage* to the *guide on the side*, helping students to discover and synthesize the learning materials instead of simply being the distributor of information in a teacher-centred classroom.

Mode 3: fully online (FOL)

At the moment the fully online (FOL) mode of online learning, where all face-to-face delivery and interaction between students and tutors is abandoned and replaced by virtual delivery, is unlikely to be utilised to any great extent at a modular or award level within the UK's HE landscape. It might be used to deliver sub-components of a unit of study but, at this level of usage, it is probably best described as a mixed mode of online learning as there will be other components that are still delivered using traditional face-to-face techniques.

Mode 4: mixed mode (MM)

The mixed approach extends the compulsory element of web usage beyond the WDOL mode but contains many of the same features. Rather than explaining these again, a case study has been used to demonstrate what is involved. It is vital to start with a framework and some ground rules for the design of any package. The next section will explore how to do this.

Tools for analysis

A series of straightforward diagnostic tools can be used to define what shape new provision should take, or how existing provision can be modified to accommodate e-learning. These can simplify the decision-making process and indicate how to proceed. They can also provide a useful justification for whatever you decide to do.

Features dashboard

By modifying the Heppell dashboard we can create a useful template for analysing teaching and learning and decide what features any new provision should have, and the balance between them. See Figure 7.2.

Simply determining where your activities fit on the nine-point scale for each of the key features gives a clear indication of the journey you may or may not have to make. Circumstances could dictate that the characteristics of new or existing provision stay firmly to the left of the template, or a radical shift to the right is necessary. Either way, it provides a basis for what any e-learning package needs to focus on.

Mode dashboard

The mode dashboard can be used to identify what form of online learning you currently employ (From) and how you would like it to evolve (To), as in Figure 7.3.

Any transition should be determined by the needs of the students. Moving from web-supplemented to fully online clearly represents the most dramatic change and should not be undertaken lightly. In order to demonstrate how best these tools can be employed, a case study charting a typical transition is explored in the next section.

	1	2	3	4	5	6	7	8	9	
Subject-based										Project-based
Delivered wisdom										User-generated content
One size fits all										Customised
Individualised										Community
Single learning mentor										Many learning mentors
Interactive										Participative
Facts										Analysis
Teaching										Learning

Figure 7.2 Features dashboard

	From	To
No e-learning		
Web-supplemented		
Web-dependent		
Mixed mode		
Fully online		

Figure 7.3 Mode dashboard

Case study

Year 1 of a three-year degree course with a placement element consists of a module which explores the theory underpinning professional studies and a work placement in a school, work-based experience (WBE). There are also series of additional modules in which the content of the core of the course is studied. The ICT module is the focus of this case study. An analysis using the features dashboard (Figure 7.4) reveals the profile of current provision.

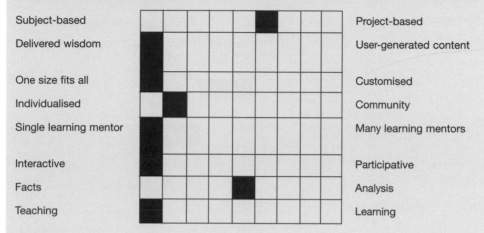

Figure 7.4 Analysis using the features dashboard

Although this indicates a tutor-centred approach with an 'expert' at the heart of delivery, some aspects such as project work and analysis are more in line with current trends. For the youngest students, who form the majority of this cohort, new technology has been part of their education throughout their schooling. At the same time there have been two striking developments in teacher training: the advent of a TV channel for the profession and the explosion in the number of dedicated subject-related websites offering advice and resources. The objective therefore is to create a more learner-centred module in which open and distance learning can take place at a differentiated pace; full account is taken of the social and professional. See **www.ferl.becta.org.uk.display.cfm?page=636&variation=101**.

The desired profile is indicated in Figure 7.5.

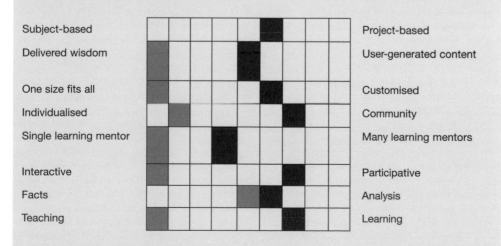

Figure 7.5 Desired profile

Interestingly, student evaluations of the existing provision indicate that greater account should be taken of prior learning, more time should be available for individual coaching, and flexible working patterns should be possible. This aligns neatly with the information in Figure 7.6.

Using the mode dashboard reveals the shift in the application of e-learning that is required.

The transition is a significant one and requires considerable care in how it is undertaken.

	From	To
No e-learning		
Web-supplemented	■	
Web-dependent		
Mixed mode		■
Fully online		

Figure 7.6 Shift in the application of e-learning

Response

A managed learning environment (MLE) has been created using a combination of an internet site, and the university VLE as a response to the Heppell analysis. The layout of the main page of the internet site has been kept simple and easy to navigate. It contains:

- **module aims;**
- **session themes;**
- **links to themed resource pages;**
- **hyperlinks to key sources including the VLE.**

The module is delivered in a variety of ways. In sessions 1 and 2 attendance at the university is compulsory because they involve an introduction to the VLE and audit of skills. In other sessions students can choose to attend or not, based on their existing skills, knowledge and understanding. This is tested through a series of sessions of related tasks which they must complete successfully. At least four sessions have a distance-learning element and require no presence at all. The MLE can be used as a self-teaching pack to foster independence and to cater for students who miss elements of the module through illness or for other reasons. However, it does not stand alone entirely. It has been a deliberate policy to make some form of direct contact in the classroom between tutor and student necessary. Consequently, tutors can model the kind of teaching behaviour they would like students to develop. In this context it is essential that the toneless quality of digital communication is counteracted by face-to-face contact. Each resource page has a similar format. An introductory passage outlines the key issues associated with the theme. Session objectives are listed. Hyperlinks to useful sites are provided. The segment on lesson resources includes information sheets on how-to-do activities and tasks.

The other essential part of this MLE is the virtual learning environment. The VLE offers a variety of tools and resources that are not readily available through the website alone. It enables learners and staff to interact through communication tools such as email and bulletin boards and collaborate using online forums. One of the first tasks students are asked to undertake in the ICT module is to engage in a synchronous discussion forum on a relevant theme. This is done in the university to teach them how to use the technology effectively. As the module progresses, additional forum-based discussion is required. The session-related tasks are submitted electronically through the VLE. This enables online formative and summative assessment and tracking of student activity to take place. Access to specific curriculum resources is controlled by placing them within the VLE. Extra support outside normal operating hours is also possible.

Conclusion

Heppell (2006) suggests that we should regard this as the age of the learner, rather than the digital age. With this mindset, it is easier to understand the need to embrace e-learning. The question of where and how the boundary between the virtual and physical classroom in higher education should be established is central. We need to ask what parts of the tactile, visceral and ever-changing environment, which we are preparing our students to live and work in, can, or should, be done virtually. The theoretical elements and the case study have, hopefully, helped to illustrate the complexities involved in developing e-learning packages. There are no shortcuts. All the skills, knowledge and understanding we currently possess need to be applied with the same vigour to traditional approaches to the development of e-learning packages. It is essential that we employ sound pedagogical reasoning in their design. Inappropriate use of the technology can be highly counterproductive. When unbalanced, there is a real danger that the tutor can become marginalised and the only relationship the student has with the institution is two-dimensional.

In order to avoid this, it is useful to reflect on whether, and to what extent, you have undertaken the following. Have you:

- **considered how your pupils (and tutors) learn best in the design of your e-learning package;**
- **developed a package that suits the specific learning context;**
- **made user needs paramount;**
- **considered sustainability;**
- **planned to measure and compare the quality of the learning experience with more traditional approaches;**
- **made the most appropriate use of the technology available;**
- **evaluated your technical infrastructure for suitablility;**
- **considered training needs, particularly those of support staff in relationship to developing web skills and e-pedagogy;**
- **considered the twenty-first-century workplace (see Tinio, 2003, p7) in your design;**
- **considered the need for good communication in developing this package;**
- **explored the cost in relationship to the perceived benefit of this development?**

And finally and most importantly:

1. Is what you are proposing to do based on sound pedagogy?
2. Do you have a backup plan for when the power fails?

References

Bates, A.W. (2005) *Technology, e-learning and distance education*. London: Routledge.

Brown, D. (ed.) (2000) *Teaching with technology*. Bolton, MA: Anker Publishing Company.

Clegg, S., Hudson, A. and Steel, J. (2003) The emperor's new clothes: globalisation and e-learning in higher education. *British Journal of Sociology of Education*, 24 (1), 39–53.

Ehrmann, S. and Chickering, A.W. (2006) **www.tltgroup.org/programs/seven.html**.

Gray, C. (2006) *Blended learning: Why everything old is new again but better.* **www.learningcircuits.org/2006/March/gray.htm**.

Heppell, S. (2006) **www.rubble.heppell.net**.

Horton, W. (2001) *Leading e learning*. Alexandria, VA: American Society for Training and Development

Learnometer (2006) **www.learnometer.net/**.

Oliver, M. and Trigwell, K. (2005) Can blended learning be redeemed?. *E-Learning*, 2 (1), 17–26.

Salmon, G. (2004) *E-moderating: The Key to Teaching and Learning Online* (2nd edition). London: Taylor & Francis.

Sigala, M. (2002) The evolution of internet pedagogy: Benefits for tourism and hospitality education. *Journal of Hospitality, Leisure, Sport and Tourism Education*, 1 (2). **www.hlst.ltsn.ac.uk/johlste/vol1 no2/academic/0004.pdf**.

Tinio, V. (2003) *ICT in Education*. E-Primers produced by UNDP's regional project, the Asia-Pacific Development Information Programme (APDIP), in association with the secretariat of the Association of Southeast Asian Nations (ASEAN). United Nations Development Programme Bureau for Development Policy, 304 E. 45th Street New York, NY 10017 **www.eprimers.org/ict/index.asp**.

University of Warwick (2006) Centre for Academic Practice **www2.warwick.ac.uk/services/cap/resources/pubs/eguides/elearning/**.

University of Western Australia (2006) **www.catl.uwa.edu.au/elearning/online/definition**.

Further reading

Ashwin, P. (2005) *Changing higher education*. London: Routledge.

Bates, A.W. (2005) *Technology, e-learning and distance education*. London: Routledge.

Becta ICT Research Network (2003) *A review of the research literature on the use of managed learning environments and virtual learning environments in education, and a consideration of the implications for schools in the UK*, **www.becta.org.uk/page_documents/research/VLE_report.pdf**.

Chickering, A.W. and Gamson, Z.F (eds) (1991) Applying the seven principles for good practice in undergraduate education. San Francisco, CA: Jossey-Bass.

Cole, J. (2005) *Using Moodle: Teaching with the popular open source course management system*. Sebastopol, CA: O'Reilly.

Cuban, L. (2001) *Oversold and underused: computers in the classroom*. Cambridge, MA: Harvard University Press.

Druin, A. (1999) *The design of children's technology*. San Francisco, CA: Kaufman.

Dupuis, E.A. (2003) *Developing web-based instruction: planning, designing, managing and evaluating for results*. London: Facet Publishing.

Fallows, S. and Bhanot, R. (2005) *Quality issues in ICT-based higher education*. London: Routledge.

Gee, J.P (2006) *Don't bother me mom – I'm learning!* Paragon House Publishers.

Laurillard, D. (2002) *Rethinking university teaching: a conversational framework for the effective use of learning technologies* (2nd edition). London: Routledge Falmer.

Valiathan, P. (2004) Can blended learning be redeemed?. *E-Learning*, 2(1), 2005 **www.learning circuits.org/2002/aug2002/valiathan.htmlDfES**.

Useful websites

There are a huge number of websites that offer support but listed below are a few of the better ones.

Becta (2006) British Educational Communications and Technology Agency **www.becta.org.uk**

Digital Divide (2006) **www.digitaldivide.org/digitaldivide.html**

E-learning Centre (2006) **www.e-learningcentre.co.uk/**

FERL (2006) Further Education Resources for Learning **www.ferl.becta.org.uk/**

Learnometer (2006) **www.learnometer.net/**

Heppell, Stephen (2006) web log, **www.rubble.heppell.net**

JISC Joint Information Systems Committee (2006) **www.jisc.ac.uk/**

National Statistics (2006) **www.statistics.gov.uk/**

ULTRALAB (2006) **www.ultralab.anglia.ac.uk/**

University of Warwick (2006) Centre for Academic Practice **www2.warwick.ac.uk/services/cap/resources/pubs/eguides/elearning/**

University of Western Australia (2006) www.catl.uwa.edu.au/elearning/online/definition.

Appendix

Definitions

The technical language associated with e-learning is rapidly expanding but some key terms are explained below.

Asynchronous	In the context of e-learning, asynchronous means communication that is subject to time delays
Bandwidth	The capacity of a communication network such as the internet to transmit data, which is often measured in bits or bytes per second
File compression	A process that reduces the size of a file without altering its contents
Computer-mediated communication (CMC)	Any form of communication between two or more individuals who interact and/or influence each other through computer-supported media
Computer network	A term used to describe two or more computers that are linked together that can share information such as files, text, pictures and video
Intranet	A computer network that is not linked to the internet. A local area network (LAN) is an Intranet
Internet	A global computer network that links computer networks and individual computers though the use of common protocol and a variety of different types of connections including radio, satellite and telephone
Learning community	A group of individuals who share common learning goals. E-learning community members can be located anywhere there is access to a computer
Managed learning environment (MLE)	Includes a whole range of information systems and processes (including a VLE) that contribute directly, or indirectly, to learning and the management of that learning
Online learning	A term used to describe internet-based learning experiences
Streaming	A technique for transferring video and audio files between the internet and a computer so that it can be processed as a steady and continuous stream
Synchronous	Refers to situations in which all e-learning participants are connected and communicate at the same time
Technology-mediated learning (TML)	Learning facilitated by the use of electronic resources
Threaded discussion	One of a series of messages in an internet discussion group commenting on or replying to a previous message
Virtual learning environment (VLE)	Refers to the online interactions of various kinds which take place between students and tutors
Wide-area network (WAN)	A network of computers and peripheral devices linked by cable over a broad geographic area

For a full glossary of terms see **www.learningcircuits.org/glossary.html.**

Chapter *8*

Beyond e-learning: can intelligent agents really support learners?

Chris Beaumont

Introduction

This chapter is rather different from the others in the book since it aims to build awareness of work that has been done over several decades in applying artificial intelligence (AI) to education. In so doing, the aim is to ask the reader to reflect on their own practice and in the light of the evidence presented here, consider whether or not such an approach might benefit their students.

When we build computer systems that interact with learners, we are attempting to develop effective environments which provide student support and guidance. This requires a thorough understanding of the student learning experience and building such a system involves all six areas of activity in the national Professional Standards Framework, especially assessment and giving feedback to learners. It is also striking to see the correspondence of knowledge required when constructing a system to the core knowledge areas in the standard, notably the extensive research conducted on student learning, evaluation and use of appropriate technologies.

AI is an enormous field, and a single chapter cannot do it justice, though it is possible to chart major developments and explore how effective the latest approaches can be for promoting learning. However, there are greater benefits for the reflective practitioner: AI in education has prompted a good deal of research into principles of tutoring, especially dialogue, and as such it has provided insights into pedagogical practices which can be applied in the classroom as well as in intelligent tutoring systems (ITS).

Most books on pedagogy and learning and teaching do not acknowledge that this subject even exists. At best it seems to be regarded as a rather idiosyncratic offshoot of computing and education. However, technology changes rapidly, and these developments, together with a wider view of how AI techniques can be applied, mean that there are considerable advances in the field. It is therefore quite possible that software that assists learning and employs elements of machine intelligence will start appearing on a wider scale and emerging from research laboratories. Some are reaching school classrooms already.

This chapter begins by exploring the background concepts and will trace the development of intelligent tutoring systems together with recent research into learning companions, using agent technology. Now this chapter could explain the technical aspects of ITS in some detail, and those readers who just happen to be computer scientists may well delight in that approach. However, my guess is that such readers will be few and far between. Consequently I have chosen to analyse the relationship between pedagogy and technology in such systems and discuss aspects important for achieving success. Finally, the chapter will discuss the contribution of ITS to HE and provide a brief comparison of ITS and e-learning.

The holy grail of ITS

Intelligent tutoring systems originate in the artificial intelligence (AI) movement of the late 1950s and early 1960s. At that time, the subject of computing was new and was developing rapidly, and researchers such as Alan Turing and Marvin Minsky thought that it might be possible for computers to 'think' as humans do. Turing (1950) proposed a now-famous test in which a machine and human conduct a dialogue: if the machine cannot be distinguished from the human then it is said to have passed the test. It seemed reasonable to assume that, once we created machines that could think, they could perform any task we associate with human thought, such as instruction.

Now there is considerable evidence to show that one-to-one human tutoring is more effective than traditional classroom teaching (Cohen et al., 1982) and in 1984 Benjamin Bloom published a study which reported that students working with a 'good' human tutor obtain average achievement levels that are two standard deviations higher than students in conventional instruction. That is, the average students in the individual tutoring condition obtain test scores as high as the top 2 per cent of students in the comparison condition. Thus, the challenge was made, and has been taken up with enthusiasm by ITS researchers: to design systems that are as effective as individual human tutors, but affordable enough to disseminate on a wide basis.

The development of intelligent tutoring systems

The first computer-aided instruction (CAI) systems were built in the 1960s. They are known as generative systems (Uhr, 1969), since they generated a set of problems, which students responded to, primarily in arithmetic and vocabulary recall. They were largely stimulus–response systems, with an assumed behaviourist model of learning, but took no account of the student responses in determining the next step in the interaction.

The next stage in development of CAI was the development of programmed learning systems that incorporated Crowder's intrinsic programming (1960). The students' behaviour (in terms of the history of their responses) was used to determine what activity occurred next. In this approach the system designers had to anticipate all possible responses. The programmers had to know in advance what types of student responses were possible and decide what information the system would subsequently present. The systems represented subject domain knowledge, but the process was very tightly coupled to the procedural logic that determined the steps to be taken. There was no attempt to model the students' knowledge states, and the systems could not respond in any way to student questions. Other severe problems in these systems identified by O'Shea (1984) were the lack of natural language dialogue with the user, and lack of real and deeper understanding of the subject being taught or students' mistakes. Consequently these systems used fixed dialogue schemes which were unable to cope with unexpected responses.

According to Otsuki (1992), the first elements of artificial intelligence were included in CAI systems by Carbonell (1970). The 'intelligence' was provided by introducing an inferential function based on a knowledge representation, in place of the procedural representation of the traditional CAI systems. Separating the knowledge base from the decision-making about student responses meant that systems could be much more flexible. Including inference rules to process the user responses provided the system with some ability at problem-solving.

Carbonell proposed the following were necessary in an ITS:

- **inferential technique for problem-solving;**
- **student modelling by diagnosing error origins;**
- **representation method for teaching expertise;**
- **mixed-initiative knowledge communication.**

This work proved highly influential in the succeeding research and led to the (now classic) architecture of intelligent tutoring systems, which involve the following components: the domain module, the student model, the pedagogical module, and a learning environment or user interface module, as shown in Figure 8.1 (Freedman, 2000; Lin, 2005).

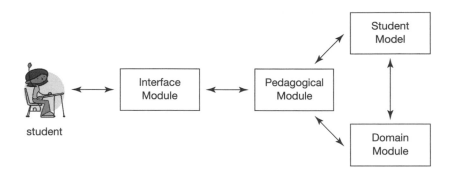

Figure 8.1 Components of an intelligent tutoring system (Lin, 2005)

The student model is the explicit way in which the progress of the student is represented for reference by the system. Clearly there is opportunity to collect a huge variety of data and interpret it in many ways. The model can vary from simply keeping a record of test scores through to sophisticated schemes of representing the ways in which the student has used various concepts and even metacognitive strategies and psychological attributes (such as learning style or motivational level). The model can be used to diagnose errors in student understanding and suggest the next appropriate step.

While complex models can be constructed, it is worth pointing out that we are really modelling the tutor's view of the student, rather than what the student actually thinks. This is still analogous to human tutoring, where the tutor builds an (incomplete) model of student understanding and uses it to determine how next to proceed. The information recorder must also be practical and useful by the system and must make a difference: there is little point in keeping information that is not used or does not improve student learning.

Early systems only modelled student domain knowledge; however, more recently there has been a focus on affective factors in using ITSs. These systems take account of student learning styles and incorporate motivational strategies (Lin, 2005, p170) in the pedagogical strategies.

A common approach to representing information about a student is the overlay model (Carr and Golstein, 1977), where a student's knowledge is modelled as a subset of an expert's knowledge. However, Ally (2005) points out that there are significant difficulties with this approach. Firstly, if there can be alternative (valid) problem-solving approaches that are not represented in the expert model, procedural modelling is very difficult to capture. In particular, novice students often do not take the same approach as experts: experts frequently use 'compiled knowledge' and consequently take shortcuts. A system needs to capture correct approaches of novices and semi-experts.

A further issue with the overlay model is that it does not account for students who have misconceptions that are not part of the expert's knowledge base. These misconceptions are often known as 'bugs' in student knowledge and an ITS can represent this mis-learned knowledge as a 'buggy model' (Brown and Burton, 1978). It is much more difficult to correct a misconception than to correct a gap in a student's knowledge and ITS often incorporate specific pedagogical patterns or procedures to attempt to correct these misconceptions. Even so, dealing with bugs is fraught with difficulties, and concepts must be broken down to a very fine level of granularity to diagnose them correctly. Evens and Michael (2006) describe how dialogue between expert tutors and students can be analysed to determine bugs a system may encounter and also the strategies taken by expert tutors to remedy the misconceptions. They further describe how multi-layer models of the student can be constructed in order to inform the ITS of the next move it should make.

A major difficulty in modelling students is uncertainty. The system builds a model from a small amount of information gleaned through a (usually short) period of interaction. The model therefore has a large amount of uncertainty, and the ITS has to make a decision about its next move on the basis of that uncertain information. A relatively recent approach to managing this uncertainty in a student's knowledge is a Bayesian network. A Bayesian network represents knowledge about a student (such as if a student knows a particular fact, or has performed a particular action) as nodes on a directed graph. Each node in the network has a probability indicating the likelihood of the student knowing that piece of knowledge. These networks reason probabilistically about a student's knowledge state based on his interactions with the tutor.

Given this brief overview of the difficulties in representing student models, it would be pertinent to ask, 'Why bother?' Indeed, it has been suggested that this is too difficult to be worth the trouble. However, it can be argued that there is always a model implicit within any system that interacts with a student. In essence this is the rationale for the approach to reflective practice as advocated in this book, where the university teacher adapts to the student and her/his learning. If the system is to adapt its responses to the student's individual inputs then it is essential to develop such a model. Systems without such models are no different to simple CBT and CAI systems that did not customise output for learners.

Not only will it assist the ITS, but research in this area helps us understand what is going on at a fine-grained level in the learning and tutoring process.

The Domain module (see Figure 8.1), which is also called the knowledge base, is the information that the system knows about its subject domain. This knowledge includes declarative knowledge (facts, concepts and principles), together with procedural knowledge (the application of that knowledge to solve problems). It is regarded as critical that the ITS can display to the learner how a problem is solved, that is, to display the reasoning that an expert would have used (Wenger, 1987). There are numerous ways of representing the domain model; for example, it can take the form of linked clusters of concepts and facts, as in a semantic network.

The pedagogical module uses information from the student model to determine what aspects of the domain knowledge should be presented to the learner, and the strategy and tactics to be used. This information, for example, may be new material, a review of previous topics, or feedback on the current topic.

In many ways the pedagogical module is the heart of the ITS. It is the part of the system that implements pedagogical theory, making use of the information in the student model to determine the next move that the system will take. The aim of an ITS is to behave as an expert tutor, ideally providing the same kind of dialogue and learning gain. If an ITS is to behave in this way, we need to understand and capture the knowledge and procedures used by expert human tutors when helping students to learn and the principles that lead to effective dialogue.

This desire to understand what human tutors do, in considerable detail, has spawned a good deal of research into this area and it is instructive to discuss some of this in detail.

One-to-one tutoring is essentially about dialogue, and the strategies and tactics that tutors use in these situations. Andrew Ravenscroft's extensive (2001) review of e-learning and its relationship to pedagogical theory highlighted that learning is a social activity and that knowledge is socially constructed. However, the dialogue must be purposeful; it must be with someone more knowledgeable, so that the learners are pushed into their zone of proximal development (ZPD). The tutor's role is to help move the learner from the concrete to the more abstract concepts. This raises the issue of what constitutes purposeful and effective dialogue. Robin Alexander's work has been in the area of primary teaching, but there is considerable commonality between his proposals for dialogic teaching (Alexander, 2005) and the findings of researchers in higher education. He identifies a repertoire of teaching talk, consisting of rote drilling; questions to stimulate recall; exposition of information; discussion and dialogue. He points out that each technique has its place, but emphasises the place of dialogue:

> *achieving common understanding through structured, cumulative questioning and discussion which guide and prompt, reduce choices, minimise risk and error, and expedite the 'handover' of concepts and principles.* (p12)

Evens and Michael (2006) emphasise strongly several aspects of dialogue that support learning, such as learning the language of the discipline, self-explanation and elaboration by the student. Fox (1993) identified collaborative construction of meaning in tutorial dialogues and Graesser et al. (1993) attributed success in tutoring compared to class teaching to be the greater number of deep questions raised by tutor and student. Chi et al. (1989) provided evidence that constructing self-explanations of new material during the learning process is an effective strategy, and that pushing students to employ this approach can be effective in producing learning gains.

Graesser et al. (1995, p497) suggest that the following components are important in tutoring.

- **Active student learning. Instead of the student being a passive recipient of information, the educational experience should encourage active student learning.**
- **Sophisticated pedagogical strategies. A good teacher/tutor should implement sophisticated pedagogical strategies that are effective in promoting learning such as the Socratic method (Collins, 1985), inquiry teaching (Collins, 1988), and modelling-scaffolding-fading (Collins *et al.*, 1989).**
- **Anchored learning in specific examples and cases. A good teacher/tutor should anchor the material in specific examples and cases rather than relying on didactic, declarative information.**
- **Collaborative problem-solving and question-answering. A good learning experience involves a balanced collaboration between the teacher/tutor and the student while they solve problems and answer questions.**
- **Deep explanatory reasoning. The teacher/tutor and student should focus on deep conceptual models and explanations rather than superficial facts.**
- **Convergence toward shared meanings. The teacher/tutor and student should achieve shared knowledge, a 'meeting of the minds'.**
- **Feedback, error diagnosis, and remediation. A good teacher/tutor should quickly give feedback on the quality of student contributions. When a student makes an error, the teacher/tutor should identify the error, correct the error, diagnose the misconception that explains the error, and rectify the misconception.**
- **Affect and motivation. A good teacher/tutor bolsters student motivation, confidence, and self-efficacy while mastering the material.**

Analysis of human expert tutors strategies and tactics reported by Evens and Michael (2006) shows that tutors employ all the approaches identified by Graesser et al., but also (unsurprisingly) that they vary the approach and dialogue depending on the student responses and the tutor's perception of how well the student is understanding. They studied problem-solving tutorials with medical students, and discovered a number of tactics were used by tutors, including:

- **tutor via causality (forward or backward reasoning);**
- **showing contradiction;**
- **exploring anomalies;**
- **tutor via deeper concepts;**
- **request explanation, push to answer original question;**
- **summarise;**
- **analogy.**

Evens and Michael also highlight that the use of hints is a major method of scaffolding *excellent ways to provide unobtrusive support during problem solving process* (Evens and Michael, 2006, p138) and further classified hints as those that *convey* information and those that point to what's important. Further analysis of expert vs. novice tutors showed that experts don't ask questions such as 'Do you understand', whereas novices do. Experts are more likely to ask follow-up questions to probe understanding. Novice tutors also used a much more limited range of Graesser's components; activities 3,4,5 are commonly employed, but the rest are underused (Graesser et al., 1995). Despite these differences Fantuzzo et al. (1992) showed that peer tutors often do an excellent job and it is interesting to note that Cohen et al.'s (1982) meta analysis of 52 studies showed that the impact of tutoring on learning is not significantly related to the amount of tutor training or age difference.

Discussion point |

Review Graesser's components (p83) and reflect upon a situation in your practice of what aspects you use with your students. Are there any ways you can use the information given to improve the level of purposeful dialogue?

I have found this challenging in my problem-based learning classes, where I have tried to analyse the dialogue used and push students into more detailed elaboration, using a Socratic method.

Clearly, becoming an effective and expert tutor requires considerable knowledge (subject and pedagogy) and skill at interpreting and responding to students. Building these into an ITS is an enormous task. But that is not the end of it. There are additional factors in the tutor–student interaction that are not considered above: the affective factors; tutors make decisions all the time about what is and is not appropriate, depending on the affective state of the student. Furthermore, we need to recognise that the student's model of the ITS will affect his/her approach to interacting with it. Students respond differently to computer systems than they do to human tutors in dialogue (Evens and Michael, 2006, p64). Moreover, the research above considered face-to-face tutoring, and it could be that there are differences in one-to-one tutoring using e-learning (for example synchronous conferencing) which impact on the effectiveness and approaches used. The research reported in Evens and Michael's book provides an in-depth study of expert face-to-face tutoring, but their sample size of tutors was very small; consequently the generalisability of the findings may be questionable. However, it is comforting to know that their results are not dissimilar to conclusions of other researchers such as Graesser. A literature is also developing around 'gaming' behaviour of tutoring systems, with students using the tutor's hints to get to answers as quickly as possible (Aleven and Koedinger, 2000).

Implementing these strategies in an ITS has proved a significant problem. Most ITSs do not explicitly identify the strategies they are using for teaching and implicitly implement one of the well-known strategies. Adaptation to the needs of the student could, in principle, be achieved using knowledge in the student model; however, most systems do not have multiple teaching strategies, so student models have not been designed to provide selection information. Thus, representing multiple strategies explicitly and the control knowledge to select among them is beyond the capabilities of most current systems.

Despite these difficulties, some significant benefits have been reported. For example, Cognitive Tutors, developed by Carnegie Learning, enhanced secondary school pupils' maths learning by as much as a full standard deviation over control conditions (Koedinger and Anderson, 1997) and experiments on AutoTutor (Person et al., 2001) have produced gains of .4 to 1.5 standard deviations depending on the learning measure, the comparison condition, and the subject matter. This would place AutoTutor somewhere between an untrained, effective human tutor and an intelligent tutoring system with sophisticated pedagogical tactics but no natural language dialogue. Untrained human tutors enhance learning with an effect size (sigma) of .4 standard deviation units, which translates to approximately half a letter grade (Cohen et al., 1982).

The Interface module of an ITS is responsible for receiving student input and co-ordinating interaction with the components of the ITS. To manage effective dialogue, a number of interface actions are required: analyse the grammar and structure of the input and interpret it; send the input and receive responses from the pedagogical module; and then generate natural language output. Screens in ITS systems are often arranged in a number of windows, presenting various parts of information (for example see Figure 8.2).

The output can be in a number of forms, for example as text, audio or graphical, or as a combination. The study of how students interact with the presentation of information is a topic for a book in itself, for example, project AdeLE (**http://adele.fh-joanneum.at/**) incorporates eye-tracking technology to research how students interact with presented outputs. This could enable the system to adapt its responses depending on the information the student has viewed.

As multimedia technology has progressed, it has been natural to include animated and somewhat lifelike images in tutoring systems and this, in turn, has led to a focus of research on affective factors involved in tutoring, and the option to endow the animated characters with personality traits. Such characters are often referred to as animated pedagogical agents.

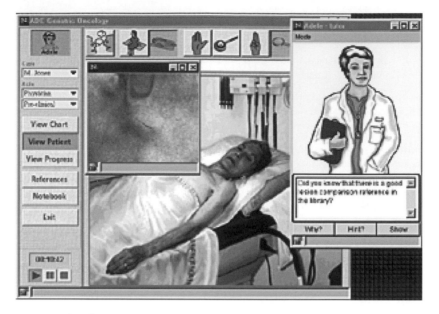

Figure 8.2 Example of ITS screen

Pedagogical agents

Pedagogical agents are autonomous software agents that occupy computer learning environments and are intended to assist learning by interacting with students (and possibly with other agents). Pedagogical agents have been designed to produce a range of roles and behaviours, for example to act as a peer, co-learner, or competitor (rather than as a tutor) and the animated characteristics now make it possible to explore other characteristics, for example:

> *These lifelike autonomous characters cohabit learning environments with students to create rich, face-to-face learning interactions. This opens up exciting new possibilities; for example, agents can demonstrate complex tasks, employ locomotion and gesture to focus students' attention on the most salient aspect of the task at hand, and convey emotional responses to the tutorial situation. Animated pedagogical agents offer great promise for broadening the bandwidth of tutorial communication and increasing learning environments' ability to engage and motivate students.*

(Johnson et al., 2000, p47)

If Johnson's vision of animated pedagogical agents, and the promise of intelligent tutoring systems, is realised, university educators might begin to worry that they will no longer be needed as teachers. However, since we are not swamped with these systems in our schools and colleges, there are evident difficulties in realising this scenario. Nevertheless, research in this area has revealed a number of interesting insights and possibilities, which broaden the appeal of agents outside the normal confines of tutoring systems. Kim and Baylor (2006) claim that interacting with one or more pedagogical agents with human-like personae can introduce social elements into learning with computer systems and the agents may provide information or encouragement, share menial tasks, or collaborate with the learner.

A number of studies show that users prefer learning environments with animated agents over those that do not have agents; that is, they perceive their learning experiences to be considerably more positive than participants assigned to learning conditions that do not include animated agents. This is known as the 'persona effect' (André et al., 1998; Baylor, 2001). However, although studies indicate that students show increased preference for such agents, it does not necessarily follow that a student's learning is more effective. There are rather mixed findings in studies of the learning achieved (Person and Graesser, 2002). For example, Graesser et al., (2003) conducted a systematic evaluation of the effectiveness of using AutoTutor, with interactions using a variety of media: text only; synthesised speech; talking head and talking head with text. The results of the study showed that the tutor increased learning but that the different media had no effect at all on learning outcome. Another study concluded that learners exposed to an environment with a pedagogical agent demonstrated deeper learning and higher motivation than learners without an agent (Moreno et al., 2001). Students in a voice-plus-agent environment outperformed those in a text-only environment, and those in a voice-only environment, on both process and product measures of learning. Given the complexity of environmental and affective factors that could make a difference to student performance, it is perhaps unsurprising that there are mixed data in this area, and more detailed research is needed to determine the precise conditions and agent attributes that make a significant difference.

It is worth stressing at this point that pedagogical agents do not just have an application as an attractive interface to an ITS. The model of agents collaborating within a learning environment, having different functions and different personae, widens the scope of application of these techniques. When intelligent tutoring systems were first developed, there was no real notion of distributed learning – certainly not in the form that the internet and world wide web now provide. Thus, we are beginning to think in terms of distributed models for such systems, built out of components. Such components communicate through standard protocols to share information; for example, the Sharable Content Object Model (SCORM) is a collection of specifications that enable interoperability, accessibility and reusability of web-based learning content. Agents could in principle communicate to assemble a collection of resources and use a distributed knowledge base.

The availability of standardised components will reduce the effort and expertise needed to develop tutoring systems and could lead to much more widespread use. The client–server model of providing the interface via a web browser and the back-end ITS on a remote server can also improve accessibility and scalability of systems. It is not difficult to see why there has been much interest generated in pedagogical agents.

The development of agents with different roles also shifts the focus from a tutoring system to alternative paradigms where the agent is not a tutor. Such systems are becoming known as intelligent learning systems (ILSs). Exploring the effects of changing the roles, personae, competency, gender and other features of pedagogical agents as learning companions (PALs) provides further insights into how such systems can be used to promote learning. For example, Kim et al., (2006) describe experiments to investigate the effect of competency (level of knowledge expertise) and interaction style (responsive vs. proactive) on student learning, attitude towards the PAL and self-efficacy in the task. A high-competency PAL was designed to simulate a more competent peer, and was (unsurprisingly) shown to improve the learner's ability to apply knowledge, compared to the low-competency PAL, and that the learners had a more positive attitude towards the higher-competency PAL. The proactive PAL was found to increase ability to recall knowledge imparted by the PAL, compared to the reactive PAL. Perhaps the more revealing finding was that, on close examination of the interactions between the learner and the PAL, the data showed that the number of their requests made by learners was less than half the total number of ideas that the responsive PAL was designed to deliver. Other studies (Dempsey and van Eck , 2003; Gay, 1986) also show that most learners do not use built-in advisor functions in computer-assisted instruction systems and that novices were more reluctant than more experienced learners. These findings would suggest that most learners are unable to realistically self-assess their progress and determine when they need assistance. If this is indeed the case, the elements of learner control need careful consideration in such systems. A further finding showed that learners working with the low-competency PAL had higher self-efficacy beliefs about completing the task than those working with the high-competency PAL. This mirrors classroom-based results which showed that when learners worked with peers who were academically weaker than themselves, their affective characteristics, such as self-esteem, confidence, and sense of responsibility, were significantly enhanced (Cohen et al., 1982).

What can the reflective practitioner learn from pedagogical agents and intelligent learning systems?

This chapter can only provide the briefest of overviews of the developments of pedagogical agents and intelligent tutoring systems. However, I hope that it has provided sufficient insight to show that the research and technology can make significant and positive impacts on student learning. Intelligent tutoring system developers have sought to simulate a particularly effective form of learning, namely the one-on-one human tutoring scenario. In order to develop computer-based tutoring systems, the interaction between student and human tutor, and the pedagogical strategy and moves employed in tutorials have been studied in considerable detail. Tutoring systems are usually developed by multi-disciplinary teams and research to develop student models and effective pedagogical modules has contributed to a more thorough understanding of pedagogy in tutoring.

Black et al., (2006) point out that e-learning and intelligent tutoring systems have largely developed along separate paths, e-learning systems comprising a collection of learning activities supported by web-technologies including conferencing and discussion systems, and rich multimedia content. Such systems are primarily pragmatically developed, without a coherent pedagogical strategy. Feedback in such systems is generally simple and pre-scripted. The systems do not attempt to understand the student input and adapt their output accordingly. There is an implicit student model, representing the progress that a learner has made. E-learning systems have, however, shown very wide applicability and have proved scalable and relatively easy to use for developers. By comparison, intelligent tutoring systems have moved away from the early models of presenting content and 'electronic page-turning' to become much more actively engaged in a student's learning. This requires detailed representation of student knowledge, domain expertise and pedagogy. Thus these systems have been specialised in their application, and are consequently limited in their scalability and application. Many modern developments focus on natural language dialogue, presenting problems for learners to solve, and actively engaging them in the dialogue by using a wide variety of moves; for example, AutoTutor, a web-based intelligent tutoring system that holds dialogues with students in natural language (Graesser et al., 2003). It is currently designed to tutor computer literacy or Newtonian physics. AutoTutor appears as an animated agent that acts as a dialogue partner with the learner. The animated agent uses synthesised speech, intonation, facial expressions and gestures, and also can present graphical displays and animations.

The questions presented by the tutor are designed to elicit explanations, justifications, procedures, elaborations, comparisons and contrasts. Students frequently respond with short answers so AutoTutor gives positive, neutral or negative feedback to the students on their answers, pumping for additional information, prompting the student to fill in missing words, giving hints, correcting misconceptions, answering students' questions and summarising answers. A complete answer is eventually constructed during this dialogue, which typically extends to about 50 conversational turns (Graesser et al., 2003).

Another example is the CIRCSIM-Tutor project, which has developed since the late 1980s, investigating human tutor–student dialogue and incorporating the principles learned to develop and evaluate an intelligent tutoring system, based on dialogue between an expert tutor and a learner. The system has been developed for a very specific domain of qualitative problem-solving for first-year medical students to learn about the reflex control of blood pressure. The tutor presents a series of problems, assuming learners already have relevant knowledge, and it uses a Socratic dialogue, presented textually with a variety of moves to assist the learner to correct mistakes in their reasoning and solution to the problem. Like AutoTutor, natural language dialogue is at the heart of the operation of the system (Evens and Michael, 2006).

AutoTutor, CIRCSIM-Tutor and other tutoring systems have been evaluated systematically to test if they improve the learning of students. These tests are often of small scale and over a short period of time, but researchers report that they do improve learning compared to a classroom situation, and can be more effective than novice human tutors in some circumstances. Studies have also shown that using an ITS can also reduce student time on task.

In a complex domain such as student learning, this kind of quantitative evaluation can never present the whole story, and there are difficulties such as the 'gaming ' behaviour of students with ITS and the problems of effectively processing natural language dialogues. However, it can be argued that the body of research knowledge about these systems is sufficient to show that their light should no longer be hidden under a bushel in a specialised research community. As Kurt VanLehn says:

> *In principle, the dream of having tutoring systems for every student in every course is within our grasp. Although human-computer interaction has limitations, especially in understanding spoken language and visual input, and these limitations restrict the ability of computer tutors to interact with students, even within these limitations, many more tutoring systems could and should exist than do now.*

(VanLehn, 2006, p254)

One of the major barriers to widespread use of ITS is the bespoke nature of the systems and the huge amount of effort required to construct them. Fortunately, there are signs that this may change with the emergence of authoring tools which provide the capability to construct prototypes rapidly (Aleven et al., 2006). The development of animated pedagogical agents as learning companions (PALs) using web technologies also helps to extend the use of intelligent learning systems. This approach is providing opportunities for the development of distributed intelligent learning environments and the possibility of learners working with a number of different PALs simultaneously. The influence of computer gaming and virtual reality (VR) technologies can further extend this approach, for example, Shih et al. (2006) have proposed the use of VR technology to model a 3-D virtual university in which students can work.

I hope that this chapter has helped to raise the profile and awareness of intelligent learning systems in the learning and teaching community and has shown that they can indeed have benefits for student learning in the twenty-first century.

Discussion point

At this point I would encourage you to reflect on your reaction to this chapter. Are you horrified at the prospect of using computers as tutoring systems? Are they so complex to build that you think it is completely impractical? Do pedagogical agents have a role to play in higher education in the twenty-first century? What more would you like to know?

There is an enormous literature on this field, much of which explores specific aspects in detail. If you are interested in finding out more, a particularly good and readable starting point is Evens and Michael (2006). There are also useful websites that draw together resources and provide links to more detailed sources. For example:

http://ctat.pact.cs.cmu.edu/ A website providing free software to help create cognitive tutor authoring tools, the simplest of which can be created without programming knowledge.

www.aaai.org/home.html The American Association for AI, this site includes a wealth of information on all aspects of AI, including intelligent agents.

References

Aleven, V. and Koedinger, K.R. (2000) Limitations of student control: Do students know when they need help?, in G. Gauthier, C. Frasson and K. VanLehn (eds) *Proceedings of the 5th International Conference on Intelligent Tutoring Systems*. pp292–303. Amsterdam: IOS Press.

Aleven, V., Sewall, J., McLaren, B.M. and Koedinger, K.R. (2006) Rapid authoring of intelligent tutors for real-world and experimental use, in Kinshuk, R. Koper, P., Kommers, P. Kirschner, D.G., Sampson and Didderen, W. (eds) *Proceedings of the 6th IEEE International Conference on Advanced Learning Technologies* (ICALT 2006), pp847–851). Los Alamitos, CA: IEEE Computer Society.

Alexander, R.J. (2005) *Culture, dialogue and learning: notes on an emerging pedagogy*, Keynote at International Association for Cognitive Education and Psychology (IACEP) 10th International Conference, University of Durham, UK.

Ally, M. (2005) Intelligent tutoring systems for distributed learning, in Lin, F.S. (ed.) *Designing distributed learning environments with intelligent software agents*. Hershey, PA: Information Science Publishing.

André, E., Rist, T. and Müller, J. (1998) Integrating reactive and scripted behaviors in a life-like presentation agent. *Proceedings of the Second International Conference on Autonomous Agents*, pp261–268, Minneapolis-St.Paul, MN.

Baylor, A.L. (2001) Investigating multiple pedagogical perspectives through MIMIC (Multiple intelligent mentors instructing collaboratively). *Proceedings of Artificial Intelligence in Education* (AI-ED) International Conference, San Antonio, Texas.

Bloom, B.S. (1984) The 2 sigma problem: The search for methods of group instruction as effective as one-to-one tutoring. *Educational Researcher*, 13 (6) 4–16.

Brooks, C., Greer, J., Melis, E. and Ullrich, C. (2006) Combining ITS and elearning technologies: Opportunities and challenges, in M. Ikeda, K. Ashley, and T.-W. Chan (eds): ITS 2006, *Lecture Notes in Computer Science*, 4053, 278–287. Berlin, Heidelberg: Springer-Verlag.

Brown, J.S. and Burton, R.R. (1978) Diagnostic models for procedural bugs in basic mathmatical skills. *Cognitive Science*, 2, 155–192.

Brown, J.S., Burton, R.R. and deKleer, J. (1982) Pedagogical, natural language and knowledge engineering techniques in SOPHIE I, II and III, in D. Sleeman and J.S. Brown (eds) *Intelligent tutoring systems* (pp227–282). New York: Academic Press.

Burton, R.R. (1982) Diagnosing bugs in a simple procedural skill, in D. Sleeman and J.S. Brown (eds) *Intelligent tutoring systems* (pp157–183). New York: Academic Press.

Carr, B. and Goldstein, I. (1977) *Overlays: a theory of modeling for computer-aided instruction*, Technical Report, AI Lab Memo 406, MIT.

Carbonell, J.R. (1970) 'AI in CAI': An artificial intelligence approach to computer-assisted Instruction. *IEEE trans. Man-Machine Systems*, 11 (4), December, 190–202.

Chi, M.T.H., Bassok, M., Lewis, M.W., Reimann, P. and Glaser, R. (1989). Self-explanation: How students study and use examples in learning to solve problems. *Cognitive Science*, 13, 145–182.

Cohen, P.A., Kulik, J.A., and Kulik, C.C. (1982) Educational outcomes of tutoring: A meta-analysis of findings. *American Educational Research Journal*, 19, 237–248.

Collins, A. (1985) Teaching reasoning skills, in S.F. Chipman, J.W. Segal and R. Glaser (eds) Thinking and learning skills (Vol. 2, 579–586). Hillsdale, NJ: Lawrence Erlbaum Associates.

Collins, A. (1988) Different goals of inquiry teaching. *Questioning Exchange*, 2, 39–45.

Collins, A. and Brown, J.S. (1988) The computer as a tool for learning through reflection, in H. Mandl and A. Lesgold (eds) *Learning issues for intelligent tutoring systems* (1–18). New York: Springer-Verlag.

Collins, A., Brown, J.S. and Newman, S.E. (1989) Cognitive apprenticeship: Teaching the craft of reading, writing, and mathematics, in L.B. Resnick (ed.) *Knowing, learning, and instruction: Essays in honor of Robert Glaser* (453–494). Hillsdale, NJ: Lawrence Erlbaum Associates.

Corbett, A. (2001) Cognitive computer tutors: Solving the two-sigma problem. *Lecture Notes in Computer Science*, Volume 2109/2001. Springer Berlin/Heidelberg.

Crowder, N.A. (1960) Automatic teaching by intrinsic programming, in A.A. Lumsdaine and R. Glaser (eds) *Teaching machines and programmed learning: A source book* (286–298). Washington, D.C.: National Education Association of the United States.

Dempsey, J.V. and van Eck, R. (2003) Modality and placement of a pedagogical adviser in individual interactive learning. *British Journal of Educational Technology*, 34 (5), 585–600.

Evens, M. and Michael, J. (2006) *On-on-one tutoring by humans and computers*. Hillsdale, NJ: Lawrence Erlbaum Associates.

Fantuzzo, J.W., King, J.A. and Heller, L.R. (1992) Effects of reciprocal peer tutoring on mathematics and school adjustment: A component analysis. *Journal of Educational Psychology*, 84, 331–339.

Fox, B. (1993) *The human tutorial dialogue project*. Hillsdale, NJ: Lawrence Erlbaum and Associates.

Freedman, R. (2000) What is an intelligent tutoring system?. *Intelligence*, 11 (3), 15–16.

Gay, G. (1986) Interaction of learner control and prior understanding in computer assisted video instruction. *Journal of Educational Psychology*, 78 (3), 225–227.

Graesser, A.C. (1993) Dialogue patterns and feedback mechanisms during naturalistic tutoring, in M. Polson (ed) *Proceedings of fifteenth annual meeting of the cognitive science society* (pp127–130). Mahwah, NJ: Lawrence Erlbaum Associates.

Graesser, A.C., Person, N.K. and Huber, J. (1993) Question asking during tutoring and the design of educational software, in M. Rabinowitz (ed.) *Cognitive science foundations of instruction* (pp149–172). Hillsdale, NJ: Lawrence Erlbaum Associates.

Graesser, A.C., Person, N.K. and Huber, J.P. (1993) Collaborative dialogue patterns in naturalistic one-to-one tutoring. *Applied Cognitive Psychology*, 9, 1–28.

Graesser, A.C., Moreno, K., Marineau, J., Adcock, A., Olney, A. and Person, N. (2003) AutoTutor improves deep learning of computer literacy: Is it the dialog or the talking head?, in U. Hoppe, F. Verdejo and J. Kay (eds), *Proceedings of Artificial Intelligence in Education* (pp47–54). Amsterdam: IOS Press.

Johnson, W.L., Rickel, J.W. and Lester, J.C. (2000) Animated pedagogical agents: Face-to-face interaction in interactive learning environments. *International Journal of Artificial Intelligence in Education*, 11, 47–78.

Kim, Y. and Baylor, A.L. (2006) Pedagogical agents as learning companions: The role of agent competency and type of interaction. *Educational Technology Research and Development*, 54, 3, 223–243.

Koedinger, K.R. and Anderson, J.R. (1997) Intelligent tutoring goes to school in the big city. *International Journal of Artificial Intelligence in Education*, 8, 30–43.

Lin, F.S. (2005) *Designing distributed learning environments with intelligent software agents*. Hershey, PA: Information Science Publishing.

Moreno, R., Mayer, R.E., Spires, H.A. and Lester, J.C. (2001) The case for social agency in computer-based teaching: Do students learn more deeply when they interact with animated pedagogical agents?. *Cognition and Instruction*, 19 (2), 177–213.

O'Shea, T., Bornet, R., du Boulay, B., Eisenstad, M. and Page, J. (1984) Tools for creating intelligent computer tutors, in Elithorn, A. and Banjerjii, R. (eds) *Human and artificial intelligence*. Amsterdam: North Holland.

Otsuki, S.(1992) Discovery learning in intelligent tutoring systems. *Lecture Notes In Computer Science*; Vol. 743 Proceedings of the Third Workshop on Algorithmic Learning Theory, pp3–12.

Person, N.K., Graesser, A.C., Bautista, L., Mathews, E.C. and the Tutoring Research Group (2001) Evaluating student learning gains in two versions of AutoTutor, in J.D. Moore, C.L. Redfield and W. L. Johnson (eds) *Artificial intelligence in education: AI-ED in the wired and wireless future* (pp286–293). Amsterdam: IOS Press.

Ravenscroft, A. (2001) Designing e-learning interactions in the 21st century: revisiting and rethinking the role of theory. *European Journal of Education*, 36 (2), 133–156.

Shih, T.K., Wang, Y. and Chen Y. (2006) A VR-based virtual agent system, in F.O. Lin (Ed.) *Designing distributed learning environments with intelligent software agents*. Hershey, PA: Information Science Publishing.

Sleeman, D. and Brown, J.S. (1982) Introduction: Intelligent tutoring systems, in D. Sleeman and J.S. Brown (eds) *Intelligent tutoring systems* (pp1–11). New York: Academic Press.

Turing, A.M. (1950) Computing machinery and intelligence. *Mind*, 59, 433–460.

Uhr, L. (1969) Teaching machine programs that generate problems as a function of interaction with students. *Proceedings of the 24th National Conference*, pp125–134.

Urban-Lurain, M. (1996) *Intelligent tutoring systems: An historic review in the context of the development of artificial intelligence and educational psychology*. (Available online at **www.cse.msu.edu/rgroups/ cse101/ITS/its.htm**, accessed 25 January 2007).

VanLehn, K. (2006) The Behavior of Tutoring Systems. *IJAIED*, 16 (3).

Wenger, E. (1987) *Artificial intelligence and tutoring systems: Computational and cognitive approaches to the communication of knowledge*. Los Altos, CA: Morgan Kaufmann.

Chapter 9

Using assessment to promote quality learning in higher education

Lin Norton

Introduction

Assessment and giving feedback to learners is one of the six specified areas of activity, core knowledge and professional values articulated in the UK Professional Standards Framework for teaching and supporting learning in higher education. Such recognition of the centrality of assessment to the learning process means that all who teach and facilitate student learning need to reflect critically on assessment practices in higher education. Paradoxically, in the National Survey of Student Satisfaction assessment and feedback is also one of the key areas that scores less well right across the higher education sector, and in most disciplines with one or two notable exceptions. Something is clearly amiss.

Meeting the Standards

This chapter will meet the UK Professional Standards Framework in the following ways:

- **by developing practice assessment and in giving feedback to learners;**
- **by developing effective environments and student support and guidance (Areas of activity 3 and 4);**
- **by using models for evaluating the effectiveness of teaching (Core knowledge 5);**
- **by demonstrating a commitment to learning communities;**
- **by enhancing continuing professional development and evaluation of practice.**

(www.heacademy.ac.uk/professionalstandards.htm)

In this chapter, I intend to explore this situation in today's context where many students are strategic and define the curriculum by what is assessed rather than by what is taught. I will argue that if universities are driven down the path of just pleasing the student, through market forces, league tables and an increasingly competitive global market, then the concept of quality learning is under serious threat. Drawing on some of my own practice and research over the past 15 years, I hope that readers will be encouraged to look at their own assessment practices with a fresh eye by exploring what can be done in a practical and pragmatic sense. In so doing, my aim is to encourage a reflective approach to assessment and feedback practice, based on an identification of personally held professional values together with a basic understanding of how university students learn.

The chapter is structured in two main sections: 'Assessment and its effect on student learning' and 'Assessment criteria and feedback'. In each section, I begin by posing some questions to you as the reader, followed by a brief theoretical overview, and then illustrate my own experience and reflections through a case study. The chapter ends with some final thoughts on how espoused theory or what we believe in, as first propounded by Argyris and Schön (1974), does not always translate into what we can actually do in our assessment practices and what we might do about it.

Assessment and its effect on quality learning

Assessment in higher education is a difficult area to write about as everyone has a view and many assumptions are commonly expressed such as 'assessment drives the learning', 'students are more strategic and marks-orientated than they were'. Interestingly, though, assessment is sometimes the last thing that we think about when designing our courses. We tend to think about the curriculum and what should be covered and only when that has been determined do we turn our attention to how we might assess what our students have learned. If we accept the principles of constructive alignment expounded by Biggs (2003), then we should start curriculum design with the question of 'What is it that I want my students to have learned by the end of this course, module, or programme?' (frequently referred to as the learning outcome). The concomitant question is 'How will I know that they have learned it?' Thinking about these two basic questions gives us a simple framework with which to design our assessment tasks and might help us to avoid potential problems with assessment's not doing what we wanted it to do. An example might be the innovative tutor who wants to incorporate online assessment in her course but finds that, because computers are good at delivering multiple-choice tests, her assessment task encourages surface and rote learning rather than a critically analytical approach. (Of course, this is a somewhat simplified and stereotyped view of the potentials of computer-aided assessment, but I am using it to make a point. For a full and helpful discussion of the potentials, I would recommend you to read Bull and McKenna (2003)). Thinking at a deeper level about these questions also gives us the opportunity to reflect on our own assessment practice, which is the underlying theme of my chapter. Before expanding on some of these ideas, I would ask you to pause for a moment and consider the following questions.

Discussion point

1. What do you mean by quality learning?
2. Is it about:
    a. providing a transformational experience?
    b. understanding the subject?
    c. demonstrating your knowledge/mastery of a specific subject?
    d. learning how to learn (sometimes called lifelong learning, sometimes called meta-learning)?
    e. thinking about the world, yourself and the discipline in a different way?
    f. having an easy and pleasurable experience?
    g. performing well and achieving high grades?
    h. acquiring skills that will aid employability?

These questions are not mutually exclusive, nor do they incorporate everything, but they do give us a flavour of how we define this commonly used term of 'quality learning' and what it personally means to us. Articulating this goes some way to expressing our values and our pedagogical beliefs (espoused theory) in a way that will determine how we view assessment.

Theoretical background

A systemic approach to assessment

Everyone who writes about higher education is influenced by a set of values and beliefs about teaching and learning so, from the outset, I want to state my own influences. I am convinced that the most useful way of thinking about learning is to think of it in terms of a system rather than taking a deficit model approach. This has been eloquently explained by Biggs (1994, 2003). What he meant by a deficit approach was that if we feel that students are not learning as well as we would hope, then we may blame the students (e.g. they are not motivated enough; they come from a widening participation background; they have to work); or we might blame ourselves as teachers (we did not explain the concept sufficiently; the learning objectives were not clearer). Both these models are based on a deficit view of learning: there is something going wrong so we need to find someone or something to blame. The systemic model of learning argues instead that what students learn and how teachers teach is part of a system, which is itself constrained by the subject discipline, the institution and ultimately by the government agenda. The point about a system is that if you change one part of it, everything else must also change, otherwise it will not work. To illustrate this, I will take a simple example: I want to change the assessment criteria for essays in a course I am teaching in third-year psychology to include a criterion in which I specify that, in order to pass, students must show evidence of having critically analysed relevant research. This is a perfectly valid and reasonable pedagogical aim. Suppose then, that 90 per cent of the class write creditable essays but have not complied with this essential criterion. I should fail their essays, but to do so would raise questions at the subject, and at an institutional, level where we could not be seen to be failing large numbers of students. Put very simply, on my own, I cannot change a norm-based marking system to a criterion-based marking system, even though my pedagogical reasons are sound. One small change in an individual module means that bigger changes have to be made in the assessment of the subject and may ultimately affect degree classification.

Taken at face value, the systemic model of learning might seem stifling and without the opportunities for change, indeed there are principles of being at an unadaptable institution (Bransford, 2006) where because of processes put in place to safeguard quality, to make even the most minor of changes to assessment practice takes an inordinately long time. In a recent study carried out with new lecturers, this was expressed as a common frustration (Norton et al., under review). However, the reality of the current context in higher education is that everything must be scrutinised, accounted for and documented in a paper trail. Given this situation, our recognition that assessment is part of that bigger context means we cannot be readily satisfied by simple, straightforward answers to assessment problems. By appreciating the complexity, we can work to improve our assessment practices to improve the learning experience but not to provide a failsafe method.

Approaches to learning

Today it is generally accepted that assessment is at the heart of the learning process (Boud, 1990; Brown *et al.*, 1997; Gibbs and Simpson, 2004; Ramsden, 2003) but what research has also shown is that how we assess our students is one of the most powerful influences on what approach to learning they will take. By approach to learning I mean whether they take a deep or a surface approach (Marton and Saljo, 1976). Many traditional types of exams encourage a surface approach where the intention is to memorise and regurgitate – this is passive learning (Elton and Johnston, 2002; Scouller, 1998). Assignments such as problem-based ones are argued to encourage a deep approach where the intention is to make sense of the subject in terms of your own understanding and your own prior knowledge – very much an active, transformative and constructivist approach to learning (see Chapter 4 by Tessa Owens for a full discussion of problem-based learning). Much effort in recent years has gone into designing assessment tasks that reward a deep rather than a surface approach and creating innovative and authentic types of assessment. But the paradox is that assessment can so often do the opposite of what we intend it to do – it encourages strategic learning, competitiveness, and students to focus on those things that are assessed at the expense of those that are not. But no matter how fair, reliable, consistent and just the system is, it will not help learning if students themselves have rather different perceptions. There is quite a body of research to suggest that they do, such as our own research on 'rules of the game' which are tactics that students adopt in their essay because they believe that it will get them higher marks (Norton et al., 1996a, b). Since the main purposes of assessment are still conceptualised by most lecturers to certify and to grade students (Samuelowicz and Bain, 2002), it is not surprising that students tend to use assessment criteria in a strategic, marks-orientated approach, nor is it surprising that plagiarism and cheating behaviours are such a common occurrence (Norton *et al.*, 2001). This is what is meant by taking a systemic view of assessment where problems and solutions cannot be thought of in isolation without looking at the broader impact and consequences.

Case study

Psychology Applied Learning Scenarios (PALS)

This case study is an account of how I have tried in my own practice to address the problem of setting an assessment task which is authentic and discourages students from taking a strategic, marks-orientated approach.

Counselling psychology was a third-year module that I taught for many years and which underwent several iterations. At first it was a single module which combined the theoretical and the applied and then it was subdivided into two modules where I became responsible for the theoretical module which was designed to help students to understand the contribution that psychological theory and research have to the discipline of counselling. Students were told from the outset that this was not a module that led to a counselling qualification but what I did hope they would gain from it was a robust and rigorous approach to some of the so-called counselling approaches that continue to be offered to vulnerable people without regulation. Third-year psychology students in our university have been through two years of quite intensive research methods training in their psychology course, so my assumption was that students would apply their research methodological skills to evaluating research which underpinned some of the theoretical claims of counselling. This turned out to be a somewhat misguided assumption and is one of the reasons why, to this day, I still question our widely held belief that skills are transferable.

In order to offer a module that provided a high-quality learning experience, I was unashamedly seeking to equip my students with the wherewithal to challenge what I see as a sometimes corrupt practice. I also wanted to equip them with the power of knowledge so that if they, or their loved ones, ever needed counselling they would know the criteria with which to judge what was being offered. This was my transformational aim. In addition, in the context of the discipline of psychology, I wanted them to have confidence in their research understanding to be able to weigh up the evidence and come to an informed decision as to whether or not it was convincing. I was told by an external examiner at one point that this was too lofty an aim for third-year undergraduates but, nevertheless, I forged ahead because I believed that you can get the best out of students if you set high goals. The full account of how I devised and used vignettes, which I called Psychology Applied Learning Scenarios, is fully described in a tutor pack available from the HEA Psychology Subject Network resources (see Norton, 2002). Briefly, these were text-based hypothetical cases which I designed in order to give my students the opportunity to apply their theoretical understandings of different psychological theories to a range of counselling cases. These were designed in order to represent situations which professional counselling psychologists typically face.

...courses which are applied in nature such as this one raise real ethical dilemmas; the students are not being trained as counsellors and therefore cannot be allowed to try out their understandings on other people. The same principle applies to 'counselling' each other. All too often, students who have unresolved issues tend to be attracted to this type of course, so letting them loose on each other is equally unethical. For all these reasons, using hypothetical case studies or scenarios works well.

(Norton, 2004, p690)

Case study continued

Given the use of PALS in my course, I used them as the pivotal method of assessment. There was no examination in my courses and coursework consisted of:

- a team presentation of a PALS case, counting for 30 per cent of the overall module marks (made up of a mark for an individual research critique and a mark for the team presentation);

- a 3000-word essay exploring a PALS case in greater depth, counting for 70 per cent of the overall module marks.

In this way the assessment formed the formative and summative part of the course. In the course, I used the assessment task to drive the whole learning experience. This was a gradual process of curriculum development over several years, the culmination of which is reported in Norton (2004) where I put not only the PALS but the whole assessment task at the centre of the learning experience by using the assessment criteria as learning criteria. To explain, the team presentation was foregrounded by an individual research critique where the assessment criteria stressed the use of up-to-date journals, critically evaluated in terms of the research methods used and appropriateness to the students' selected PALS case. This was then reinforced in the team presentation where the students shared their resources from the critique assignment, and this in turn gave them the opportunity to get further feedback and guidance from me in a way that would help them with their essay. Of course, such initiatives are of little use unless they have the desired effect of improving student learning, and I was able to demonstrate through my analysis of the feedback that I gave students on their essays that there was qualitative evidence of a more sophisticated application of theory to practical case study. Nothing is ever an endpoint, though, and in my paper I highlighted the fact that using PALS in this way is a complex process that challenges able students but might possibly overstretch the less able ones.

Assessment criteria and feedback

My second big question in this chapter is: 'What part do assessment criteria and feedback play in improving student learning?' There has been considerable emphasis in the sector on making assessment fair and transparent. The Quality Assurance Agency for Higher Education in their revised code of practice for the assessment of students say: *Principle 7 Marking and grading: Institutions have transparent and fair mechanisms for marking and moderating marks* (QAA, 2006). Yet how do we practically ensure this deceptively simple precept applies to our own marking practices? Presumably we need to make sure that the assessment tasks are clear and that the assessment criteria are transparent, for that is how students realise what we require and what they are aiming at. Again, I would like to pose a few questions before looking at some of the theoretical issues.

Discussion point

1. How do your students know what they are supposed to do in assignments?

2. Do fellow lecturers in your subject all mark similarly?

3. Do lecturers share the same understandings of assessment criteria as:

   a. their students?

   b. their fellow lecturers in the same subject? (If, for example, I were to ask you to define 'critical evaluation', would your answer be the same as that of your colleagues?)

4. Is your written feedback generally consistent with the assessment criteria?

5. Do your students understand your feedback?

6. How do you know?

Theoretical background

General principles of feedback

It is a general learning principle that feedback improves performance (Gilbert, 1978), indeed the whole world of coaching in sports and all other fields of human performance activity, be it operatic singing or learning to drive a car, revolves round this simple principle, which owes much to Skinner's theory of operant conditioning which, put simply, is the theory of learning by consequences (Skinner, 1938). Underlying this basic premise lies a host of caveats. One of these is that the feedback needs to be swift, as soon after the performed behaviour as possible – think of improving a golf swing: the golfer will learn more if the coach is there with her rather than if she has to wait to see a video of her swing, or even more distantly read about golf swings a week later. To be effective, feedback also needs to be incremental, targeted at distinct areas where the learner needs to improve – in the golf swing, work might first need to be done on how the learner holds the golf club. It should be constructively critical – telling your nascent golfer that her swing is terrible does not motivate her to want to improve. All these aspects of effective feedback seem perfectly obvious, so why in higher education do we give feedback to students usually at the end of a module and sometimes as much as more than four weeks later? By then there is no reason for the student to bother with our comments at all, as they have moved onto another module or, even if not, the gap is too long, and they have gone 'off the boil' and no longer care about their work and performance in the same passionate way they do when they hand in a piece of work. Why do we, in our feedback on an essay, make general comments such as 'Good effort, but you need to write more academically'? What is the student to make of this? What do we mean by 'academically'? Do we mean avoid slang, use long words or present in a format that is appropriate to the discipline? The feedback simply does not indicate how the student is to improve. Are we always sure that we write constructive criticism when giving feedback? I would be surprised if I were alone in having sometimes seen harsh and offensive comments on students' work, such as 'rubbish' and 'drivel'. As well as falling foul of being non-targeted feedback, such comments are damaging to students' often quite fragile feelings of competence and confidence.

Research on student understandings of assessment criteria

The role of assessment criteria in helping university students improve their writing has been extensively researched in a consortium project called *Assessment Plus: Using assessment criteria to support student learning* (**www.assessmentplus.net**) funded by the Higher Education Funding Council for England. Part of this research consisted of an interview study which showed that tutors generally believe that students do not understand the assessment criteria, particularly in their first year (Norton et al., 2004). Our findings confirmed those of other studies which have shown that students have difficulty with understanding assessment criteria (see, for example, Elander, 2002; Merr et al., 1998, 2000). This might suggest a lack of effort on the students' part, given the emphasis that most tutors put into making assessment criteria explicit, but this does not appear to be the case. Some of our further research using student focus groups and one-to-one interviews showed that students made significant efforts to seek feedback and to actively understand what their tutors were looking for when marking their work (Harrington et al., 2006). There has been a body of valuable work carried out by Price et al., which suggests that students need to explicitly work with assessment criteria in order to fully understand them, and this can be done in a number of different ways (see, for example, O'Donovan et al., 2001; Price et al., 2003). For readers who are interested, there is a series of workshops with many suggestions for practical exercises available from the Assessment Plus website which can be adapted for your own students' needs. The effectiveness of these workshops is reported in Norton et al. (2005). Another way of helping to make criteria more accessible is to ask students to mark their own or fellow students' essays using your given criteria. There has been a great deal of discussion about the pros and cons of self- and peer assessment (see Dohy et al., 1999, for a review), but one of the key benefits is that it does help students understand the marking process. Perhaps though, one of the easiest ways of helping students is to give feedback which is directly and explicitly related to each of the assessment criteria. One way of doing this is suggested in the following case study.

Case study

The Essay Feedback Checklist (EFC)

The search for a way of helping students better understand my feedback has resulted in a series of action research studies which ultimately culminated in the design and use of a very simple tool called the Essay Feedback Checklist (Norton and Norton, 2001a, b; Norton et al., 2002; Norton et al., 2002). A version of this tool is presented at the end of this chapter and readers are invited to adapt this to use with their own students.

The principles of the tool are very straightforward in that the assessment criteria are listed and students are asked to use the checklist while they are preparing for and writing their essays, so as to have a constant reminder of what the demands of the task are. They are also asked to check their final draft against each of the criteria before submitting it to make sure they have not forgotten an important criterion, such as referencing, for example. Finally, they are asked to rate their own essays for each of the listed criteria using a three-category response system:

C = I feel completely confident that I have met this criterion.

P = I feel partially confident that I have met this criterion.

N = I feel not at all confident that I have met this criterion and would appreciate some advice.

Students are then requested to attach the completed EFC to the back of their essay and they are assured that the tutor will not look at the EFC until after s/he has marked their essay, when s/he will look at the EFC and put her/his own ratings underneath that of the student using the same three-category response system. The idea of this is that where there is a mismatch between a student's and a tutor's rating, there is a particular need for the tutor to target her/his feedback. In our research studies the EFC was found to be popular with students and they thought that it did enhance the feedback they were given, though some students thought that even more guidance and clarification should be given. This was a finding that was echoed in our later work with assessment criteria workshops where some students wanted more guidance and more advice than was given in the workshops. Again, there is never an endpoint when improving one's own assessment practice, and the EFC is a tool which could be further adapted and modified to take note of students' suggestions for more detailed guidance. But this is a point on which I reflect in my last section of this chapter.

Espoused theory and theory in use: some final thoughts

Ever since reading about the difference first put forward by Argyris and Schön (1974) in espoused theory (the mental model which people will say they hold if asked to explain or justify a given pattern of activity) and theory in use (the mental model that is implicit in the performance of that pattern of activity), I have been intrigued by the differences between what we think we believe in and what we actually do as lecturers in higher education. In assessment, I believe that assessment and feedback should be about encouraging independent learning (my espoused pedagogical theory) and yet I find myself striving to make my assessment criteria more transparent in the hope that this will enable my students to engage with the learning task (my theory in use). However, the action research studies I mentioned previously have led me to worry about this having the unintended and paradoxical effect of making students more, rather than less, dependent on me. For example, they ask me questions such as '*How many journal papers should I include in my essay?*' and '*Am I allowed to use bullet points in the essay?*' (Norton, 2004). Such a concern with squeezing out of me every last detail is counter to what I am hoping to achieve in attempting to give my students a better understanding of the assessment criteria. This is to set them free to explore the learning task that the essay assignment sets them. More and more I worry that the assessment and my explication of the assessment criteria take them away from the learning task. So what might be going on here? I am not suggesting abandoning the principle of making assessment criteria clear, but perhaps at some deep level, my espoused theory is at odds with my theory in use. Perhaps what I really want my students to do is to do what I tell them, so I emphasise what is important to me rather than setting them free to express and answer in the way that is important to them.

There are, of course, no easy answers to this particular conundrum, but thinking at this level about assessment and learning is how I perceive the role of the reflective practitioner. I hope that this chapter will help you to think about your own assessment practice and to use such reflection not only to adapt and develop strategies to support your students, but actively to question the establishment and your institutional policy around assessment. This, I think, is the only way we can move towards a system of assessment that genuinely does promote quality learning.

The Essay Feedback Checklist (EFC)

This checklist is designed to help you with your essay writing in THREE WAYS:

1. By making sure you have taken account of all the assessment criteria BEFORE you hand in your essay; it also helps while you are writing the essay by reminding you of the important elements.
2. By signalling which areas you would like me to concentrate on when giving you feedback.
3. By giving you more practice at self-assessment.

I will not look at this checklist until AFTER the essay has been marked, so for you to get the most benefit from it, I want you to be completely honest so I can give you the feedback you need. I do this by giving you my tutor rating under your own rating. Where there are differences between your rating and mine, I will give feedback that is more detailed. This will explain why I think you have done either better or not as well as you yourself think you have done.

Before you hand in your essay, please give a rating of how confident you feel about having met each of the assessment criteria:

C = Confident – I think I have met this criterion to the best of my ability.

P = Partially confident – I have tried to meet this criterion but would appreciate more feedback.

N = Not at all confident – I do not understand this criterion and need more guidance.

	C	P	N
Shown knowledge and understanding of theoretical approaches to the case study?			
tutor feedback			
Organised the essay clearly with a structure that supports a considered conclusion?			
tutor feedback			
Referenced according to psychology requirements (i.e. the Harvard system)?			
tutor feedback			
Presented your essay in an acceptable academic style (including grammar and spelling)?			
tutor feedback			

Addressed the question throughout the essay?

tutor feedback

Put forward a reasoned argument which shows evaluation and analysis?

tutor feedback

Are there any other feedback comments you would like me to make about your essay? …

References

Argyris, C. and Schön, D. (1974) *Theory in practice: Increasing professional effectiveness*. San Francisco, CA: Jossey Bass.

Biggs, J. (1994) Student learning research and theory – where do we currently stand? Available at **www.city.londonmet.ac.uk/deliberations/ocsd-pubs/isltp-biggs.html** (accessed 14 January 2007).

Biggs, J. (2003) Aligning teaching and assessing to course objectives, Teaching and learning in Higher Education: New trends and innovations, University of Aveiro, 13–17 April 2003. Available at **http://event.ua.pt/iched/main/invcom/p182.pdf#search='at%20http%3A%2F%2Feven t.ua.pt%2Fiched%2Fmain%2Finvcom%2Fp182.pdf'** (accessed 14 January 2007).

Boud, D. (1990) Assessment and the promotion of academic values. *Studies in Higher Education*, 15 (1), 101–111.

Bransford, J. (2006) Emerging views of expertise, transfer and assessment impication for guiding our collective scholarship on teaching and learning. Keynote paper at the 3rd conference of the International Society for the Scholarship of Teaching and Learning (ISSOTL), Washington DC, 9–12 November 2006.

Brown, G., Bull, J. and Pendlebury, M. (1997) *Assessing student learning in higher education*. London: Routledge.

Bull, J. and McKenna, C. (2003) *A blueprint for computer-assisted assessment*. London: Routledge.

Dohy, F., Segers, M. and Sluijsmans, D. (1999) The use of self, peer and co-assessment in higher education: a review. *Studies in Higher Education*, 24 (3), 331–350.

Elander, J. (2002) Developing aspect-specific assessment criteria for essays and examination answers in psychology. *Psychology Teaching Review*, 10, 31–51.

Elton, L. and Johnston, B. (2002) Assessment in universities: a critical review of research. LTSN Generic Centre January 2002. Available at **www.heacademy.ac.uk/resources.asp?process= full_record&section=generic&id=13** (accessed 14 January 2007).

Gibbs, G. and Simpson, C. (2004) Conditions under which assessment supports student learning, *Learning and Teaching in Higher Education* 1, 3–29. Available at **www.glos.ac.uk/shareddata/ dms/2B70988BBCD42A03949CB4F3CB78A516.pdf** (accessed 14 January 2007).

Gilbert, T.F. (1978) *Human competence*. New York: McGraw-Hill.

Harrington, K., Elander, J., Lusher, J., Norton, L., Aiyegbayo, O., Pitt, E., Robinson, H. and Reddy, P. (2006) Using core assessment criteria to improve essay writing, in Bryan, C. and Clegg, K. (eds) (2006) *Innovative assessment in higher education*. London: Routledge.

Marton, F. and Saljo, R. (1976) On qualitative differences in learning: 1. Outcome and process. *British Journal of Educational Psychology*, 46, 4–11.

Merry, S., Orsmond, P. and Reiling, K. (1998) Biology students' and tutors' understanding of 'a good essay', in C. Rust (ed.) *Improving student learning. Improving students as learners*. Oxford: The Oxford Centre for Staff and Learning Development.

Merry, S., Orsmond, P. and Reiling, K. (2000) Biological essays: how do students use feedback?, in C. Rust (ed.) *Improving student learning. Improving student learning through the disciplines*. Oxford: The Oxford Centre for Staff and Learning Development.

Norton, L. (2002) PALS: A practical introduction to problem-based learning using vignettes for psychology lecturers. Available at **www.psychology.heacademy.ac.uk/docs/pdf/p20040422_ pals.pdf** (accessed 14 January 2007).

Norton, L., Aiyegbayo, O., Harrington, K., Elander, J. and Reddy, P. (paper under review) Becoming a university teacher: Factors that influence new lecturers' beliefs about learning and teaching.

Norton, L.S., Dickins, T.E. and McLaughlin Cook, A.N. (1996a) Rules of the Game in essay writing. *Psychology Teaching Review*, 5 (1), 1–14.

Norton, L.S., Dickins, T.E. and McLaughlin Cook, N. (1996b) Coursework assessment: What are tutors really looking for?, in G. Gibbs (ed.) (1996) *Improving student learning. Using research to improve student learning*. Oxford: The Oxford Centre for Staff Development.

Norton, L., Clifford, R., Hopkins, L., Toner, I. and Norton, J.C.W. (2002a) Helping psychology students write better essays. *Psychology Learning and Teaching*, 2 (2), 116–126.

Norton, L.S., Hopkins, L., Toner, I. Clifford, R. and Norton, J.C.W. (2002b) The essay feedback checklist: helping psychology students to write better essays and tutors to give better feedback. Paper presented at the Psychology Learning and Teaching Conference (PLAT 2002), University of York, 18–20 March 2002.

Norton, L., Harrington, K., Elander, J., Sinfield, S., Lusher, J., Reddy, P., Aiyegbayo, O. and Pitt, E. (2005) Supporting students to improve their essay writing through assessment criteria focused workshops, in C. Rust (ed.) *Improving Student Learning 12*. Oxford: Oxford Centre for Staff and Learning Development.

Norton, L.S. and Norton, J.C.W. (2001a) The essay feedback checklist: How can it help students improve their academic writing? Paper and workshop given at the first international conference of the European Association for the Teaching of Academic Writing across Europe (EATAW), Groningen, The Netherlands, 18–20 June 2001.

Norton, L.S. and Norton, J.C.W. (2001b) Essay feedback: How can it help students improve their academic writing? ERIC abstract No ED454530.

Norton, L.S., Tilley, A.J., Newstead, S.E. and Franklyn-Stokes, A. (2001) The pressures of assessment in undergraduate courses and their effect on student behaviours. *Assessment and Evaluation in Higher Education*, 26 (3), 269–284.

Norton, L.S., Ward-Robinson, H., Reddy, P., Elander, J. and Harrington, K. (2004) Exploring psychology lecturers' view on assessment criteria. Paper presented at the Psychology Learning and Teaching Conference (PLAT 2004), University of Strathclyde, 5–7 April 2004.

O'Donovan, B., Price, M. and Rust, C. (2001) The student experience of criterion-referenced assessment through the use of a common criteria assessment grid. *Innovations on Learning and Teaching International*, 38 (1), 74–85.

Price, M., Rust, C. and O'Donovan, B. (2003) Improving students' learning by developing their understanding of assessment criteria and processes. *Assessment and Evaluation in Higher Education*, 28, 147–164.

QAA (2006) The Quality Assurance Agency for Higher Education. Code of practice for the assurance of academic quality and standards in higher education. Section 6. Assessment of students (2nd edition). Available at **www.qaa.ac.uk/academicinfrastructure/codeOfPractice/section6/COP_AOS.pdf** (accessed 14 January 2007).

Ramsden, P. (2003) *Learning to teach in higher education* (2nd edition). London: Routledge.

Samuelowicz, K. and Bain, J.D. (2002) Identifying academics' orientation to assessment practice, *Higher Education*, 43, 173–201.

Scouller, K.M. (1998) The influence of assessment method on student's learning approaches: multiple choice question examination versus assignment essay. *Higher Education*, 35, 453–472.

Skinner, B.F. (1938) *The behavior of organisms*. New York: Appleton-Century-Crofts.

Chapter *10*

Formative assessment of the practice-based element of degree work

Deirdre Hewitt and Deborah Smith

Introduction

Anything can be an experience but anything need not be a learning experience.

(Elmer, 2002, p249)

Nowadays, it is quite usual for degree pathways to contain some sort of work placement. It can be a way for 'real-life' experienced practitioners to pass on their knowledge which they have gained through their own working practice. It can also be a way of facilitating staff development in the workplace as individuals take on the role of mentor or coach to the incoming student. During work placements, students require high-quality mentoring to encourage them to gain the most from the experience. The employer, student, and university staff are all stakeholders in the work experience, seeking to develop the student's skills and knowledge by providing a valuable learning experience. It is our belief that, as professionals, we should be integrating formative assessment into this process for the maximum learning to be achieved in this context.

Meeting the Standards

The UK Professional Standards Framework for teaching and supporting learning in Higher Education highlights this *understanding of the student learning experience and the ability to promote student learning in all areas of activity ... through mentoring* as being a requirement of the educator within higher education (Standards 2 and 3). On examining the areas of activity, core knowledge, and professional values within the Framework, a common thread around effective assessment can be seen. In brief, it is expected that the higher education lecturer will be involved in the areas of activity expanded on below.

- **Supporting student learning (activity 2).**
- **Assessment and giving feedback to learners (activity 3).**
- **Developing effective environments and student support and guidance. (activity 4).**
- **Promoting a core knowledge base that includes, understanding how students learn, both generally and in the subject (core knowledge 3).**
- **Enabling students to demonstrate respect for individual learners (core knowledge 1).**

This chapter will explore how successful work placements should involve an element of formative assessment and how all stakeholders can be involved in this process. Good practice will be highlighted from our own field of teacher education and the issues and relevant transferable skills, principles and/practices discussed. The idea that it is possible to offer some generalisations of good workplace practice, with reference to the place of formative assessment, will be put forward. Specific reference will be made to both the tutor and student experiences of formative assessments within the work placement. Their views on the value of formative assessments will be highlighted and analysed with reference to empirical research as appropriate.

As our understanding of how we learn changes, so too must our practices. The key historical difference lies in the essence of a passive view of learning as opposed to a more modern, constructivist approach. There must be active student involvement in their learning, but there are two questions: 'How?' and 'Is there enough going on?' The answer to the latter question seems to be negative. The current view sees the learner as an active constructivist based on particular experiences as a student (Biggs, 1999). In order for this to happen, the student must be given the opportunity to analyse her/his learning. But it is what is done with the analysis that becomes the important feature. If a student is to construct learning which is positive and enables a degree of development, then there must be conversation and quality feedback.

> ## Discussion point |
>
> Consider for a moment your understanding of 'quality feedback'.
>
> Does formative assessment simply mean criticism from a more experienced person within the workplace? If this is the case, then researchers such as Elmer (2002) would argue that this is not true formative assessment. We would agree, but realise that, unfortunately, it is the experience of some students.

To begin the discussion it is worth considering the value of the practice-based element of degree work. If no value to the learner were to be found or demonstrated, then there would be no need for it to be included, especially since what is required is an expensive investment in terms of financial, personal and professional commitment of time and effort on the part of all stakeholders. The National Committee of Inquiry into Higher Education (NCIHE) suggested that all undergraduates should be able to access work experience placements, recognising its value to the learner (NCIHE, 1997). Others would argue that work placements are invaluable as they provide the student with a real experience of their future career. It can be an opportunity for individuals to try out their suitability for their chosen career within a supportive environment. Purcell et al. (1999) reported that of the graduates they studied, up to 48 per cent identified their work experience as being a contributory factor in obtaining employment. This factor can also be seen to feature in the study by Little and Harvey (2006), as outlined below.

The value of work placements was recently researched by Little and Harvey (2006), who identified that work experience was supposed to cover a range of skills, which included problem-solving, organisational skills, creativity, personal and social skills as well as communication skills. What Little and Harvey discovered was that work experience did not cover all the above skills, which would virtually be impossible, as any one placement is so different from any other. Instead, according to the students, a much more holistic experience was gained. Nevertheless, it is acknowledged by employers that students do in fact develop certain skills, and it is this very fact which makes these particular students more sought after by employers (Bowes and Harvey, 1999; Mason et al., 2003). But what has received little attention is the transfer of learning between the placement and the university course. Little and Harvey's research involved an exploration of this transfer of learning. Many of the students interviewed stated that their work experience deepened their focus on the achievement of a good degree in order to secure employment. For a number of students their assessment of the work placement was the added experience they gained, hence once again increasing their employability. Furthermore, the students on the whole were able to formulate their learning and link it with their course work. Among their beliefs were that their work experience had allowed them to appreciate the links between theory and practice, while other students had an increased confidence, allowing them to question what university lecturers were telling them. Moreover, self-motivation was highlighted by many as a very positive outcome of work experience. Importantly, the students in this study felt more equipped to contribute to seminars and discussions. Overall, the research revealed that the advantages to students of work-based experience certainly outweighed any disadvantages. This point is extremely important and one that should be heeded by all who are assessing the value of work-based placements. Lamenting on the decline in the number of students being offered work-based placements, Little and Harvey conclude their study by saying:

> *However, given the tangible benefits that students gain from placements ... it would indeed be unfortunate if those benefits were increasingly more likely to be available to certain students (and less likely to be available to those who arguably might derive even greater benefit).*

(Little and Harvey, 2006, p59)

In order that the holistic experience which is referred to by Little and Harvey can be deepened and appreciated by all the people involved in the strands of delivery, formative assessment must play a vital role. If we are to appreciate the way in which a student learns (core knowledge 3) then an understanding of the individual student is required. On a practical note, in most cases it is difficult for lecturers to know each individual student, but this becomes even more difficult particularly when the lecturer visiting the student on placement is unknown to the student. Hence, in this scenario, the employer becomes the key link in the triangulation of university, student and employer. In order for triangulation to work effectively, there must be good-quality communication between all parties involved.

Let us now look at a case study of a third-year student who is on a four-year course (see page 104). As you are reading this case study, examine it in the light of the triangulation model.

Work placement experience in teacher education

The work experience undertaken by our fourth-year students involves a 'curriculum enrichment' module, during which, the students work on a project based on their specialist subject within a school. This experience was cited by many head teachers as a definite contributory factor in the employment of that student. (Again note the reiteration of the HEA study.) This module also involves a great degree of formative assessment. In the words of one tutor, *The depth and breadth of this course, when good quality formative assessment is used, allows the student to almost visibly grow before your eyes.*

Please note that the tutor uses the phrase 'good quality' formative assessment. As research shows, there is a great difference in the quality of assessment, but the benefit of high-quality assessment cannot be denied, and all parties involved should strive for this. Cowan (1998) explores the idea that the quality of student reflection is vital to the success of a work placement. We would add to this the view that higher education tutors have a role to play in teaching the students how to reflect appropriately, in order to maximise their learning. One method of doing this is through 'modelling' within the process of formative assessment. Blackwell et al. (2001, p281) were concerned with exploring *what can be done to increase the opportunities for undergraduates to gain work experience and how the learning from these experiences can be maximised*. It is the second part of their focus that is important to our debate, regarding the use of formative assessment in the practice-based element of degree work. Blackwell *et al*. report how students recognised the value of support from academic staff, in so far as it *helps students to consider how they can learn from work and articulate learning* (ibid).

It is appropriate here to note, in particular, two of their six themes, as they are concerned with student views on the value of feedback and assessment during work placements. One of these themes was how students expressed the view that quality monitoring was vital to a successful learning experience. This included the need for ongoing reflection to be facilitated as well as debriefing and the identification of outcomes. Secondly, linked to this, was the view that any assessment must be *fair and trustworthy* (Blackwell et al., 2001, p292). Students developed this idea further by expressing the opinion that formative assessment can be viewed as a *basis for dialogue that can shape the process of learning from work experience* (ibid.).

Having considered what Blackwell *et al*. believe to be important elements of assessment, unfortunately, as the following case study illustrates, not all students receive such good-quality feedback. The following is an extract from an interview conducted by the first author in 2006; the interviewee is a student at Oxford Brookes University. It is informative to consider the points raised by the interview with Anthony and reflect on how his experience could be deepened.

Case study

Anthony completed a year-long work placement in industry. During the year there were two appraisals. The first took place after week 20, and the second at the end of the year. The appraisal took place in the manager's office and the brief conversation was mainly between the manager and the placement officer (this person was unknown to Anthony and no further connection was made on return to university). In addition to the two appraisals a monthly presentation occurred. The use of the word 'presentation' is very revealing; in his own words, Anthony states that:

> It was a presentation given by myself to the manager, the conclusion being an acknowledgement of the presentation. No further discussion ensued; it was simply a case of my presenting an aspect of his work. There was no formal feedback session.

Discussion point |

Is this formative assessment? What might you do as a university lecturer to extract some formative feedback for Anthony out of this rather arid experience?

I then asked Anthony what he did when he made an error on placement:

What if you did something wrong whilst on placement?

Well I am not being bigheaded but I did not come across it really. I worked on my own using trial and error. I suppose I could have gone to a manager if I really felt the need. I had no mentor and no targets were set. (Anthony)

Well how did you measure your progress?

I was given more responsibility as the year progressed, so I suppose that is how I knew that I was doing OK. (Anthony)

Would you have preferred discussion on your progress at intervals?

Oh yes, it would have been much better to get better feedback. (Anthony)

In this case it would appear that the employer is failing to offer good-quality feedback to the student. Consequently, the question arises whether the employer know and understand his/her role. To quote Antony again: *Even when the manager had to complete a graded sheet, this was not discussed or reviewed.*

Biggs (1999) believes that there should be consistent collaboration and discussion so that the student can actively construct learning from the formative assessment. In Anthony's placement, he experienced monthly reviews with the manager, but a valuable learning opportunity was missed. The student gave a presentation of work covered in the previous month but it was merely an acknowledgement. No discussion took place and certainly no targets were set. When asked how he assessed his progress, the given response was: *I presumed I was doing OK, otherwise I would have been told.*

There are obvious opportunities throughout this placement for formative assessment. Unfortunately for this particular student's experience, they were being overlooked.

Discussion point |

- What would quality formative assessment look and sound like for Anthony?
- Are your students receiving quality feedback with discussion when they are on work placements? If not, what prevents this from happening?
- What strategies might university teachers use to alleviate any restraints to good formative feedback in the workplace?
- Is the feedback being provided enhancing your students' experience, and what is the evidence?

This last reflective question relates to another issue about how we, as university educators, know that our students are learning at a deep level when they go on work placement. In many instances, the student and placement office simply complete an evaluation at the end of the experience. If, as educators, we truly believe in constructive learning, then this appears to be an opportunity that is sadly missed. The reason given by one university lecturer was, *It is not for the want of asking. We know how important formative assessment is, and we believe this is an ideal opportunity to work with the students on a practical level. But there simply is not the time permitted on our timetables* (Lorraine, 2006, Liverpool Hope University).

There is an obvious lament for the lack of a learning opportunity which is recognised by the tutors. Interestingly, this issue was highlighted by Elmer (2002) in his study. Similar to Anthony's experience in industry, the core activity was a presentation, but as noted by Elmer, and experienced by Anthony, university tutors did not normally visit students on a placement. As a consequence, *There was a restricted opportunity to give direct feedback on the experiences of the placement and no opportunity to give a 'coaching' dimension to it* (Elmer, 2002, p248).

This appears to be a fundamental error, but why are such obvious opportunities missed? As the work of Joyce and Showers (1988) illustrates, if the practice and theory are not connected by the student and not seen to be valued, the impact on learning is low. However, Joyce and Showers believe that with quality feedback and coaching, the impact on learning moves from low to high.

Anthony's case study supports the view of Elmer, who observes:

> Learners need to feel that they are undertaking authentic activities within their placement settings, that there are opportunities for closure of learning cycles and that there is strong linkage of learning process with learning support.

(Elmer, 2002, p239)

One of Anthony's concluding statements was: *The placement had no link with our course content. It was completely separate*. Maybe Anthony may have felt that he would have had a deeper learning experience if the links between the placement and the university had been stronger or more explicit. Jamieson (1991) argues that students' learning on placements depends, not only on their own capacities and the structure and organisation of the workplace, but on the curriculum frame in which the placement is located (cited in Elmer, 2002).

Work placement for trainee teachers

There appears to be a considerable contrast between the students' experience in industry and student teachers' experience in schools. Trainee teachers generally appear to appreciate the direct link between their course and their school-based practice. Within this experience much stress is placed on assessment, both formative and summative. *Assessment is learning. The idea of learning without some form of assessment is inconceivable* (Brown and Knight, 1994, p36). This view is supported and extended by Brown et al. (1997), who suggest assessment is of vital importance to the student experience. They continue by stating that, in fact, *Students take their cues from what is assessed rather than from what the lecturers assert as important* (Brown, et al., 1997, p7). The following case study highlights what occurs at Liverpool Hope University. You may wish to reflect on whether and how the student/lecturer relationship allows assessment to be a meaningful experience in their school-based practice.

Case study

Final-year students are about to embark on their final school-based practice. An initial meeting is convened between tutor and student. The meeting is set in order to discuss clear targets to be achieved during the practice. This is a very important meeting which should be given time and attention by both parties. When a considerable amount of time has elapsed since the previous school block experience, memories can be 'fuzzy'. Consequently, it is vital to allow the students time to transport themselves back into a school situation. Ideally a student should have advanced warning about the tutorial and the expectations for the meeting.

Case study continued

The student is asked to identify:

- three areas of development;

- how s/he is going to address these areas;

- what will be the outcome?

From personal experience, we appreciate that to some students these questions are very challenging, suggesting that their learning on previous school block experience may not have been as effective as it could have been; otherwise their future targets would be quite clear. Nonetheless, another opportunity is created; in this instance for the student to receive good quality formative assessment.

Dorfman et al. (2006, p231) reviewed a system of assessment used within teacher training degrees, reporting that student teachers were better able to develop their own assessment skills when they experienced placements in which assessment was ongoing. This would seem to be relevant to all degree students not just those on work placements.

Within a teaching degree pathway, students are often assessed by completion of several periods of school block experience (SBE). During this time they are expected to take on all aspects of a teacher's role for up to 80 per cent of the teaching time, depending at what level they are up to in their degree. The hope is that students are able to use the theory they have learnt in university in a practical situation. Whilst out on SBE, they are assessed via lesson observations undertaken weekly by their school-based tutor, and their university-based tutor. Within some teaching degrees, this teaching block has no credits awarded for it but students must pass in order to proceed to the next academic level of the degree pathway. In our experience, we have found that feedback from these experiences is often very positive as students relate the knowledge and skills they have learnt in university to a practical setting. Jackson (1994) would support this claim as he recognises the value of real-life tasks. These tasks have meaning and purposes apart from the assessment context and often aid students' intrinsic motivation to learn:

Teaching, learning and assessment is linked with all being equally valuable. Teaching and feedback (formative assessment) merge and assessment are a necessary part of helping students to learn.

(Brown et al., 1997, p13)

In our efforts to understand the value of the school-based experience, we questioned a group of 143 second-year teacher training students who had just completed their school work placement. The results are interesting to note. All the students agreed that the period of school-based experience was very useful or useful for demonstrating knowledge and skills. This was surprising in itself, as not all had had a positive or successful school-based experience. In fact, of this particular cohort, just above 10 per cent of the students had had, for one reason or another, an unsuccessful experience, where they had been deemed to have failed this part of their course. However, as this assessment allows them to act as practising teachers (which after all is their overall aim on completion of their degree with Qualified Teacher Status), maybe we should not be surprised by their responses. Students traditionally find this experience extremely challenging as they take on the role of classroom teacher within a primary school for at least 75 per cent of teaching time across a minimum six-week period. Through informal conversations with them, on return from their teaching block, they report that it felt worthwhile, and was a chance to put the theory learned into practice. Indeed many students express a sense of personal achievement on completion of this form of assessment, purporting to now feel like 'real teachers'. Students were aware that they had achieved much more than what can be recorded with a numerical or literal grade or credit award. This concurs with the view of Brown and Saunders (1995, p97), who recognise the need for this *balance between the extrinsic motivation from marks achieved and intrinsic motivation and satisfaction in learning*. The use of this method of assessment refers to Brown and Glasner's (1977) ideas on the need for tutors to make sure our assessment methods are the most appropriate to assess what we *really want students to demonstrate* (Brown and Glasner, 1977, p9). Two of the main purposes they see for assessments are that they enable individual differences between students to be celebrated and that they provide meaningful and useful feedback. In the case of the school-based experience, each student received verbal and written feedback on lessons taught by them during the placement as well as weekly reviews and a final written report by their placement-based tutor. Throughout, their individual achievements, and qualities, are acknowledged and celebrated. These written records can then form the basis for future target-setting. This method of assessment is obviously respected by students as the purpose of it is clear to them; it has a direct impact upon how they perform in their chosen career. This idea is supported by Knapper (1995, cited in Norton et al., 2001, p281), where it is argued that:

> *Higher Education should be about lifelong learning, so lecturers need to design courses that prepare students for life beyond the university and not just teach them how to jump through academic hoops.*

Use of ICT to improve formative feedback in school-based experience

We are currently undertaking a pilot study to examine how effective the use of a tablet personal computer (PC) is during a placement-based visit. Apart from the interest shown by the children, which, in fact can often prove to be quite a distraction, the tablet is limited in its use of formative assessment. We have the observation form on the screen and use it in the same way we would use a hard copy, the obvious advantage being the fact that any written elements can be easily erased and rectified. So, for example, in one instance the student was being criticised for not planning for the extra adult in the room. When this was discussed during the feedback session, it was discovered that the extra adult was in fact a parent helper who just happened to be available that morning. Hence, the remarks were easily rectified and removed by the tutor from the student's personal record. This is a simple example of how effective use of information technology tools can aid the process of formative assessment whilst ensuring the student is fully engaged in this process. Another, more sophisticated, example is where a tutor used the tablet to great effect, using a video connection. A student was having difficulty with the use of effective questioning; consequently, he videoed her teaching and used it as a discussion tool. As a result, this student was able to appreciate the effect of the use of open and closed questions. This is certainly a way forward and should be seriously considered as a tool for formative assessment, particularly if a student were borderline or in danger of failing. Such information technology tools could be used to aid the tutor in both formative and summative assessment to great effect. However, once again, we would want to argue that it is still the quality of feedback and student/teacher interaction that is a vital ingredient. If we accept the theory that language and thought are interrelated (Vygotsky, 1978), then the importance of quality feedback cannot be underestimated. But it must, as has already been suggested, be a two-way conversation; a conversation in which the experienced person can appreciate where the student is at, and then, in the words of Vygotsky (1978) expand *the zone of proximal development*. To express this in another way, the teacher looks for the learning potential of a student, which, as we are all aware, is different for each individual; and then aims to take the student beyond his/her present level to a deeper understanding. It is through well-chosen words that students' thoughts and conceptual understandings can be developed.

It would now be useful to look at how a particular teacher views her role in formative assessment.

A teacher's point of view

Within teacher training degrees, the idea of a dialogue as a means of formative assessment is seen as a strength of the experience. Evidence can be found as to the value placed on the role of the tutor during a student teacher's work placement within the programme handbooks for such honours degrees. Tutors are trained to observe students on placement and how to present feedback as a means of formative assessment. Many practising teachers would also view this as a part of their role when they have a student teacher on placement in their particular classrooms. The discussion that occurs between the classroom teacher and the student is generally highly valued. Most teachers agree that they have day-to-day discussions with the student; however, in our programme we initiated a 'weekly review' that was formalised and recorded in the student's file. It appears that this was a welcome step in the right direction. This was because a set time was fixed between the teacher and student and the focus was on formative, quality feedback. As one teacher observed, *This is quality time with the student where real discussion and learning can take place. During this time I would expect students to reflect on their teaching and the children's learning; I would expect comments to be prefaced with such phrases as: I think that ... But I feel that ... a genuine dialogue should follow*. It is extremely interesting that this teacher uses such vocabulary as 'reflective', as this is exactly the language used by Schön (1983) in his seminal work on the role of the reflective practitioner. We would add that it is not simply the student who needs to reflect; so too does the teacher, and tutor, if what follows is to be an open, supportive, and respectful conversation. In this way, both parties will move forward. Just as children's learning develops through situations which make real demands on them, so too will a student's, but it has to be in a supportive environment.

When the teacher in question was asked what she expected the outcome to be, she said that both she and the student should have reached a better understanding, enabling more enriched teaching and learning to take place the following week. There are of course sensitivity issues; therefore, the need for compassion and understanding is vital. As this teacher points out, even though she is experienced, she suffers from nerves when being observed and when getting the feedback. It is always important to remember that the student is probably feeling the same. In order to be sensitive, this teacher, and we believe many other teachers, and lecturers, begin the discussion with praise for the positive aspects of the teaching that has been witnessed. As we all know, it is through joy and praise that true growth and learning take place. In the words of a final-year student, *You can only go forward and build on the positive feedback*. We could rephrase this. Using the language of Bruner, it could be said that the formative assessment is the 'scaffold' given by the teacher in order for the student to climb the ladder of success.

Conclusion

We make no apologies for the fact that parts of this chapter have relied heavily on practical examples from teacher training degrees; we would argue that these examples have much to teach us about the value of formative assessment within degree work. We have chosen examples that will promote debate and discussion amongst academics and students alike. We believe that some elements of good practice can be drawn from them.

- **The work placement elements of degree work should be seen as an integral part of the student learning experience.**
- **Formative assessment needs to fully engage the student in the learning process.**
- **The dialogue between student and tutor is vital to the learning context.**
- **The link between the theory and practice should be clear and able to be fully appreciated.**

We believe that students have a right to expect the very best from their university tutors in terms of teaching and assessment. These expectations do not change whilst the student is on placement. It is the university tutor's responsibility to ensure they are equipped with the necessary teaching skills required. As we stated at the beginning of this chapter, it is a requirement as set by the Higher Education Academy (2006) in their Professional Standards Framework. These standards apply to all university academics and we would hope that as professionals we would all strive to be fully equipped to meet them. After all, the satisfaction for most university teachers tends to be the achievements of our students whatever their learning context may be.

References

Biggs, J. (1999) *Teaching for quality learning at university*. Birmingham: Open University Press/Society for Research into Higher Education.

Blackwell, A., Bowes, L., Harvey, L., Hesketh, A.J. and Knight, P. (2001) Transforming work experience in higher education. *British Educational Research Journal*, 27 (3), 269–285.

Bowes, L. and Harvey, L. (1999) *The impact of sandwich education on the activities of graduates six months post graduation*. Birmingham: University of Central England in Birmingham, Centre for Research into Quality.

Brown, G., Bull, J. and Pendlebury, M. (1997) *Assessing student learning in higher education*. London: Routledge.

Brown, S. and Glasner, A. (1977) *Assessment matters in higher education: Choosing and using diverse approaches*. Buckingham Open University.

Brown, S. and Knight, P. (1994) *Assessing learners in higher education*. London: Kogan Page.

Brown, S. and Saunders, P. (1995) The challenges of modularization. *Innovations in Education and Training International*, 32 (2), 96–105.

Cowan, J. (1998) *On becoming an innovative university teacher*. Buckingham: Open University Press.

Dorfman, A.B., Galluzo, G.R. and Meisels, S.J. (2006) Learning to teach: Developing assessment skills when program and placement are aligned. *Journal of Early Childhood Teacher Education*, 27, 231–247.

Elmer, R. (2002) Learning from a shift of context? Student teachers on non-school placements. *European Journal of Teacher Education*, 25 (2–3), 239–250.

Higher Education Academy (2006) *UK Professional Standards framework for teaching and supporting learning in Higher Education*. York: HEA.

Jackson, M. (1994) Assessment issues, in *Modular higher education in focus*, pp94–95. London: Higher Education Quality Council.

Jamieson, I. (1991) Evaluations, in A. Miller, A.G. Watts and I. Jamieson (eds) *Rethinking Work Experience*, pp260–280. London: Falmer.

Joyce, B. and Showers, B. (1988) *Student achievement through staff development*. London: Longman.

Knapper, C. (1995) Approaches to study and lifelong learning: some Canadian initiatives, in G. Gibbs (ed.) *Improving student learning through assessment and evaluation*. Oxford: The Oxford Centre for Staff Development.

Little, B. (2000) Undergraduates' work based learning and skills development. *Tertiary Education and Management*, 6, 119–35.

Little, B. and Harvey, L. (2006) Learning through work placements and beyond. A report for HECSO and Higher Education Academy's Work Placements Organisation Forum Centre for Higher Education and Research and Information, Open University.

Mason, G., Williams, G., Cranmer, S. and Gulie, D. (2003) *How much does higher education enhance then employability of graduates?* **www.hefce.ac.uk/pubs** (accessed January 2007).

National Committee of Inquiry into Higher Education, (NCIHE) (1997) *Higher Education in the Learning Society*: London: HMSO.

Norton, L.S., Tilley, A.J., Newsted, S.E. and Franklin-Stokes, A. (2001) The pressures of assessment in undergraduate courses and their effect on student behaviours. *Assessment and Evaluation in Higher Education*, 26 (3), 269–284.

Purcell, K., Pitcher, J. and Simm, C. (1999) *Working out? Graduates' early experience of the labour market*. Manchester: Higher Education Careers Service Unit (CSU).

Schön, D. (1983) *The reflective practitioner*. London: Temple Smith.

Vygotsky, L. (1978) *Mind in society. The development of higher psychological processes*. Cambridge, MA: Harvard University Press.

Chapter *11*

Building on vocational competence: achieving a better workforce by degrees

Moira McLoughlin and Ann Marie Jones

Introduction

This chapter will explain the nature and purpose of Foundation degrees, which have provided a route to degree-level study for practitioners in a wide range of disciplines and employment settings. Whilst these degree programmes do not usually draw upon the traditional university entrant group of 18-year-old students with A level points or the equivalent, there are many features of Foundation degree study which may well benefit all students. In particular, there is an obligatory study-skills element which underpins the student's entire university experience. For this reason, its hoped that this discussion will prove relevant to lecturers in higher education, both to enable a better understanding of Foundation degrees and because they too need to bear in mind the varying level of academic skills and experience with which their own students arrive.

It may well be that lecturers reading this text will find themselves teaching on Foundation degree courses. The demands of widening participation and the saturation of the student recruitment market with traditional students point in this direction. When Foundation degrees came into being, the participation of young, full-time students with good A level grades was in excess of 80 per cent and yet less than 20 per cent of school-leavers in the lower socio-economic groups go to university (Liverpool University, 2001). In addition, the HEFCE strategic plan (2006) states that:

> nearly 55% of students starting undergraduate studies are 21 or over and 45% study part-time ... Despite the expansion of student numbers, some groups are under-represented in HE. We cannot afford to waste talent simply because of a reluctance to foster it.

Foundation degrees

Foundation degrees were introduced in 2001 as vocational higher education qualifications which combine academic study with work-based learning and experience. They are the equivalent of the first two years of an honours degree and are classified at level 5 in the QCA National Qualifications Framework (DfES, 2004). Graduates may then progress to relevant honours degrees or other professional qualifications. They provide employers with the opportunity to become involved in the design and/or delivery of the programmes and hence offer a way to fill the workforce skills gaps and shortages as well as increasing the educational achievements of the UK workforce. Generally, employers need to make the commitment of releasing their employee for the required part-time study arrangement of one afternoon per week over two to three years. However, some programmes run entirely in the evenings or weekends and some are available online. By 2003–4 more than 21,000 students had registered on Foundation degree programmes and since then there has been a 160 per cent increase in applications (QAA, 2006). Whilst much provision has been offered in further education (FE) settings, there has been a 23 per cent increase in the number of higher education institutions (HEIs) offering these programmes (QAA, 2006). Some foundation degrees (Fds) are sector-endorsed: for instance, the Health Services FdA, which has been designed for staff working as health-care assistants. This means that fees may be paid and financial help may be available to students. This has not been the case with the Foundation degree on which this chapter centres.

The Foundation degree in special needs

This chapter will draw on materials from the Foundation degree in special needs at Liverpool Hope University, which was specifically developed for students who had some experience with people with special needs and a real interest in the subject. Opportunities to explore attitudes, ethics and concepts related to special needs at that time were, and still are, limited in the local area. Teacher training courses for Early Years practitioners and social work training offer elements of disability and special needs within their curricula. However, for practitioners with long experience of working in the field of special needs or disability, but with few qualifications, there were only a few short, work-related courses. The course has attracted practitioners from the fields of education, health, social services and the voluntary and private sectors. Indeed, some of the students have themselves been carers for family members.

It was decided to develop the Foundation Degree Special Needs alongside the BA Combined Honours (BAC) and BA Qualified Teacher Status (BA QTS) pathways during 2002–03. The belief was that a programme which examined the ways in which disability and special needs are conceptualised and addressed in our society was long overdue. Thus, the aim was to establish a rigorous academic programme, but also to ensure that it was strongly rooted in practice. In this it was hoped that students would be able to graduate with an ethical, enquiring approach to their work with people with special needs and to empower those who had practised for many years and longed to discuss and refine their views and to increase their knowledge. Interestingly the Developing Learning Skills (DLS) module has informed the review of the curriculum for level 1 undergraduates, as its approach to integrated academic development has now been incorporated into the other pathways.

Students study alongside the full honours degree students for all modules, but in addition they study two modules upon which this chapter will focus: these are Developing Learning Skills (DLS) and Work Practice (WP). As their names suggest, DLS facilitates students in gaining or refreshing the skills required to study successfully at HE level, whilst WP uses the students' work settings as the basis of examining and reflecting upon practice. Since this is our own reflection on practice, we have written occasionally in the first person. The programme is still quite new: the first cohort, which began in September 2003, completed the degree in May 2006 and have just graduated. But whilst numbers remain relatively small, the programme gained a very successful QAA review in 2005, which endorsed:

- **the programme itself which is unique in the North West;**
- **the enrolment of students who would otherwise not have engaged with higher education;**
- **the multidisciplinary team involved in programme design and delivery.**

It also recognised among the programme's strengths:

- **the realistic and staged chronological and incremental approach to learning that promotes success;**
- **the integration of academic and work-based elements in teaching, learning and assessment (QAA, 2005).**

Other key features

The programme is not designed simply around a predetermined academic curriculum, but is also informed by practice issues and sector skills. Of course this is also a challenge, but one well worth accepting. A great deal has been learned about how to facilitate students to succeed in HE during the last three years, and much of this has been just as relevant to the honours degree students as it has to the Fd students.

The programme has been revised with the Higher Education Academy (HEA) Professional Standards Framework in mind to ensure that vocational and academic aspects are considered and carefully integrated into the curriculum. These will be indicated at various points within the chapter. The chapter will explain the design and delivery of what we consider to be an innovative and dynamic learning experience for our Fd students.

Lecturers can tend to feel that unless they are centre stage, performing or informing, they are failing their students. However, in examining the links between practical and professional experience, we would argue that a much more subtle approach is what truly opens up the minds of many students, particularly those who come to higher education with grave doubts about their chances of success. The links between their everyday working lives and their academic writing is what needs to be emphasised. The reasoning they employ in the moment-to-moment decisions they are called upon to make each day, for instance, can be used to illustrate the complex ethical issues with which they instinctively grapple. Turning that instinctive response to a more considered decision not only gives them more confidence in coping with their work, but hopefully helps to build a more aware workforce of staff who know why they are doing a certain task in a particular way and feel pride in doing so. This approach is endorsed by the HEA Standard 6 in Areas of Activity and Standard 5 in Professional Values, which require evaluation of practice and continuing professional development (HEA, 2006). This is an aspect of the course that we, as lecturers, can relate to, having moved into the academic world from a practitioner background ourselves, one a nurse/health visitor and one a teacher.

> *Discussion point*
>
> Consider the skills which you might bring to your teaching from your previous experience, particularly those which relate to practice.

The Developing Learning Skills module

Despite four years' experience of teaching undergraduates and many more years of teaching adults, we still found that Fd students had the capacity to present every variation in terms of student difference; literally no two are alike. They range from a significant proportion who do not even possess level 2 qualifications (GCSE equivalent), to one or two who already have degrees or equivalent qualifications in other disciplines. For some, entry to university presents them with their first academic challenge for years and for others it is the next step on a pathway that began with a return to study several years earlier. One thing that they do have in common is a wealth of vocational experience and in many cases work-related learning, but even this is extremely varied in depth, breadth, duration and mode of study.

For the majority, the demands of an academic course are daunting and all have some anxieties. It was also daunting to have responsibility for a module that would underpin their studies and provide them with knowledge and skills which could be transferred into all other modules of the course and into the workplace, knowing that their needs were so diverse.

The knowledge and skills they require cover a range of areas including reading, writing, time management, oral presentation, proofreading, referencing, but the most important factor was meta-learning, i.e. knowledge of how they actually learn. Biggs (1985), who is credited with creating and defining this concept, was of the opinion that meta-learning was not only about knowing how one learns but also with managing one's own learning. Upon reflection, a teaching style within higher education, as opposed to that when teaching children, relies heavily on facilitation of self-reflection and evaluation. Previous experience with teachers on a master's degree indicated that they came with the notion that they would receive tips for teachers and completed modules with statements such as 'It made me think'; I have found that this approach can also prove successful with undergraduates, but more so when in the small-group situation involving well-motivated practitioners, such as those on FdAs. In addition, TMP Worldwide Research (1998, cited in Cottrell, 2003) ascertained that employers value 'soft skills', which include listening, sharing knowledge, influencing others and networking, all of which were found to be in short supply by this research but are developed by this approach. This also accords well with HEA Standards 1 and 2 of Areas of Activity (2006), which relate to design and planning of learning and supporting the students.

A sound starting point for teaching is always the known, but yet again this presents difficulties – the students were not known nor did they know what was going to be expected of them. They would even be likely to make mistakes without knowing they were wrong or, to use Howell's terms, they were *unconsciously incompetent or they don't know what they don't know* (Howell, 1982). So, how to set off on this journey which would take these students to a point where they could be capable and confident learners?

> *Discussion point* |
>
> What, if anything, did the Foundation degree students require that was different from other undergraduates?

The Work Practice module

The Work Practice module begins in a similar way as students are asked to write an account of a 'typical' day, to accustom them to writing as well as speaking about their work from the very beginning. Many students find this quite difficult as they have never before been asked for such an account. Given the nature of their roles as the staff members who work most closely with children, adults or elderly people with disabilities, this was surprising. As might be expected, workers who are mostly used to simply being given tasks or instructions do not easily develop the facility to discuss their experiences. As Bolton (2005, p43) points out, some people are probably more at ease just *getting on with the job and leaving the thinking to others*. This raised consciousness of the need to facilitate the development of the skills to explore, enquire and search below the surface of the students' own subjective views and then to develop the tools to see from others' perspectives: i.e. to become reflective practitioners. Such activity truly supports HEA Standard 4 within Professional Values (2006) which expects *commitment to encouraging participation in higher education, acknowledging diversity and promoting equality of opportunity.*

Resources

Over the following few weeks the students would, according to the usual formula, be introduced to using the university library and some of the applications of information and communications technology (ICT) essential to the course, namely email, the library catalogue and the virtual learning environment (VLE). One advantage of aspects of these sessions is that although some may have experience of at least email they do not have any knowledge of the system used in our university and the VLE is new to all, so all have a similar starting point. Frequently, when the group is asked if they have any knowledge of something and nobody indicates that they have, it is almost always followed by an audible sigh as they then know they are not at a disadvantage.

> *Discussion point* |
>
> How well are undergraduate students introduced to the ICT requirements of their course?

Meta-learning

In order to introduce the students to meta-learning one of the first topics of study is learning styles (Fleming, 2005). The students complete questionnaires to ascertain their own style and apply this new-found knowledge to their own learning. Although Loo (2004) feels that learners match learning styles to tasks, and that skilled learners are not tied into particular styles, consideration of styles starts the process of development of meta-learning. Students quickly see the value of this in relation to other aspects of the course. For example, the main module of study, which is common to students on all three pathways, is delivered by means of a lecture, complemented by seminars. The students examine the effectiveness of this mode of delivery as an opportunity for learning, and select the aspects of the lecture that they find helpful or otherwise. This does of course provide useful feedback for the lecturer, but the main aim of this task is to enable the students to get the most out of the lecture, acknowledging that it may not suit all learning styles. In addition to helping them to determine how they could learn best, the sharing of this in discussion enables them to learn from each other. The knowledge that one may have an idea that somebody else is interested in, and may even copy, provides a tremendous boost to self-esteem and, as it was not always the most able students who had the novel ideas, the boost was frequently given where it was most needed.

Relevant skills

For topics such as reading, note-taking and note-making, time management and conditions for study, experience of being taught reveals how best to carry out these tasks. It is not appropriate to provide a list of dos and don'ts for discussion. Instead, exploration of a lengthy set of questions is designed to prompt introspection in relation to each aspect of study. Even in the first discussion, students are openly acknowledging their shortcomings and strengths, although sometimes there is an element of misplaced pride, such as the student who stated loudly that she never reads; it proved difficult to motivate her to consider aspects of reading such as how, what and why. Presumably, she must never have seen the introductions in 'University Challenge', but thankfully it was revealed that she did read, but books were going to present her with her own university challenge.

Group discussion

Another important feature of these sessions is the quality of discussion. Most tutors must have experienced the seminar when generating interaction is more like pulling teeth, but this has never been the case with the Fd groups. The students develop strong relationships within these groups for a number of reasons – the groups are small, they are all mature students, the majority are working full-time and they, therefore, have similar demands on their time both personally and vocationally. They tend to have a higher level of self-confidence, although of course this does not necessarily translate into self-belief in relation to their studies, and they study together for a period of three years. In addition, they build up a tremendous amount of respect for their peers, having listened to accounts of their working experiences, and this enhances their openness to learning from each other and respect for each other.

It is a considerable advantage that the majority of students who work in the caring services are always interested in the human element of a situation and are therefore more than willing to listen to other students' stories. This can facilitate students in developing a capacity to take a step back, to consider the facts and the possible different points of view of those involved. So, early on in the course, there is a session which is entirely devoted to each student giving a short account of their working life up to that point and crucially explaining their choice to embark upon their course of study.

This is when the revealing comments emerge: *No one seems to even notice what I do, but I know I'm making a difference; I have no say in what happens to her, I'm just there to occupy her time and feed her; I know I can do more.* There have been moments when an individual's revelations have had all the members of the group holding their breath and waiting for the conclusion. What is fascinating is the reluctance at the start of the session and then the inevitable over-run as students realise they have a respectful and genuinely interested audience.

From the point of view as a lecturer – able to command attention by virtue of position or the occasional use of the 'gimlet eye' – this is very revealing. Such respect has an immensely enabling and liberating effect upon students who are often poorly paid, yet highly responsible adults with a multitude of roles.

My belief is that an enquiring and respectful lecturer can facilitate both the less traditional and the more typical student to dare to speculate about their experiences. No matter how widely students read, they must still learn to take this personal risk. A recent study of the differences in achievement between traditional and non-traditional students revealed that *students who have not come via the direct entry route are more likely to drop out. But those who see their courses through are more likely to notch up a higher class of degree* (Kingston, 2006, p4). What this might tell us is that students who bring all their life experiences to bear upon the course they undertake can, with the right support, develop a more critical and reflective approach to their studies and emerge from being at times the scourge of a lecturer's day to being a positive delight to accompany on their journey.

The aims of examining work practice then are these.

- **To clarify meaning: to consider for example why a particular client is difficult to support.**
- **To move from using simple descriptions to more precise and accurate terms: this could be moving from *I just feel that he never really responds very much to me*, to. *Since he has difficulty making eye contact anyway and I am only in that unit once each week, I wonder if he actually recognises me and so our relationship never moves on.***
- **To be more objective when discussing difficult situations: this is the topic of an early session where students, in groups of three, discuss a challenging situation each has faced and try to analyse why the problem arose. The tutor needs to be constantly monitoring each group to help discussions develop and to show a real involvement. These discussions provide wonderful material for future sessions. One student, for instance, talked of her feeling of vulnerability when working with very aggressive young men and women who have been excluded from school, when there is no clear management policy on handling such behaviour.**
- **To become reflective. Much has been written on this topic: Kolb's beliefs about learning through the cycle of analysis and reflection (1984) are still much quoted. For Bolton (2005, p23), the stories we tell when we write reflectively about practice are *data banks of skill, knowledge and experience: much of our knowing is in our doing* and *sharing reflective writings and discussing them in depth enables practice development because the outcomes of reflection are taken back into practice.* Indeed, the continued willingness to reflect is seen as a way to contain the distress of some work situations and to keep alive a spirit of optimism about improvement. Skovholt (2001) believes it actively promotes resilience and can actually prevent burn-out – a useful tip for lecturers as well as students. Asking students sometimes to first write and then discuss a particular incident or situation can encourage the development of the first three aims given above, as well as improving writing style as students process their stories for consumption by others, aiming for clarity and balance. Such an approach to enabling students to learn is embedded within HEA Standards 2 and 3 of Core Knowledge (2006), which consider providing appropriate teaching methods and recognising how students learn.**

Discussion point |

Consider the influence on your approach of someone who has helped you reflect on your experience.

Assessment

The assessment for the DLS module has, of course, been designed to ascertain if the learning outcomes have been met, but also forms part of the process of learning. The first assignment is an audit of students' learning and an action plan for learning in both academic and vocational settings, but the students require a great deal of preparation in order to tackle this. This preparation begins in the first session when they are asked to write a passage about themselves with set criteria for content. This is not an unusual icebreaker but it is intended to get them writing straight away, introduce the notion of audience, give clear guidance about content and to make them focus on themselves. (As the majority have been women who are working full-time, while juggling busy home lives, the latter is often a new experience.) They then present this to the rest of the group, which for most means reading from the script, thus providing an opportunity to consider if this is the best way to present information orally.

The second piece of work was originally designed as an open-book examination to test the basic skills required for academic writing, including proofreading, Harvard referencing, summarising and reading critically. This approach was followed by an examination, despite concerns about its suitability, but the evaluation of its success was that students performed well but did not transfer their learning effectively to subsequent assignments. Brown et al. (1996, p74) suggest that *questions that require students to make use of their knowledge* test what students have learned rather than what they have been taught. The following year saw me frequently modelling the skills in class and setting a series of tasks, some class based and some home based, and the anxiety levels seemed to be reduced without compromising the outcome. I feel strongly that such skills either need to be practised frequently to develop or, as in the case of Harvard referencing, do not need to be memorised, as it is always possible to consult a reference document just as one would a dictionary if spelling were proving problematic. The HEA Standard 3 of Areas of Activity (2006) concerns assessment and feedback, and Standard 5 of Core Knowledge relates to evaluating the effectiveness of teaching: both of these were considered and are addressed by the approach taken to this assignment.

In the Work Practice module, the first assignment students undertake is to keep a diary of their working day for ten days, attempting to give both a factual account and then a more evaluative discussion. Whilst we often think, perhaps quite profoundly, about what we are doing and why during a busy working day, unless we become accustomed to recording these thoughts, they and any insights they might have provided can be lost. Thus when writing their discussions, students are directed to think about the professional values of the sector within which they work. These could be from the social care, health or education sectors and again this supports the *commitment to continuing professional development and evaluation of practice* required by the Higher Education Academy Standards Framework.

Students are next asked to complete an analysis and comparison of two tasks they perform in their place of work: one is to be an everyday task and the other a more unusual one. The comparison requires students to think very carefully about how important this task is to them and whether or not this matches the view of the person they are supporting. For instance, a trip to the shops for a young adult with learning difficulties who is in a residential setting, can be fairly routine for the support worker, yet may confer a huge sense of achievement on clients who can choose what they would like to eat or the clothes they would like to buy and can pay for it themselves. In their conclusions, students must refer to texts or government papers on good practice in their particular field: in the example just given, this might include *Improving the life chances of disabled people* (2005) from the Prime Minister's National Strategy Unit. Since this paper covers a much wider field than learning disabilities, it also serves to extend the students' reading, which in turn helps makes their writing less subjective. This form of assessment meets the expectations of HEA Standard 5 of Areas of Activity (2006) which requires *Integration of scholarship, research and professional activities with teaching and supporting learning*.

The third assignment is a reflective conclusion to the first two pieces of work, a review of their work experience over the past year. It is limited to 1000 words to encourage clear focus and also because each student must read the essay to the others as if presenting a paper. Whilst they are a little nervous, it clearly promotes their sense of self-worth as the implicit message is that their thoughts are worth hearing. It is a great personal opportunity to learn about different work situations and often allows for the sharing of some wise practical advice. For students to feel safe to share their thoughts, they must be carefully prepared and supported. As Mortiboys (2002, p8) points out, universities may readily become places which lack emotional literacy. Yet true learning from experience cannot happen if lecturers are unaware of their students' emotions. I would strongly endorse Mortiboys' belief that *learning by reflection, developing students' motivation, frequent constructive feedback and interactive learning are bound up with encouraging and building upon a positive emotional response from the students*. The safer the students feel to admit to problems, mistakes and express their feelings about these matters, the deeper the level of reflection that can be achieved in a session where lecturer and students work together. Hinett (2002, p2) offers a powerful recommendation for introducing reflection into learning programmes in higher education, seeing it as *both a structure to aid critical thinking and improve existing understanding and a method for promoting autonomous and deep learning through enquiry*.

As the next assignment for DLS is an essay on theories of learning, students have yet another opportunity to showcase what they have learned about the mechanics of academic writing while developing an understanding of how theory relates to their own practice, thus continuing their academic development and enabling them to make links between this module and WP.

The final assessment is in two parts: a group presentation offering a critical analysis of three articles on special needs disability with a common theme and an individual written critique of one of the articles. Although such activities, namely the presentation and reflection upon articles, form part of Conceptualising Special Needs (the module studied by all students, not just those on the FdA), DLS provides the opportunity to undertake these activities with a greater level of support – another benefit of the small-group teaching afforded the FdA students. As Race (2004) asserts, *small groups are ideal contexts for students to make sense of things – digesting information to turn it into knowledge through experience.*

Discussion point |

How might it be possible to foster this 'digestion' in larger groups?

Conclusion

Biggs (2003) considers that being a reflective teacher consists of three elements: to use one's experience to find the solution to a problem which has arisen in the classroom; to possess a thorough subject knowledge so that when students question or misunderstand, we can find a clearer way to explain a concept; to be prepared to consider why learning is not taking place and find a way to engage the students in a more active way. Biggs reminds us that this is an ongoing cycle in which *you keep looking at what they do, what they achieve and link that with what you are doing. You get to know your students as learners very well* (2003, p251).

Overall, these two modules enable us to get to know our students very well, both as learners and as practitioners. Moreover, it generates an atmosphere of mutual respect with tutors perceived as practitioners facilitating their learning, rather than lecturers who focus only on the academic aspects, rather than their professional roles. Our belief is that using this teaching approach brings into sharper focus both our own and the students' awareness of what they are learning, as opposed to what we are teaching. As a consequence we are better able to monitor the extent to which they are applying what they are learning to their professional lives. In this regard we have also found that students feel affirmed in the good practice they were involved in, or perhaps more importantly, empowered to change what they come to perceive as poor practice. In the light of both the HEA standards, and of our own aims for this Foundation degree, this is a matter of major significance.

As lecturers, we too must reflect upon the successes and failures we experience. When to allow a student more time to finish the story being told, when to interrupt and give some direction to the narrative, how to link the points made to the issues raised in another student's tale and how to draw some conclusions, are skills we must develop. I remember having great faith in using a model of the human eye to enable students to understand visual problems children have. It took me three years of repeating this module to realise that for the vast majority, it was not helping them at all. I thought I was drawing upon the learning theory which advocates teaching in such a way as to enable the visual, auditory and kinaesthetic learners. It was certainly an impressive visual aid and it provided a hands-on experience. But all that students were really learning was how the model came apart and could be reconstructed, and incidentally having some fun. A far better approach was the use of a clear, short video about human vision followed by a quiz. We should not be afraid therefore to fail, but must be prepared to try to change.

References

Biggs, J.B. (1985) The role of metalearning in study processes. *British Journal of Educational Psychology*, 55, 185–212.

Biggs, J. (2003) *Teaching for quality learning at university*. Buckingham: Open University Press.

Bolton, G. (2005) *Reflective practice – writing and professional development* (2nd edition). London: Sage Publications.

Brown, S., Race, P., and Smith, B., (1996) *500 tips on assessment*. London: Kogan Page.

Cottrell, S. (2003) *The study skills handbook* (2nd edition). Basingstoke: Palgrave Macmillan.

Cowan, J. (undated) *Facilitating development through varieties of reflection*. Higher Education Academy.

DfES (2004) *The employer guide to foundation degrees*. London: DfES.

Fleming, N. (2005) *Teaching and learning styles: VARK strategies*. Christchurch, NZ: Fleming.

HEFCE (2006) HEFCE Strategic Plan 2006–11 available at **www.hefce.ac.uk/widen** (accessed 12 December).

Higher Education Academy (2006) National Professional Standards Framework for Teaching and Supporting Learning in Higher Education. Available online at **www.heacademy.ac.uk/reganaccr/|Standards Framework(1).pdf**.

Hinett, K. (2002) *Improving learning through reflection-part one*. The Higher Education Academy.

Howell, W.S. (1982) *The empathic communicator*. Prospect Heights, IL: Waveland Press.

Kingston, P. (2006) The changing face of success, *The Guardian*, 1 August.

Kolb, D.A. (1984) *Experiential learning: experience as the source of learning and development*. Englewood Cliffs, NJ: Prentice-Hall.

Liverpool University (2001) Widening participation policy.

Loo, R. (2004) Kolb's learning styles and learning preferences: Is there a linkage?. *Educational Psychology*, 24 (1), 99–108.

Mortiboys, A. (2002) *The emotionally intelligent lecturer*. SEDA Special No.12.

Prime Minister's Strategy Unit (2005) *Improving the life chances of disabled people*.

QAA (2005) *Foundation Degree Forward* Issue 7. Available at **www.fdf.ac.uk**.

Race, P. (2004) *Facilitating learning in small groups*. Available at **www.heacademy.ac.uk/embedded_objcct.asp?id=21685&filename=Race01** (accessed January 2007).

Skovholt, T. (2001) *The resilient practitioner. Burnout prevention and self-care strategies for counselors, therapists, teachers and health professionals*. Boston, MA: Allyn and Bacon.

Chapter 12

Combining service learning and social enterprise in higher education to achieve academic learning, business skills development, citizenship education and volunteerism

John Patterson and Colleen Loomis

Introduction

Over the years there has been a growing concern in the Higher Education Academy (HEA) about how to address the need for educating citizens and developing a capable workforce, yet few models exist for simultaneously accomplishing these twin goals. An overarching concern that seems universal (as reported in the results of an international survey of HEA by Berry and Chisholm, 1999) is how we should educate students to have an ethic to serve. Addressing these needs is important for sustaining democracy and civic life as well as maintaining a position within a global economy. We believe that educating the next generation to serve is part of the equation for creating a more just world, locally and globally.

In the past, industry often carried the responsibility for training workers. This adult educational model is effective for developing trade-specific skills. One limitation of this approach, however, is an absence of attention to developing an ethic of care for others. Addressing the need to educate the masses on ethics has often been conducted through religious institutions. An obvious limitation of a religious approach to developing an ethical society is the historical evidence of the creation of in-groups who are treated with compassion and out-groups who are excluded. Alone, industry and ecclesiastical institutions only partly fulfil society's need to foster youth's vocational and ethical development, facilitating their contributions to political, social and economic life.

It is suggested that this complex set of needs can be met by the HEA from both faith-based and secular institutions. The HEA is distinct in its ability to meet both needs of developing employees and citizens. For example, citizenship education (CE) and volunteerism guide our work in HEA. Focusing on delivering these outcomes has often left lecturers wondering about the curriculum content and the tools for delivering that content. Clearly our course designs affect how well we deliver CE, as well as whether volunteering is part of the course work or beyond it. As educators, often we have not had the resources and tools for resolving conflicts between curriculum content and employing a pedagogical approach that includes volunteerism. Additionally, we are also challenged to attend to another educational agenda: the use of the HEA to produce entrepreneurs. How do we teach CE while encouraging volunteerism and educating future entrepreneurs? We do not profess to have a solid, tried and true method, but we have some evidence from a recent project (directed by the first author) that suggests that integrating service-learning (SL) with social enterprise provides a unifying framework for developing academic knowledge, work skills, citizenship education and volunteerism.

Before discussing the project as an example, let us examine why we need a unifying framework for education delivery. Not having a framework to deliver the content of various curricula translates into missed opportunities. The course of educational history reflects periods of attention to academic achievement often without concern for personal outcomes such as social and emotional development (e.g. feelings of empathy, conflict-resolution skills and helping behaviours). A narrow focus on individuals' academic outcomes excludes attention to community and social outcomes; for example, not asking how individuals who graduate from our institutions impact the larger society. Other challenges include our working within a context in which we sometimes feel overworked and under-resourced when implementing many different learning objectives and agendas. Without a guiding framework, lecturers often are at their wits' end about which approach is better and easier to use, as well as whether the one selected will accomplish the intended outcomes. In the end, educators may feel confused about quality assurance in the implementation and delivery of various curricula separately derived. Having a framework that integrates work skill development, citizenship education and volunteerism advances educational process and outcomes. This framework exist within (and is influenced by) history and educational policies.

History and policies as context of curricula development in the UK

As we strive to provide the very best for students through our own fields of expertise, the educational arena is suffering from torrents of new, robust and empowering directives, strategies and targets, woven-in, bolted-on, added to or having synergy with cross-cutting themes their strands and outcomes. In a mind-mapping exercise it is looking rather like a large and somewhat cold bowl of spaghetti. As we dive right into that bowl each new academic year, armed with a dictionary of new buzzwords, searching to pull all the strands together and make sense of it for students, it's not surprising for people to lose focus on the reason they jumped in the first place. For many of us our personal values drew us to higher education. Now, the role of values in education is receiving attention from the government and our professional standards. We would argue that an integrated SL approach, as noted, has much to offer, through the provision of opportunity to engage our values within our teaching, and alongside our students.

The call for values as an important aspect in the planning of educational provision is evidenced through the emergence of a wide range of publications around the subject, such as Haldane (2004). The students we are just receiving are amongst the first to be effected by the *Every Child Matters* agenda (DfES, 2004) which has followed hot on the heels of the United States version, *No Child Left Behind*. In asking young people, products themselves of the very attainment as opposed to achievement-led constraints of the national tests, *Every Child Matters* (ECM) concluded that our youth wanted the following: to be healthy, stay safe, enjoy and achieve, make a positive contribution and achieve economic well-being. How does our course provision embrace these areas of influence for new students and indeed move them forward in learning experiences towards employment?

As the government seeks an outcome of new innovative industry born from the creativity of motivated young people, we are tasked to draw together a multi-agency approach to facilitate this development across education. To the more cynical, it's a case of shrinking budgets and centralising pots of money we must all fight for; at best it is an attempt to generate new employment in what is now a very service industry-led UK; providing systems to ensure all young people are given opportunity. Nonetheless, one way to meet the challenge is to create settings and pathways for equal opportunity for all youth. The new National Professional Standards Framework (HEA, 2006) provides values for direction, particularly standards numbers 3 and 4: *Commitment to development of learning communities* and *Commitment to encouraging participation in higher education, acknowledging diversity and promoting equality of opportunity*. In this chapter, we present arguments from a belief that it is practical involvement which brings a better understanding of these areas and their links, providing in turn a pathway towards an informed and enhanced understanding of most, if not all, of the areas of activity, core knowledge and professional values noted in the Standards Framework. Furthermore, we would argue that involvement as a tool of learning is at its most powerful when it engages the individual student's emotional intelligence (EI). First proposed by Salovey and Mayer (1990) and popularised by Goleman (1996), EI suggests that new insights into brain function can be used to nurture and positively affect such areas as self-awareness, persistence, motivation, empathy and social deftness. It may be argued that EI has a key role to play in attracting people into activity in the first instance, providing the critical mass needed for research and the generation of a well-rounded workforce of tomorrow.

The ECM agenda addresses physical, mental and economic well-being. It is arguable that although the government seems to place a greater emphasis on economic outcomes, as was the case under Margaret Thatcher's administration, these three facets are highly interrelated. The HEA can (and does) attain these seemingly lofty goals by employing experiential learning, citizenship education and volunteerism, which is indeed service-learning (as defined below). A few examples of service-learning exist in the UK and there are many more models to learn from throughout the world. We propose building on existing models of service-learning and adapting these to local contexts, embracing social enterprise, distinct from other forms of entrepreneurial learning, as part of a fluid movable-feast model for communities of learning. We shall discuss each of these issues in turn, followed by an illustration of integrating service-learning and social enterprise with a recent example implemented by the first author at Liverpool Hope University. The chapter will close with suggestions for practice and research.

Service-learning throughout the world

Definitions of SL and models for service delivery as well as approaches to assessing its impact vary widely. SL is delivered in many ways, by, and for, various groups of individuals in many different settings with wide-ranging goals. Nonetheless, SL has a common thread. As the name suggests, the primary objective is to connect and balance service with learning. This focus on balance between service and learning is relatively new.

Traditionally, the focus was on learning. Students were to learn course content by hands-on service work that would bring the classroom or lecture room material to life. This pedagogical approach is referred to as experiential learning. An underlying assumption of this definition is that the university environment lacks the necessary resources to provide a comprehensive learning experience for students. To fill this gap, various approaches have been used such as co-ops, vocational and technical programmes and indeed SL. These approaches focused on learning knowledge and skills, but did not teach students to serve; nor did it attend particularly to outcomes for the community or agency where students were having their 'real world' experiences. This approach has often been referred to as a practicum. Historically, practica were meant to provide students with an advantage over others through placement in a prestigious setting. Value might be seen as coming from a *curricula vitae* inclusion once students graduated and found themselves searching the job market (Berry and Chisholm, 1999).

The narrow focus on academic and intellectual learning was broadened to include learning about oneself and learning how to serve others. This experience is distinct from volunteer work, which is an act of charity alone without an explicit learning agenda. Around the globe, volunteer work with a focus on learning about oneself and caring for others when it is attached to a curriculum is called service-learning. This international consensus came about independently in the 1990s driven by social problems in many different countries (see Berry and Chisholm, 1999, for a full report of their international survey on service-learning in higher education).

The most comprehensive definition of service-learning is offered by the National Service-Learning and Assessment Study Group in the USA:

SL is a teaching and learning strategy that combines the principles of experiential learning with service to the community … students develop as citizens, learn problem-solving skills, and experience a sense of social responsibility by engaging in thoughtful action to help their communities. Students … deepen and reinforce their newly acquired content knowledge and skills by using them to address real community needs. They experience themselves — and are perceived by others — as competent, contributing members of the community.

(The National Service-Learning and Assessment Study Group, 1999, pp1–2)

Using similar definitions, most SL research has focused on examining impact on student outcomes such as academic achievement, personal satisfaction (Root et al., Giles, 2003), time management, problem-solving skills (Weinreich, 2003), civic skills (Niemi et al., 2000), intent to volunteer in the future (Giles and Eyler, 1994), and fostering care for others in the community (Hinck and Brandell, 1999). Most research findings support the hypothesis that participation in SL is related to enhanced student development outcomes. There are very few studies investigating the impact of SL on service recipients, and the community organisations and agencies which serve them, or the mechanisms that make service-learning work. However, findings from an international survey (Berry and Chisholm, 1999) across Thailand, India, Korea, the Philippines, Liberia and the United States, reported that SL is related to community development, being adapted to promote such development in many different political contexts.

A key question lies in how we engage students in the power of SL in the first instance. There is certainly a need for rigour in developing what we do, how we do it and what we research as this new field develops. This holds particular importance as HE is encouraged by central government to engage ever-increasing numbers in learning. As noted by Butcher et al. (2003) in studying community service learning and student efficacy for community engagement, the diversity of student backgrounds calls for wider understanding of different people's worlds. SL may indeed offer itself as a means to connect students to a place where knowledge and skills are enhanced, facilitating wider and deeper understanding; a place where students can learn through their own preferred learning styles, whilst maturing in emotional intelligence alongside their peers from diverse backgrounds.

Citizenship education and volunteerism

Education for the purpose of promoting citizenship has been part of the HEA agenda in the United Kingdom since 1998, when the Crick Report made citizenship development the focus of the National Curriculum. The National Curriculum was changed with an explicit focus on citizenship content. Active citizenship was specified with six clear components: (1) awareness and knowledge; (2) interests and motivation; (3) decision-making ability and skills; (4) peaceful action; (5) collaborative action and community building; and (6) reflection (Qualifications and Curriculum Authority, 2004). The Crick Report (QCA, 1998) was clear that education has a role to play in preparing the next generation to be stewards of society:

We firmly believe that volunteering and community involvement are necessary conditions of civil society and democracy. Preparation for these, at the very least, should be an explicit part of education.

(QCA, 1998, p10)

The role of volunteering has certainly generated interest in recent years. The opening of an online gateway, *Participation Works*, by the Children's and Young People's Partnership (CHYPP), believing in new collaborative approaches to youth engagement, is certainly of interest. Supported by the Department for Education and Skills (DfES), CHYPP is a connection of several leading organisations involved in children and young people's participation. The British Youth Council, Carnegie Young People Initiative, Children's Rights Alliance for England, the National Children's Bureau and the National Youth Agency have drawn their efforts together to improve:

the way practitioners, organisations, policy makers and young people access and share information about involving children and young people in decision making.

(CHYPP, 2005)

A point of synergy across each organisation would be the importance placed on the engagement of the individual, in their community, through participation. The new National Framework for Youth Action and Engagement (Russell Commission, 2005) posed a challenge for youth volunteering within communities. In asking searching questions, Russell hoped to establish how a step change could be made towards youth volunteering in the UK. He asked what could be done to encourage more young people to get involved in their communities and how their contribution could be recognised. Russell saw the generation of a new national framework as a tool to facilitate volunteering of worth and quality. He recommended a series of campaigns to promote volunteering stating that:

it should be commonplace for young people to volunteer whilst they are at school, college or in higher education. All education institutions should have a volunteering ethos ... a stronger emphasis on volunteering within the citizenship curriculum and training for citizenship teachers.

(Russell Commision, 2005, p14)

As Russell makes reference to establishing frameworks and structures around volunteering, questions must be asked whether a point comes when volunteering ceases to be so and whether SL frameworks remove benefits as volunteering becomes mandatory. Recent research in Canada (Brown *et al.*, 2005) examined this issue by comparing secondary school students who were mandated to participate in community service to those students who were not mandated. The findings show that mandating service still leads to higher civic engagement and future volunteerism than not mandating students. The ongoing Public Education Leadership Project (PELP 2005) by the Harvard Business School (HBS) in the United States is worth noting at this point as a good example of balancing volunteer activity within community partnerships. An ultimate target in our HEA endeavours is to take our students through to employment where they can contribute. The pressure is upon us to generate innovative, entrepreneurial students who will in turn create the new businesses of tomorrow and, furthermore, to be stewards of their communities. One way to achieve these goals, we would argue, is to integrate service-learning with social enterprise.

From enterprise to social enterprise

Before exploring how social enterprise can be integrated with SL, we need a view on what social enterprise (SE) is. The words 'enterprise', 'enterprising', 'entrepreneur', 'entrepreneurship' and 'entrepreneurial learning' are appearing more and more in the directives, targets and missions of the agencies who are expected to act on the ECM agenda. This has been influenced by work from the Organisation for Economic Co-Operation and Development (OECD) and the Council Resolution by the European Commission (1998). Enterprise was seen as fuelling a drive for new economic opportunity in a globalising economy, entrepreneurship being viewed within the context of a formula to *reconcile economic success with social cohesion* (OECD, 1998). Head teachers across the UK, for their part, will soon be inspected on their enterprise provision. We should expect our students, therefore, to be coming through to us with increasing levels of understanding of the need to focus their time in higher and further education towards employment and new employment generation, especially as we consider that future students will have come through some significant input at school level. The Government's White Paper *Excellence in Schools* (1997), followed closely by a White Paper for *Enterprise Opportunity For All in a World of Change* (2000), for example, focused on ensuring that *creativity and enterprise and the ability to innovate are at the heart of the education and skills we provide to our young people* (DTI/DFEE, 2000).

These variable definitions are manifest in our local context as well. On a regional note, the Cheshire Programme Enterprise Group (PEG), set up through the North West Development Agency to encourage new enterprise, stated:

there is no wide agreement about how to define 'enterprise'. Similarly, there is no agreement about the most appropriate approach to adopt in trying to encourage entrepreneurship.

(NWDA, 2000)

The studies of Burley and Huzyka (2000) reinforce the NWDA view. Reference is made in their work to a wide spectrum of enterprise understanding, from those seeing enterprise as linked to high-technology companies alone, to those seeing enterprise as linked to community change. In the most simplistic of terms, we have 'stack it high and sell it cheap/profit at all costs' at one end of an understanding scale, with 'give something back to your community' at the other. It's perfectly clear therefore that everything is unclear! To clarify, we suggest grounding our course structures in community-based enterprise, and in doing so address the values of ECM.

In addition to the lack of consensus about what entrepreneurship is and how we direct students to that goal, we, as educators, are challenged by another factor; that of current practices in secondary schooling. One particular challenge we face is secondary schools teaching to the test. We would strongly suggest this practice negatively affects the creativity of our new student intake. The late Ted Wragg (Emeritus Professor of Education at Exeter University and *Times Educational Supplement* columnist) and many of our schoolteaching colleagues, would argue that the drive to secure high Standard Assessment Task (SAT) level scores for league tables and Ofsted inspections has adversely affected the creativity of pupils taught to regurgitate facts for examinations. Creativity is the very essence for generating new ideas and industry: in other words, enterprising thought. Consequently, HE must play an increasingly important role in moving students coming from a limited test-taking framework to one in which creativity is valued and nurtured. Our challenge is to make sense of what our students have already experienced, unravel that 'bowl of spaghetti' and, taking students from where they are at as individual learners, equip them for the future with a pair of 'enlarging binoculars'. How are we to develop our courses to cover bursting input requirements (i.e. 'facts in'), maintain enthusiasm for our subject areas for it to percolate down to students, and sustain the 'bigger picture' aims of ECM? This is a big question for us all in HE. It is here that we champion the value of social enterprise experience for students within a SL activity framework.

As a starting point, a recent conceptualisation of entrepreneurship places people at its centre (Ma and Tan, 2006, p716). Their model for entrepreneurship comprises the following four aspects: pioneer, perspective, practice and performance. According to Ma and Tan, combining passion with perseverance develops a pioneering attitude. This passion must be directed; generating a place where perspective comes into play, providing clear purpose and the informing of policy. At this point the action of the individual matters, whereby practice in the art of persuasion encourages further involvement of individual passion. Finally, performance can be determined, being measured both in terms of profit and impact on people. Ma and Tan conclude that, ultimately, *entrepreneurship is about serving people*.

When pioneers are passionate about addressing social issues and enhancing the quality of life for individuals, they are commonly referred to as social entrepreneurs (Bornstein, 2004; Thompson *et al.*, 2000). In other words, individuals engaged in social enterprise are those whose pioneering ideas result in promoting social justice; they are social entrepreneurs. This entrepreneurial spirit is values-based. People matter.

Social enterprise in itself has increasingly appeared across public, private and voluntary-sector debates in recent years. Studies by Merton et al. (2003, p119) in their guide for local authorities within the context of neighbourhood renewal and adult learning, strongly support social enterprise's influence and impact within community settings. Furthermore, its relevance to the individual, community empowerment and to economic development is underlined by Gray et al. (2003, pp141–154) in their study of marginal activities amongst community social workers. Social enterprise itself is best described by the Development and Education Programme for Daughters and Community (DEPDC) (2004) in the United States. Established to educate leaders by the integration of SE-related research via reporting on individuals who have successfully alleviated poverty and illness, or combated unemployment and violence, whilst bringing *education, light, opportunity and freedom to poor and marginalized people around the world*, DEPDC defines social enterprise as activities which *solve social problems*; the social entrepreneurs themselves acting as:

> *change agents for society, seizing opportunities others miss in order to improve systems, invent and disseminate new approaches and advance sustainable solutions that create social value ... social entrepreneurs primarily seek to generate social value rather than profits.*

(DEPDC, 2004)

Are we not social entrepreneurs as we teach the workers of tomorrow? What can we add to our own learning community and other communities of learners both physically in course content and application, and virtually through the use of information and communication technology (ICT), disseminating our best practices? There should be some resonance for us as we reflect on the day-to-day delivery of our own duties in light of Bornstein's description of social entrepreneurs as those who:

> *identify resources where people only see problems. They view the villagers as the solution, not the passive beneficiary. They begin with the assumption of competence and unleash resources in the communities they're serving.*

(Bornstein, 2004, p21)

Harvard Business School (HBS) may offer some evidence to support such a notion, being at the 'community change' end of Burley and Huzyka's (2000) spectrum of enterprise understanding. The 'social enterprise initiative' at the centre of their mission views SE as a medium through which they: *generate and share knowledge that helps individuals and organisations create social value in the non-profit, private and public sectors.*

In viewing knowledge generation as the engine driving SE programmes, PELP has highlighted some interesting research. Working in nine urban school districts in the USA within a partnership between their Graduate School of Education and their business school, HBS engages students in schools as volunteers. Research points towards raised achievement in pupils, the generation of high-quality teaching materials amongst partners, and improvement of on-the-ground engagement.

As SE (by its nature) is about people, its key dynamic lies in its ability to generate group learning. Group learning in wide collaborations would certainly be a vision to aspire towards, especially if we can engage our own student base as volunteers in the process. The value of such learning has been highlighted in the work of Clarke (1997) and studies around designing and implementing an integrated curriculum. Amongst the benefits of group learning, Clarke lists the sense of worth individuals feel in sharing a common purpose, whilst having their own individual input valued. This chapter would suggest that volunteer activity in SE, based on their previous CE input, may assist in the generation of active citizens, providing opportunities whereby individuals participate in and contribute to their localities. Our students, we believe, are key to that process as we reflect on the National Advisory Committee on Creativity and Cultural Education's statement:

> *Britain's economic prosperity and social cohesion depends on unlocking the potential of every young person and enabling them to face an uncertain and demanding future.*

(NACCE, 1999)

Case study

Integrating service-learning and social enterprise

As an example, a citizenship education project that used service-learning and resulted in social enterprise is the Schools Intergenerational Nurturing and Learning Project (SIGNAL), which comes from Liverpool Hope University. Students from across a wide range of disciplines worked alongside *Every Child Matters* partners in primary and secondary schools generating musical performances to celebrate core value messages from citizenship assemblies delivered by the Liverpool Football Club Truth for Youth initiative. Recordings of the music under such titles as 'Show racism the red card' and 'Kick drugs into touch' are sold to parents within an enterprise. Profits from the sale of CDs are given to local charities. University students from the first author's specialty, physical education, use the experience of working alongside partners to inform their dissertations and future career choices. It is of interest to note (as yet to be fully researched) that those volunteering into such an initiative on the whole demonstrate a broader depth of understanding and a wider bibliography, suggesting that their involvement engaged an academic interest. A more detailed explanation of SIGNAL may be found on the CD order form for SIGNAL 2, which may be viewed at **www.schoolsinteractive.co.uk**. It would be worth printing this order form and reflecting on previous points made in this chapter in reading through its contents.

SE activity provides opportunities for students to see the value of their chosen studies in the context of the bigger picture, receiving an intrinsic reward as they engage their own emotional and spiritual values with that of the 'real world': a world of diverse, unique learning communities.

The SIGNAL process has three defined stages: the engagement of children's (and student) interest through explicit citizenship assemblies, cross-curricular education through the foci of engagement, and the final celebration of work through a social enterprise reinforcing the initial citizenship engagement. In England, SIGNAL is one of the first projects to combine service-learning and student emotional intelligences with business enterprise. This form of enterprise was directed at students generating funds and then their being charitable. SIGNAL's work is one small way to ameliorate social problems, but can it be replicated in diverse settings?

So what do we do?

In closing, we propose that to address the need for educating citizens and a capable workforce, various service-learning models be adopted and adapted, and that social enterprise be integrated into service-learning. The choice of a particular SL model should be driven by the learning objectives and the needs of the local community (Berry and Chisholm, 1999, p1). Service-learning also occurs where students leave their local context and serve in a different country (see the work of Hope One World, **www.hope.ac.uk**). Blending service-learning with social enterprise reignites passions for learning (and teaching), develops the skills of future workers, and addresses social problems and issues. In this endeavour, we suggest that we reflect on our own values and act on our ideas; and support those of our creative students. The call for broader learning experiences through curriculum and community to provide better outcomes is clear (EPPI, 2005; Spencer, 2005; Davies, 2002; OECD, 1998). And the scope is wide. It is down to us as lecturers, however, to engage our students with SL and its academic research in the first instance through the 'awe and wow factor' of learning and learning about learning.

Lecturing to the Education Deanery staff at Liverpool Hope University in September 2006, Professor Bart MacGettrick from the University of Glasgow underlined the role of humanity as pivotal in the design of an education curriculum. He stressed the need to view the curriculum as a means to an end, not an end in itself. MacGettrick saw the future of education as not merely informing people but forming them, proposing a model of learning to connect course content (principles, knowledge concepts, skills and ideas) with, as summarised by Susan Groundwater-Smith (2006), adjunct professor to Liverpool Hope University, *dispositions to learn, fed by relationships founded and nurtured by emotional and spiritual values.* MacGettrick encouraged the Deanery to exercise ethical courage, suggesting this could be achieved through a curriculum construction which engaged the learner as *an active participant in framing and enacting it*.

There are several ways to incorporate SL at an institution. Some readers may already be involved by having developed modules/courses and established community partners. This approach is effective; however, it is time consuming. The work of managing relationships between community partners and the institution can become competitive or redundant when these efforts are not co-ordinated within one university or college. A productive alternative is to work with colleagues in your department or programme to establish a service-learning plan for this area. Another approach is to work across departments and to collaborate with others who already have established SL within modules or a curriculum.

As a starting point, it's well worth sitting down with a large piece of paper and mind-map the elements existing in your locality which could be used to generate SL /SE activity. Consider your own institution's mission statement and that of potential partners. Where there is some common ground and unity of purpose, blessings can flow. There are clear partners who should be identifiable through their input to the ECM agenda. The police are natural partners here with clear community strategies both national and local which are easily accessed on the internet. Taking time to see who else is already out there in any locality and establishing ways of working with them is time well spent. In the UK, the Dark Horse Venture (**www.darkhorse@rapid.co.uk**, a 55-and-over volunteer organisation) and on an international scale, Rotary (**www.rotary.org**) are two excellent examples of community-focused service. Working with local school networks can provide a wide range of ideas and ongoing projects into which you may see routes to engage your students. Again, schools have mission statements and ECM responsibilities where some synergy can be identified. You may find value in spending some time researching what the government 'Excellence in Cities' (EiC) programme identified as pressure points to the schools in your area (**www.standards.dfes.gov.uk/sie/eic**). Launched in September 1999 to raise standards and promote inclusion, research into its real effects varies widely; but it can help inform your understanding of an area before undertaking an SL/SE activity. Heavily influenced by New Labour social capital theory, you should find that all local authorities and local government must establish links to a community strategy. Local aims can be investigated and linked to ideas, that lectures and students can create and deliver. It is worth exploring links in course content to what excites students and can translate into local action.

We need to learn from earlier examples in our local areas. Although service-learning is not yet as widely implemented in the UK as in the USA and Mexico, there are several service-learning programmes serving individuals in hospitals (e.g. Barnardo's hospitals), schools and residential settings such as the Linden House for the Blind. Great Britain was an early pioneer in SL when in 1975 Imperial College initiated a peer tutoring programme. This programme has evolved and grown over time, gaining support from the company British Petroleum, and developed into an international programme. In Great Britain alone over 50 universities participate in a local tutoring programme (Berry and Chisholm, 1999). These examples can provide fodder for future SL settings and types of arrangements.

In addition to these approaches we propose that further research is needed and that programme developers work closely with researchers to evaluate the pedagogy of blending service-learning with social enterprise. Filling in the gaps from the existing SL research, we need to examine the impact of SL on community partners and agencies (as well as students, faculty and HEA institutions) in addition to community capacity. Central to this should be the role of values across all engaged partners. Expanding outcome research beyond the focus of the student is a next critical step. Beyond outcomes, research also needs to focus on mechanisms of SL so we can better understand when it works and when it does not. All of these areas of research need to consider the influence of social enterprise and how it impacts the SL processes and outcomes.

We suggest that all of the efforts above work towards institutionalising SL. The support of an administration will sustain SL through tangible resources such as office space, staff to co-ordinate placements, faculty development seminars, and notably, credit for SL service. Let us share what works, and identify what can be replicated in diverse communities by our equally diverse student base. It's an exciting time. Eating spaghetti can be great fun.

References

Berry, H.A. and Chisholm, L.A. (1999) *Service-learning in higher education around the world: An initial look.* New York: The International Partnership for Service-Learning.

Bornstein, X. (2004) *How to change the world: Social entrepreneurs and the power of ideas.* New York: Oxford University Press.

Brown, S.D., Pancer, S.M., Henderson, A. and Ellis-Hale, K. (2005) *The impact of high school mandatory service programs on subsequent volunteering and civic engagement.* Research Report to the Knowledge Development Centre, Imagine Canada.

Burley, S. and Huzyka, D. (2000) *Mastering entrepreneurship. Your single source guide to becoming a matter of entrepreneurship.* Prentice Hall, Financial Times.

Butcher, J., Howard, P., Labone, E., Bailey, M., Groundwater-Smith, S., McFadden, M., McMeniman, M., Malone, K. and Martinez, K. (2003) *Asia Pacific Journal of Teacher Education*, 31 (2), 109–124.

Children's and Young People's Partnership (CHYPP, 2005) **www.participationworks.org.uk** (accessed 12 November 2006).

Clarke, E. (1997) *Designing and implementing an integrated curriculum.* Brandon, UT: Holistic Education Press.

Davies, H. (2002) *A review of enterprise and the economy in education.* London: HMSO.

Department for Education and Skills (DfES) (2004) *Every Child Matters: Change for children.* Nottingham: DfES Publications.

Department for Trade and Industry (DTI)/Department for Education and Employment (DfEE) (2000) *Opportunity for all in a world of change. A White Paper For Enterprise.* London: HMSO.

Development and Education Programme for Daughters and Community (DEPDC) (2004) **www.pbs.org/opb/thenewheroes/whatis** (accessed 12 December 2006).

EPPI (2005) *An international review of citizenship education research.* London: The Evidence for Policy and Practice Information and Coordinating Centre.

EPPI (2005) *A systematic review of the impact of citizenship education on the provision of schooling.* London: EPPI.

Giles, D.E. Jr. and Eyler, J. (1994) The impact of a college community service laboratory on students' personal, social and cognitive outcomes. *Journal of Adolescence*, 17, 327–339.

Goleman, D. (1996) *Emotional intelligence. Why it can matter more than IQ.* London: Bloomsbury.

Government's White Paper *Excellence in Schools* (1997) London: Her Majesty's Stationery Office.

Gray, H., Healey, K. and Crofts, P. (June 2003) Social enterprise. Is it the business of social work?. *Australia Social Work*, 56 (2), 141–154.

Groundwater-Smith, S. (2006) Summary of MacGettrick lecture to Liverpool Hope University Education Deanery (September 2006).

Haldane, J. (2004) *Values, education, and the human world*. Exeter: St Andrews Studies in Philosophy and Human Affairs.

Harvard Business School, Public Education Leadership project (PELP) (2005) **www.hbs.edu/social enterprise/whatis.html** (accessed 13 December 2006).

Higher Education Academy (2006) National Professional Standards Framework for Teaching and Supporting Learning in Higher Education. Available online at **www.hcacademy.ac.uk/reganaccr/ |StandardsFramework(1).pdf** (accessed October 2006).

Hinck, S. and Brandell, M (1999) Service-learning: Facilitating academic learning and character development. *National Association of Secondary School Principals*, 83 (609), 16–24.

Ma, H. and Tan, J. (2006) Key components and implications of entrepreneurship: A 4-P framework. *Journal of Business Venturing*, 21 (5), 704–725.

MacGettrick, B. (2006) Lecture to Education Deanery, Liverpool Hope University, September 2006.

Merton, B., Turner, C., Ward, J. and White, L. (2003) National Institute Of Adult Continuing Education, Leicester (England) BBB26304.

National Advisory Committee on Creative and Cultural Education (NACCE) (1999) *All our futures. Creativity, culture and education* (The Robinson Report). London: DfEE.

National Service-Learning and Assessment Study Group (1999) *Service-learning and assessment: A field guide for teachers*. Washington DC: Learn and Serve America. Retrieved 10 November 2003, from **www.servicelearning.org/filemanager/download/45/**.

New National Framework for Professional Standards in Teaching and Supporting Learning, the Standing Conference of Principals (SCOP) Universities UK (UUK), and the Higher Education Academy, 23 February 2006.

Niemi, R.G., Hepburn, M.A. and Chapman, C. (2000) Community service by high school students: A cure for civic ills?. *Political Behavior*, 22 (1), 45–69.

North West Development Agency (NWDA) Objective 3 (2000) NWDA.

Organisation for Economic Co-Operation and Development (OECD) (1998) *Fostering entrepreneurship. The OECD Jobs Strategy*. OECD.

Qualification and Curriculum Authority (QCA) (1998) *Education for citizenship and the teaching of democracy in schools* (Crick Report). London: QCA.

Root, S., Eyler, J. and Giles, D. (2003) The Bonnor Scholars Program: A study of the impact of stipends on indicators of community service ethics. *Metropolitan Universities – An International Forum*, 14 (3), 15–110.

Russell Commission (2005) *A national framework for youth action and engagement*. Executive Summary to The Russell Commission (Russell, I.M.).

Salovey, P. and Mayer, J. (1990) Emotional intelligence. *Imagination, Cognition, and Personality*, 9, 185–211.

Spencer, K. (2005) Higher Education Community Conference, 14th November. Manchester Metropolitan University Conference Centre.

Thompson, J., Alvy, G. and Lees, A. (2000) Social entrepreneurship – a new look at the people and the potential. *Management Decision*, 38 (5/6), 328–338.

Weinreich, D. (2003) Service-learning at the edge of chaos. *Educational Gerontology*, 29, 198–195.

Useful websites

Canadian Association for Service-Learning: **www.communityservicelearning.ca/en/**

(US) National Service-Learning Clearinghouse:

Learn and Serve America, A Program of the Corporation for National and Community Service: **www.learnandserve.org/**

Campus Compact: **www.compact.org/** (Example Service-Learning Syllabi)

The International Partnership for Service-Learning and Leadership, founded in 1982. **www.ipsl.org/ www.schoolsinteractive.co.uk**

www.participationworks.org.uk
www.darkhorse@rapid.co.uk
www.hbs.edu/socialenterprise/whatis.html.

Chapter *13*

Supporting students with disabilities in higher education

Wendy Hall

Introduction

The impetus for this chapter has come from the work that I and other colleagues undertake supporting students with disabilities at Liverpool Hope University. Whilst the reader may take the model used at Hope as an example of helpful practice to follow, it is intended that the issues raised will also prompt reflection on existing practice. After a discussion of the definition of disability, and some of the background, there follows a discussion of implications and issues of the Special Educational Needs and Disability Act (SENDA) of 2001 at the institution, departmental and individual tutor level. Throughout, reference is made to the national Professional Standards Framework, so readers can locate their own practice in conjunction with both these reference points. At various points in the chapter there are discussion points to help readers reflect on the provision in their own institutions. Finally, some case studies are intended to act as a stimulus for further reflection.

Meeting the Standards

This chapter will meet the UK Professional Standards Framework in the following ways and support those with learning disabilities:

- **by aiding the design and planning of learning activities;**
- **by supporting student learning;**
- **by developing appropriate feedback to learners with disabilities;**
- **enhancing the effectiveness of learning environments and student support and guidance (Areas of activity 1, 2, 3 and 4);**
- **by developing appropriate methods for teaching and learning;**
- **by developing knowledge and understanding of how students learn (Core knowledge 2 and 3);**
- **by respecting individual learners;**
- **by deepening commitment to encouraging participation in higher education, acknowledging diversity and promoting equality of opportunity (Professional values 1 and 4).**

(www.heacademy.ac.uk/professionalstandards.htm)

Some common definitions of disability

Section 1 of the Disability Discrimination Act 1995 states that a person has a disability if he or she has a physical or mental impairment which has a substantial and long-term adverse effect on their ability to carry out normal day-to-day activities. JISC Legal (undated) further indicates that:

> a student may come under the definition of 'learning difficulty' in terms of other legislation such as the Further and Higher Education (Scotland) Act 1992 or the Learning and Skills Act 2000. However this does not necessarily mean that the student is disabled under the definition as stated in the Disability Discrimination Act 1995 section 2.2 para 3.

In 2001 SENDA amended the 1995 Act, drawing in education, which had previously been exempt. Since then the Disability Rights Commission (2006a) has requested a review of the definition of disability to focus less on the medical state of the person but rather on the impact of any unfair, or unjustified, treatment, and any disadvantage resulting from such treatment.

Background

SENDA has changed the status of students with disabilities throughout education. Concurrently, there has been a groundswell of support for the moral rationale underpinning the provision of greater opportunity to people with disabilities. Since SENDA, more and more students are entering higher education and the range of disabilities has also grown, notwithstanding the following statistics provided by the Disability Rights Commission (2006b) on its site:

- *21% of disabled people aged 16–24 have no qualifications whatsoever, compared to 9% of non-disabled people of the same age – an 11% gap.*

- *Disabled 16 year olds are twice as likely to be out of work, education or training as their non-disabled peers (15% compared to 7%).*

This is a situation which is totally within our control to change, but the sheer diversity of disabilities that are now commonly encountered in higher education means that there has to be a significant re-ordering of priorities for university teachers.

In 1995 asthma was the predominant declared disability. However, currently declared disabilities include sensory disabilities, physical disabilities, autistic spectrum disorders as well as the more common specific learning difficulties including dyslexia, dyspraxia, attention deficit/hyperactivity disorder, Irlen syndrome and mental health difficulties. There are also students with medical conditions which many tutors have not heard of previously and may never meet again once that student has left. This has coincided with a time of financial contraction in many areas so that staff who are already taking on more responsibilities than previously are also being asked to provide teaching material in a variety of formats for different learning needs, and to rethink how they present to such an eclectic group. Potentially, this could create an explosion in workload and presents a challenge to all concerned in managing this situation.

The basis of this chapter is that students with disabilities are entering higher education in ever greater numbers and have a right to demonstrate their capabilities as much as other students. It is the responsibility of those who work in universities to make sure that students' disabilities do not prevent them from gaining that access to learning or prevent them from demonstrating their knowledge and understanding. We also need to keep in mind that many of our students are mature students and bring with them a history of prejudice and negative perceptions in relation to their disability. Adults also have particular ways of learning because they are adult and they have found their own methods over the years which support them in managing their disability (Rogers, 1992).

The anticipatory duty clause of SENDA places a responsibility on us to consider and reflect on an institution's provision in the event of a student with any disability applying, and not just to consider the needs of current students. Again, given the variety of disabilities, and how these are increasing daily as more is learnt about disability, this is not an easy challenge to meet. This requirement needs to be addressed at three levels.

1. Institutional level.
2. Sub-organisational level, e.g. faculty.
3. Teaching team/tutor level.

The challenges institutions and tutors to:

- **ensure support for the transition to higher education, which can be particularly difficult for disabled students, and provide ongoing social support (personal tutoring);**
- **provide for, and support access to, the subjects the students wish to study, including analysing assessment strategies to ensure equality of opportunity;**
- **use time and other resources efficiently and proportionately, and make best use of the resources available.**

HEFCE (1996) identified six success factors for effective inclusion as:

- **institutional commitments;**
- **strategic planning;**
- **staff development;**
- **learner support;**
- **embedding of any project;**
- **monitoring services.**

These factors involve raising awareness whilst auditing provision and increasing advice and information to staff, and an improvement in support and teaching for all students, as a consequence of improvements for those with disabilities. The full HEFCE report provides further details of successful implementation for supporting students with disabilities.

Institutional issues

How an institution markets itself, the location of marketing strategies and the accessibility of promotional materials are of crucial importance in the first instance in demonstrating an institutional commitment to inclusion. This may be the first aspect that Higher Education Institutions (HEIs) wish to review.

Discussion point

In your institution:

- Are you only using traditional forms of marketing or are you making use of internet sites and other resources?

- Do open days provide a quiet area for hard-of-hearing students; is there assistance for wheelchair users, and are all staff informed of available support?

- Is signage on campus suitable for students with visual difficulties and at a good level for wheelchair users?

- Is the décor of accommodation sufficiently contrasting and suitable for visually impaired visitors?

- Are Braille buttons at a height so that a visually impaired wheelchair user could use them easily?

- Is there a designated area/policy for the use of guide dogs?

- Do resources reflect the needs of all disabilities, such as subtitles for the hard of hearing?

- Can you/do you provide marketing material in a variety of formats?

All staff involved in recruitment days need to be aware of the answers to these questions, not just a few 'specialists', as this reflects the awareness and importance attached to such issues. If someone does not know the answers or has to find out, it may suggest to the potential student that this is a low-priority area.

Use of ICT

For the benefit of existing disabled students, and for consideration as a marketing point for future students, there should be a review of the technology infrastructure and how this facilitates the support of those students with disabilities.

- **Is the infrastructure capable of supporting traditional and e learning adequately? E-learning is one of the resources valued most by disabled students.**
- **Are there support facilities for staff struggling with new technology and presentations to support students with disabilities who rely on this medium of tuition?**

This review of facilities should have been ongoing in the last few years. If it has not, you may wish to bring this to the attention of the person responsible for the impact assessment of 2006.

The role of student support services

In many HEIs, all students declaring a disability on application are invited to an interview with the university student support service (SSS) prior to acceptance onto a course. This service is university wide and provided across all departments. The student support service helps students to identify their learning and support needs, devising a learning support plan which is then distributed (with the student's permission) and also assists them in completing the application forms for the Disabled Student's Allowance. Student support staff at many HEIs also act as an advocate for students, and liaise very often between a student and the local education authority. The learning support plan may detail points of contact for the student including named personnel in the library, and, for example, at Liverpool Hope, a named Disability Adviser (DA) in each department. This person forms a point of contact once students are accepted on a course and all students are advised to make contact with their DA early on.

The SSS plays a strategic role for all students with disabilities by undertaking risk assessments of teaching areas, ensuring disability compliance on field trips, ensuring accommodation needs are met and providing essential equipment such as vibrating alarms for deaf students. The SSS may also provide the main input for staff training about disabilities meeting with the Disability Advisers as a group, say, at least once a term. The level of support from SSS varies between institutions and is often a factor that influences recruitment of disabled students.

Sub-organisational issues

Feedback at a recent Training and Development Agency (TDA) conference suggested that the role of the DA in a department is uncommon, yet it is arguably integral to the support network and the efficient management of teaching and learning. There are arguably three distinct aspects to the role of the DA:

- **supervising and managing appropriate academic support, ensuring it is available across the department;**
- **keeping abreast of legislative issues and training needs of staff, i.e. providing a point of reference for information for staff;**
- **providing pastoral care for disabled students in an otherwise hectic and changing environment.**

The Disability Adviser can provide a point of reference between the SSS and the academic tutors and is crucial for agreeing how students' needs are met within any department, in accordance with their agreed Learning Support Plan (LSP). Once agreed, the DA disseminates the LSP to teaching staff and provides a point of contact for both staff and students. The DA queries the nature of any disability with which s/he is not familiar and includes this in the details for staff, and will also provide a point of contact for students who may be dissatisfied with an aspect of provision. Even good provision sometimes falls down under the pressure of a busy timetable. For example, a quick email from the DA to a group of staff reminding them of the need to provide appropriate hard copy for students who need this, often works better than the students having to make this request several times over.

If there is no DA in post, these responsibilities could fall to individual tutors, which could then create a diversity of support across the organisation both positively and negatively.

The DA may also provide a source of information, ideas and simple tips for tutors. One example of this is to email students with an electronic version of the notes/OHPs or handouts of a session before the taught session. Tutors are advised to compile a group email in their personal mailbox. In order to observe confidentiality, the tutors are advised to email this to themselves and blind copy the group into this email. This has the advantage that students can adapt notes to any font or size they wish and, using the 'sent items' facility, tutors can check who has opened the mail ready for the lecture. There are disadvantages to this system, such as compatibility of software. It also takes time to access material if the student is using a dial-up service, or has a limited mailbox which will not accommodate large attachments, while some students use this as an opportunity to not attend the lecture but still know the content of the session. Another example of support for staff is a handbook of guidance, detailing suitable amendments and presentation techniques for lectures, seminars and workplace observations across a variety of disabilities. The same (edited) guidance can be given to students for information. A website for disabled students is usual at most HEIs where students can access information relating to services and disabilities.

For such a system to work effectively within an institution, the personal skills and knowledge of the DAs need constant updating. They need to be able to demonstrate how students can adapt university-wide formats for their own purposes or how to access certain information online. They also need to be able to advise staff who have difficulty accessing relevant information from web-based sources. Although many students are eligible for specialist external tutor support, others prefer to use a familiar DA who knows the requirements of their courses.

Experienced Disability Advisers should know all the students within their remit who have learning support plans. They should also know of the support and assistance which is available through the Student Support Service, and often social monitoring can be undertaken informally between the SSS and the DA.

Finally, the DA can be the point of contact and comfort for a disabled student who is away from normal family support structures for the first time. Disability advisers can become almost like surrogate parents, coaxing students through, when the student claims s/he 'can't do this; it is too hard'. They are often the only persons who know the background of particular students. This is in stark contrast to many sixth forms which often provide a year tutor who knows the 40 or so students in that year group individually. The Department for Education and Skills (DfES, 2006) notes that some HEIs organise pre-entry familiarisation visits and actively manage the transition between FE and HE. The pastoral role of the DA, who tracks a group of students, cannot be overemphasised and was one of the recommendations made when provision at Liverpool Hope University was evaluated and audited in 2002 (Power et al., 2002).

Administrative issues related to courses

Many student notices are provided in a format and font which are not suitable for a good number of students with the disabilities of dyslexia, dyspraxia and visual disability. The positioning of some notices is not accessible for wheelchair users. Timetables may be printed off in grids of no more than font 12 and placed on noticeboards at a height of 2 or more metres from the ground, the average eye height of a standing adult. This height is not suitable for students using wheelchairs and the font is not suitable for many disabilities. A personal recommendation is that all notices are printed in bold font 14 for all students and placed no more than 1.5 metres from the ground. This should be supported by general guidance of font 14 being suitable for the needs of dyslexic students, while the height should be suitable for a wheelchair user. In addition to this, many students have the requirement to have notices emailed to them by the support staff for that course. Similarly, tutors should use standard fonts of one colour rather than some of the more artistic fonts which can prove difficult for some students.

Assessment

At your institution, you may wish to consider the following questions.

- **Do your assessment strategies use traditional exam or essay forms? Are there better ways of assessing some students with disabilities? Do your assessments present a good balance or a choice for students?**
- **Are your adjustments really beneficial – can disabled students take exams in a peaceful environment or do people taking rest breaks provide distraction?**
- **Do submissions by course work carry the same extra time allowance that exams carry or is there a detriment to students undertaking courses assessed mainly by course work?**
- **Are oral presentations balanced by another option, such as presentation of a DVD for students who are not able to present well orally?**
- **Are you clear on what you are assessing: the ability to convey information or the information itself?**
- **Do all essays need to conform to a format or can the information be presented in a variety of formats equally well?**

In respect of individual tutors one might reflect on the following.

- **Documentation and how this is prepared and distributed; the use of e-versions or hard copy; accessibility issues related to e-learning.**
- **Access to and set-up of a room – to ensure access for students with mobility difficulties and the use of a horseshoe shape to facilitate discussion activities with deaf or visually impaired students.**
- **Method of teaching and resources used – use of ICT, including interactive whiteboards, which may include individual monitors for some students, tape recorders, use of laptops, provision of individual handouts as well as group versus class teaching.**
- **Pace of delivery and range of activity – breaking the session into manageable chunks, recapping and arranging for a variety of activities to suit different needs; many students experience processing difficulties when requested to perform either single or series of tasks (Singleton et al., 2001).**
- **Assessment strategies both on course and as final assessment: does a course or module include a range of forms of assessment and choice?**
- **Tutor support for those who require particular assistance such as glossaries, proofreading and feedback on drafts. DfES (2006) details how even the most well-prepared and self-sufficient students can feel 'deskilled in the face of unfamiliar and varying academic practices'.**

Some examples of good practice

Good practice for disabled students means providing them with a high-quality learning experience. Resources invested in such practices should not be viewed as limited for the use of disabled students but should be regarded as an investment to benefit all students. The following are some practical suggestions which readers might like to consider in their own practice.

1. Where documentation is word-processed and available to staff and students from an electronic source, font 14 bold should be used to write the original. This can then be reduced easily to font 12 for general use. This is easier than enlarging. Photocopying of font 12 should not be considered as this enlarges spaces as well as the typeface. Font 14 bold serves the needs of most students requiring enlarged or adapted hard copy and is then ready when the need arises. Braille is very rarely used but can be provided by SSS through software.

2. A policy decision about the method of distribution of documentation and its implications should be applied consistently within courses, although it does not have to be the same over different courses. It is essential that, on any particular course, if a hard copy is given to non-disabled students, then an appropriate hard copy (in whatever format is required) is provided to the disabled students and they are not told to run their own copy from the electronic source. This could result in a claim of discrimination on the basis of less favourable treatment.

3. It is important, when devising courses which include trips or specific reading, that the tutor is sure that these can be accessed by all students or that reasonable adjustments can be made. Trips which are essential, but prevent some disabled students from participating, need to be evaluated and alternatives found which serve the same purpose but are accessible to all students. Issues of access can sometimes be solved by the use of alternative transport or an extra adult to assist the disabled student, funded from the Disabled Students' Allowance. Required reading, as opposed to optional reading, should be available to all students; it is therefore essential to check whether texts are available as electronic versions. Where this is not possible, visually impaired students needing a copy of the text may have the material scanned onto a CD and provided so that it can be read by appropriate software. The Copyright (visually impaired persons) Act 2002 (RNIB, 2002) allows this as long as it is not issued for general access and is limited to the use of the visually-impaired student. However, RNIB advises that it also states: *The right does not apply if an equivalent accessible copy is already available commercially*. Unfortunately, the same law does not give provision for other disabilities. Many disabled students will rely more heavily on reading than on lectures and therefore need reading lists well ahead of other students in order to benefit from the lectures (RNID, 2006). This implies that tutors are aware of this and have prepared their lists well in advance, or have updated reading lists to include e-versions of texts.

4. On course.

   a. Use of PowerPoint

   Tutors will have a variety of different needs in any one lecturing group. PowerPoint is a favoured medium for lectures nowadays. However, tutors need to be aware of some disadvantages of its use. Some of the backgrounds for powerpoint are too 'fussy' for use with students who may be dyslexic, dyspraxic or visually impaired. A simple uncluttered background provides the best backdrop for text. Tutors also need to think of the needs of deaf students when writing a PowerPoint presentation. Many deaf students lip-read and will need to have good lighting for this. When PowerPoint is used in well-lit surroundings, the contrast between text and background needs to be greater than in a dimmed environment. Yellow on dark blue is the favoured colour to accommodate the needs of most students with visual resolution difficulties such as dyslexia, Irlen syndrome, some visual impairments or lip-reading students. Deaf students should also be encouraged to sit near the front of a lecture theatre for lip-reading. Many are not aware of the difficulties of higher education and its different environment until they have struggled for half a year.

   b. Room set-up and mode of teaching

   While the needs of dyslexic, dyspraxic and ADHD students are relatively easily met through appropriate documentation, the needs of hearing-impaired and visually impaired students, however, require more thought and adaptation of style. These students need more than just their own copies of materials. Each of these groups requires a specific set-up to the room so that students can see any overhead projections, or will need their own copy of this material with time to digest the contents. They will find it very difficult to multi-task in the way we expect most students to.

   c. The lecture situation

   One might spend a few minutes reflecting on what is expected of most students in a lecture. This will include several of the following simultaneously: listening, note-taking, reading, thinking, formulating questions, acting on instructions, posing questions. Many disabled students are only able to do each of these in turn without experiencing difficulty. To listen and take notes, which is a very basic activity in most lecture sessions, is very difficult for dyslexic, Irlen syndrome and hearing-impaired students. Each group may need special consideration when teaching, as so much is conveyed through facial expression. Lip-reading students need to be able to see the tutor's face clearly with good lighting on the face. This is very difficult if tutors have a habit of walking around while talking or turning their back to point to visual displays. A well thought-out delivery helps students keep track of what is being said. Interjections and asides are not very helpful for deaf students who may be struggling with keeping up with the focus of the lecture, nor to autistic spectrum disorder students. Tutors need an understanding of the difficulties of hearing-impaired students and to adjust their method of delivery as needed. This can be achieved easily through activities in training, which can be undertaken either in-house or by requesting an input on deaf awareness from your local centre for deaf people. Sometimes it is helpful to have a friendly observer sit in to note 'bad habits' and point them out, as usually we do not know our own habits and students are often too polite to enlighten us. Visually impaired students may also need to sit near the front to pick up on any visual cues but they should be provided with either a personal copy of the material being used or they could use a copy of the material run on their own laptops. Again there is a need for vigilance and observation to see if they are keeping up with the rest of the class. Addressing them by name is particularly useful in encouraging them to join in discussion, as is directing them in group activities, as often they miss the cues which other students pick up on. Care is needed for any discussion and group work, as both deaf students and visually impaired students need special consideration in order to participate fully. Discussion groups are particularly problematic both in tutor rooms, and in the context of a large room housing several groups.

d. When several groups are engaging in discussion within a large room, it may be necessary to locate some groups outside the room so that interference noise is limited. Other suggestions for managing talk are to:
   - use a chairperson to keep order or allocate roles in a group;
   - record on a large chart what has to be achieved by whom, when, what the main points made are;
   - make sure seating is in a horseshoe so that all can see and be seen;
   - limit numbers to four in a group.

e. Looped systems need checking to ensure that the systems are working, and that all equipment has fresh batteries. The only way to do this is with a student who uses the looped system, so it is often helpful to ask a student using these facilities to arrive early so that you can check they are all working. If the student is happy to rely on other methods if the system doesn't work, then there isn't a problem but you do need to demonstrate that you have taken every effort to support his/her needs.

f. Many of the courses in HEIs are now located in virtual learning environments or through DVD or other electronic versions. Accountability (2006) cites research which found that disabled students rated the value of the internet more highly than non-disabled people. However, the same source states that they often find themselves on the wrong side of the digital divide, supporting the findings of Sloan (2001) in relation to flawed access. Whilst this is largely an institutional issue, it is one individual tutors should be aware of, and responsive to, if supporting students with disabilities.

g. Auditing ICT facilities. Below are some key guidelines.
   - Are websites accessible to all or is the design inherently flawed to limit access? (Sloan, 2001)
   - Do ICT facilities provide wide bays and lower surfaces for those using wheelchairs?
   - Is there a wide range of resources such as head pointers and blowers? (Becta, 2003)
   - Are all students expected to use standard facilities or can provision be adapted for those with limited dexterity, or limited ability, to sit for a prolonged time in front of a screen?
   - Is voice-activated software (VAS) used without thought of the difficulties it can create? Often a text reader is more useful than VAS.

h. Most ICT labs tend to be a standard design with little thought given to disability issues. The ICT itself seems to be the answer to access for disabled people. Phipps et al. (2002) provide a comprehensive overview of technology in relation to disability.

It is important always to be aware of the limitations, as well as the opportunities, of what is being offered and of any alternatives. In all cases, fitness for purpose should be evaluated. The onus should be on the provider offering a suitable adjustment, rather than waiting until the student encounters a difficulty and requests it. This is enshrined in the anticipatory duty under the 2001 Act (SENDA, 2001).

It is worth considering the research findings on learning styles (Mortimore, 2003) and multiple intelligences, when thinking about the implications of only allowing for one method of presenting information or problem-solving for disabled students. It might be helpful in cases where there are only single methods of assessment to analyse the grades. If this analysis reveals an inequity, then it may be necessary to carry out an overall review of assessment procedures.

Reflective practice means thinking carefully about how best to ensure that disabled students receive a comparably high-quality learning experience as enjoyed by their non-disabled peers. This chapter has attempted to suggest many different ways of thinking about the issues at a number of different levels as well as to give some pointers. The case studies that follow are designed to aid reflective practice and would work best in team discussions.

Case studies

1. A blind student, assisted by a guide dog, is coming to study English and history as combined honours. They wish to be resident on campus. The student has previously been accommodated in sheltered accommodation, whilst studying away from home for A levels. This accommodation has included a high proportion of elderly people who are also visually impaired.

   What are the academic and social issues at both institutional level and tutor level that this student will present?

2. A trainee teacher at secondary level has a severe visual disability. This disability requires drops to be put in the eyes each morning and it takes several hours for the eyes to adjust. The student cannot see further than about 10 feet in front even when the drops have become effective. His specialist subject is ICT and he uses an adapted screen magnifier and specialist software. He has difficulty using public transport due to his limited vision.

   Identify the training needs of this student and any potential issues arising out of school placement.

3. A student studying drama and English has been deafened in her teenage years through an accident. She has learnt Standard English as her first language and does not use sign language. However, her progress in learning to lip-read is limited. Consider the needs of this student. What resource implications are presented and how might you address this student's personal and social needs?

References

Accountability – Employers forum on disability (2006) *Disability and the digital divide. An employer's forum on disability*. Briefing for CSR Practitioners.

Becta (2003) *Physical disabilities and ICT Guidance document*. **www.schools.becta.org.uk/** (Jan 2003) (accessed 24 July 2006).

DfES (2006) *A framework for understanding dyslexia*. Available at **www.dfes.gov.uk/readwriteplus/ understandingdyslexia/** (accessed 24 July 2006).

DfES (2006) *A Framework for understanding dyslexia*. London: HMSO.

Disability Rights Commission (2006a) *We want a society where all disabled people can participate fully as equal citizens*. **www.disabilitydebate.org/about_the_debate.aspx** (accessed 24 July 2006).

Disability Rights Commission (2006b) 16 year olds. **www.drc-gb.org/newsroom/key_drc_ facts_and_glossary/16_year_olds.aspx** (accessed on 18 August 2006).

HEFCE (1996) Access to higher education: Students with learning difficulties and disabilities. Ref M 23/96 August 1996: **www.hefce.ac.uk/pubs/hefce/1996/m23_96.htm** (accessed on 24 July 2006).

JISC Legal (updated) *Accessibility disability overview* by the JISC Legal Information Service **www.jisclegal.ac.uk/disability/accessibility.htm** (accessed on 24 July 2006).

Mortimore, T. (2003) *Dyslexia and learning style; A practitioner's handbook*. London: Whurr.

Phipps, L., Sutherland, A. and Seale, J. (2002) *Access all areas: disability, technology and learning*. JISC TechDis and ALT.

Power, C., Coufopoulos, A., Torkington, P. and Evans, A. (2002) *Unique hope for students with disabilities evaluation project 2002*. The Applied Research Centre Liverpool Hope.

RNIB (2002) Copyright (Visually Impaired Persons) Act 2002 **www.rnib.org.uk/xpedio/groups/ public/documents/publicwebsite/public_cvipsact2002.hcsp** (accessed 15 November 2006).

RNIB (2006) *Teaching strategies to use with deaf and hard of hearing students – advice for lecturers in further and higher education*. Available at **www.rnid.org.uk/information_resources/factsheets/ education/factsheets_leaflets**.

Rogers, A. (1992) *Teaching adults*. Milton Keynes: Open University Press.

Seale, J. (2002) So what does this all mean for me?, in *Access all areas: disability, technology and learning*. JISC TechDis and ALT.

SENDA Special Educational Needs and Disability Act 2001 **www.opsi.gov.uk/acts/acts2001/ 10010--d.htm** (accessed 24 July 2006).

Singleton, C., Pumfrey, P., Stacey, G. and Gibberd, D. (2001) *Dyslexia in higher education: a review of progress in the UK.* Presented as a symposium paper at the BDA International conference 2001.

Sloan, M. (2001) Web Accessibility and the DDA, *Journal of Information Law and Technology.* Available at **www2.warwick.ac.uk/fac/soc/law/elj/jilt/2001_2/sloan/** (accessed 24 July 2006).

University of Greenwich (2006) *Briefings for personal tutors and their students.* Available at **greguns1.gre.ac.uk/Registry/personal.nsf/504ca249c786e20f85256284006da7ab/28ffcf 953a30d005802566c60046d693?OpenDocument** (accessed 24 July 2006).

Further reading

Ability, see the ability not the disability **www.ability.org.uk/deaf.html** (accessed 19 January 2007).

Association of Dyslexia in Higher Education **www.adshe.org.uk** (accessed 19 Janury 2007).

Directgov Higher Education – disabled students **www.direct.gov.uk/DisabledPeople/Education AndTraining/HigherEducation/HigherEducationArticles/fs/en?CONTENT_ID=4000917 &chk=MnXE84**.

Dyslexia-adults **www.dyslexia-adults.com**.

The Dyspraxia Foundation **www.dyspraxiafoundation.org.uk/** (accessed 20 January 2007).

HERO Higher Education and Research Opportunities **www.hero.ac.uk/uk/studying/index.cfm** (accessed 20 January 2007).

Higher Education Academy (2006) Embedding success, enhancing the learning experience of disabled students.

MALTS: E-Learning **www.elearn.malts.ed.ac.uk/links/external.phtml** (accessed 20 January 2007).

National Disability Authority **www.nda.ie/cntmgmtnew.nsf** (accessed 24 January 2007).

Royal National Institute for the Blind **www.rnib.org.uk/xpedio/groups/public/documents/code/ InternetHome.hcsp** (accessed 20 January 2007).

Seale, J.K. (2006) *E-learning and disability in higher education. Accessibility research and practice.* Routledge **www.eprints.soton.ac.uk/19341/** (accessed 20 January 2007).

Skill – National bureau for students with disabilities **www.skill.org.uk/info/pubs.asp** (accessed 20 January 2007).

Chapter 14

The development of reflective practice in higher education: a theoretical perspective

Lin Norton and Anne Campbell

Introduction

In this final chapter it is intended to explore some of the theoretical underpinnings of reflective practice and action research. In doing this there will be a brief outline of the context of university education and the current emphasis on autonomy and individuality. It will be argued that this has some negative as well as positive benefits when thinking about education and higher education in particular, which means a call for evidence and engaging with the scholarship of teaching and learning. In the light of the whole thrust of the book, the editors are suggesting that in order to contend with the disparate demands and pressures of being a university teacher and/or facilitator of student learning, the development of reflective practice is a way forward that can be practically realised through a form of action research or practitioner inquiry.

Meeting the Standards

This chapter will meet the UK Professional Standards Framework in the following ways:

- **by promoting the integration of scholarship, research and professional activities with teaching and supporting learning (Area of activity 5);**
- **by demonstrating how reflection contributes to developing methods and for evaluating the effectiveness of teaching (Core knowledge 5);**
- **by emphasising the role of reflection in enhancing a commitment to continuing professional development and evaluation of practice (Professional values 5)**
  (www.heacademy.ac.uk/professionalstandards.htm)

As mentioned in Chapter 1, the context is that of the 'age of the learner' where the emphasis has changed from a teacher focus to a learner focus. Seen in this light, reflective practice is also a powerful way of modelling for our students the advantages of taking a reflective approach. King and Kitchener (1994) have researched the development of reflective judgement in students for many years by investigating their reasoning about ill-structured 'real world' problems for which there are no neat solutions. This developmental progression between childhood and adulthood has profound implications for the ways students approach their study of a discipline and ultimately come to realise its epistemological foundations. By taking a reflective approach, students will be able to think more critically, but will also in a related process become aware of themselves as learners, by developing meta-learning awareness (Meyer and Norton, 2004). Meta-learning is a concept that is discussed by several authors in this book and is important for the focus it places on the learner rather than on the teacher. As Sotto (1994) suggests, no matter how effective our teaching and assessment practices are, they count for little if the students are not learning anything. Engaging students in effective reflective learning is the theme of a useful and practical guide by Cowan (2006) which reiterates some of the issues that emerge from this book, when considering the benefits of being a reflective practitioner. In so doing, there is an acknowledgment that reflective practice itself is not without its critics and these are briefly considered here. The argument that is being put forward is the driving force behind the whole book, that reflective practice can be conceptualised in different ways to suit different purposes, as demonstrated in the chapters that go to make up this book. Finally, the editors conclude with their own personal belief about the potential power that developing reflective practice can, and should have, on improving learning teaching and assessment in higher education.

Reflective practice: the origins

The phrase 'developing reflective practice' in the title of this book foregrounds the importance of the role of the practitioner in higher education, be that the experienced lecturer, the novice demonstrator or the professional librarian. All are practitioners and all have an impact on the quality of the learning experience of our students. What does being a reflective practitioner actually mean and how can those of us who work in universities ensure that our reflection and experience impact on the student experience? The word 'reflection' is crucial as the book is grounded in others' practical experience so that readers can construct their own sense from what has been shared here and begin to see how such practices might impact on their teaching and students' learning. Moon's (2004) description of reflection as an evolving capacity within individuals best captures the experience and practice described in the various chapters that constitute this book. Our fellow authors have, in their writing, exemplified many different facets of reflective practice but common to all is this sense of evolution and development.

Moon gives a clear exposition of reflection, tracing its origins and the many context-dependent interpretations of the word. She acknowledges the contributions of two philosophers, in particular: John Dewey and Jürgen Habermas, calling their thinking the *backbone philosophies of reflection*. John Dewey (1859–1952) was one of America's most influential philosophers and educators who was also a prolific writer. Dewey said that reflective thinking is caused by some difficulty, uncertainty or doubt, and he pointed out that real reflective thinking is hard and uncomfortable:

> *Reflective thinking is always more or less troublesome because it involves overcoming the inertia that inclines one to accept suggestions at their face value; it involves willingness to endure a condition of mental unrest.*

(Dewey, 1910, p13)

Most tellingly for the reflective practitioner, he also argued that reflective activity should include some form of testing out ideas derived from reflective thinking and he said that reflective thinking means suspending our judgement until we have carried out some sort of systematic enquiry. Applying these precepts to the higher education context, this means careful analysis of the issue, the uncomfortable time (enduring the condition of mental unrest) of working out what might be the causes and what might be potential solutions, and then taking action in the form of testing out the preferred solution. Such a process is not very different from hypothetical-deductive reasoning employed in positivist science.

Moon's other 'backbone philosopher' was Jürgen Habermas, who was specifically concerned with knowledge in the service of emancipatory interests. Habermas challenged empirical analytical enquiry, claiming it is not a sufficient basis for producing knowledge, as scientific interpretations are themselves subjective. Habermas has had a profound influence on the field of action research, so will be returned to later in this chapter.

Any consideration of reflective practice must acknowledge the seminal work of Schön (1983, 1987). Schön's thinking developed from his earlier work with Argyris on the distinction between espoused theories (what we believe) and theories in use (what we enact). This is mentioned earlier in Norton's chapter (Chapter 9) on assessment (see Argyris and Schön, 1974). Building on this, Schön's basic premise was a distinction between reflection-in-action and reflection-on-action. Very briefly, Schön believed that refection-in-action occurs when the practitioner, in our case the university educator, is teaching and something unplanned for occurs, such as students have not brought their prepared readings to a seminar class. In this situation the teacher will reflect and take some action but this will bear very little relation to her/his espoused theory. S/he might, for example, substitute a 'mini-lecture' in the seminar class which is in direct contradiction to her/his espoused theory of taking a facilitative, not teaching, role in seminars. Reflection-on-action is the type of reflection that occurs after the action and may well involve espoused theory. There have been many criticisms of the rather fuzzy distinction made by Schön, but what he has done is to make clear how professionals enhance their practice while they are engaging in it.

Brockbank and McGill (1998) take up these ideas and apply them to the higher education context for three main reasons.

1. It enables the teacher to learn from and therefore potentially enhance their practice and learning about their practice.
2. It enables the teacher to come to an understanding of the reflective process and so be able to make it accessible to students through modelling it.
3. Making reflective practice accessible to students enables them to become aware of the power of reflection in and on their own learning approaches (described as meta-learning in several earlier chapters).

Brockbank and McGill argue that this is not a 'bolt-on' activity but should be a core element of a teacher's work. We would go further and say that our view as expounded by our fellow authors is that reflective practice allied to continuing professional development is one of the hallmarks of professionalism. This is consonant with the view of many theorists and practitioners who work in higher education and therein lies a potential weakness. Because of this widespread acceptance of reflection and reflective practice, some critics have suggested that it is no more than a potential 'fashionable' solution to the tensions inherent in the competing demands of continuing professional development, professional autonomy and institutional and sector demands for accountability.

Reflective practice: the criticisms

When considering the nature of reflection, professional standards and the improvement of the student learning experience, it is instructive to look at the arguments of Knight (2002), who cautions against putting overmuch faith in reflection … *as a means to improve teaching or any other practice* (Knight, 2002, p29). His argument rests on several criticisms, including that of Schön's inconsistency in distinguishing between reflection-in-action and reflection-on-action. His other criticisms include those set out below.

- **The term itself has been used in different ways and this has resulted in confusion.**
- **Reflection can be easily devalued by being confused with any type of thinking (Parker, 1997).**
- **Reflection may become *closed-circle thinking which confirms one's original feeling of rightness of thoughts* (our response to this particular criticism would be to go back to the original work of Dewey, who in our earlier quote made the point that reflective thought actually is uncomfortable).**
- **Reflection is not necessarily proved to be a failsafe way of converting one's tacit knowledge into explicit knowledge.**

We would add another: reflection in itself does not necessarily lead to action, a point that is developed further in the following section.

The reflective practitioner: a pragmatic approach

To guard against the introspective passive potential of reflection, it is helpful to draw on the works of Albert Ellis (1997), the founder of rational emotive behaviour therapy, who in writing about people's problems, argues that insight on its own is not enough, that people need to constantly and consistently work and practise in the 'here and now' to change their problems by changing their thinking and their feeling in order to take action to improve the situation. By transposing reflection for insight, the implications for being a reflective practitioner in higher education become clear. Taking action is also at the heart of the action research movement where the aim is to bring about change. Given the caveats about reflective practice, it is important to make the implicit explicit. It is also vital that university educators' tacit knowledge about their teaching and their students' learning is explicitly articulated and disseminated so, where possible, good practice can be shared in the higher education community. 'Going public' is one response to criticisms as it opens up one's work to peer review (Norton et al., 2004).

This book has been, in essence, a 'public' account of how individuals make that private and individual activity explicit, accountable and testable. In the constituent chapters, the reader will have seen examples of this being done in different ways such as taking account of the student experience, course evaluation, analysing students' academic performance, discussing ideas with a trusted colleague or mentor, or through peer observation of teaching. These could all be classified as externally driven stimuli.

Other chapter authors have acted from an internally generated intellectual curiosity (see Breslow *et al.*, 2004) about some element of their teaching, or innovation, or issue around learning that has arisen and that they have decided to pursue. In so doing, they have begun to engage with the considerable literature that exists in the scholarship of teaching and learning (a key example of this is Beaumont's chapter – Chapter 8 – in which he has carefully reviewed much of the research literature on artificial intelligence and student learning). The term of 'scholarship of teaching and learning' (SOTL) is not yet widely recognised in the UK but is certainly gathering momentum in the USA, as witnessed by the establishment of the International Society for the Scholarship of Teaching and Learning (IS.SOTL) (**www.issotl.org/index.html**, accessed 28 January 2007). According to Healey (2003), the basic elements of the scholarship of teaching and learning include engaging with the literature, reflection-on-practice in the context of a subject discipline and, most crucially, disseminating the ideas, knowledge and contributions to theory. This is what we mean by going public as mentioned earlier.

Context of university education: autonomy

University teachers engage in pedagogy in many ways and the current drive is a voluntary one through the auspices of the Higher Education Academy and the National Professional Standards Framework, which lays down core areas and principles which are intended to be broad enough to allow each university to interpret and apply them according to its own needs. This acknowledgment of the importance of institutional and personal autonomy is very much a feature of the higher education landscape in the UK, and in England can be seen through HEFCE teaching quality enhancement funding, which operates at three levels, explained below.

1. At individual level, through the National Teaching Fellowship Scheme.
2. At institutional level, through quality enhancement allocations such as the support of teaching enriched by research, and the establishment of 74 Centres for Excellence in Teaching and Learning (of which Liverpool Hope University is involved in two: LearnHigher **www.learnhigher.ac.uk/** and Write Now **www.writenow.ac.uk/**).
3. Sector-wide through the Higher Education Academy. Interestingly, one of its major successes has been the continuation of the 24 Subject Centres (originally established by the Institute for Learning and Teaching in Higher Education). These centres are hosted by universities and offer learning and teaching support for practitioners, subject departments and discipline communities.

Such an emphasis on autonomy of our higher education institutions and trusting in individual teachers' professionalism does, however, throw up some serious tensions.

Where is the evidence?

One of the disadvantages of such academic autonomy is that education, at all levels, has always been prey to a tendency to adopt the latest fashionable idea, without, it seems to us, too much attention paid to the evidence or the underlying theory. This is not to say that evidence itself is 'innocent'. Indeed, as

Botha *et al.* (2006) argue, evidence can be used politically and/or personally to influence policy at a management decision-making level. It can also be used and interpreted subjectively to perhaps blind the researcher or the user of the research to what they want to believe in. Again, this is one of the criticisms of reflective practice. Botha and his colleagues challenge a simplistic or 'reified' notion of evidence that sometimes underpins the insistence on evidence-based decision-making and propose instead the use of the term 'evidence-informed' decision-making. They argue, instead, that the establishment and enhancement of a culture of evidence-informed decision-making in higher education is desirable for a whole range of reasons. It is heartening to see that the HEA is addressing this very point in the context of university teaching where there is increasing effort placed on building evidence to inform what we do in higher education to improve the quality of our students' learning experience. Much useful information, resources and reviews can be obtained from their research and evaluation website, **www.heacademy.ac.uk/Research.htm**.

However, for the busy university educator coping with many pressures, the need to engage with the scholarship of teaching and learning in terms of theoretical and empirical issues might seem daunting. This is where the concept of reflective practice and action research, in particular, has certain strengths as a link between continuing professional development and improving students' learning experience and performance. The purpose of the remainder of this chapter is to consider the part that action research or practitioner enquiry can play in the development of reflective practice.

Reflective practice through action research

Action research has had a chequered history, borne perhaps from its two distinct traditions of social reform in the USA and the education movement in the UK. Masters (1995) summarised five movements that have influenced the rise and fall and rise again of action research. These are briefly explored here.

1. The Science in Education movement, which posits that there is a stable, coherent, knowable self. This self knows itself and the world through reason which, in this movement, is viewed as the highest and only objective form of mental functioning. Knowing produced by the objective rational self is 'science', which can provide universal truths about the world, regardless of the individual status of the knower. Knowledge produced by science is seen as 'truth', and is eternal. The knowledge/truth produced by science will always lead towards progress and perfection. All human institutions and practices can be analysed by science (reason/objectivity) and improved.
2. The influence of John Dewey, as outlined above, but specifically in terms of action research, and his view that reflective activity should include some form of testing out ideas derived from reflective thinking.
3. Kurt Lewin's group dynamics movement. Lewin taught people to analyse and be leaders of change by being aware of the social forces that operate on them. In the 1940s he constructed his theory of action research in which he argued for the integration of theory with practice: *There is nothing so practical as a good theory* (Lewin, 1951, p169).
4. Post-war reconstructionist curriculum development. In the 1950s 'educational researchers' were brought in to tackle problems with the curriculum such as prejudice. This led to a bigger split between theory and practice ('them and us': the educational researchers and the educators). This had the effect of putting action research in decline.
5. The teacher-researcher movement. This is the movement that is most closely related to the themes in this book and much is owed to the influence of Carr and Kemmis (1986), who in a seminal book critiqued educational research in its failure to relate to practice. Their alternative was based on the concept of a critical social science by Jürgen Habermas (1970s). Habermas was concerned with processes involved in developing knowledge (of particular interest to us as practitioners exploring action research because he challenges empirical analytical enquiry). Carr and Kemmis developed this work to argue for a critical educational science which could impact on practice through what they called emancipatory action research.

Action research is simply a form of self-reflective enquiry undertaken by participants in social situations in order to improve the rationality and justice of their own practices, their understanding of these practices, and the situations in which the practices are carried out.

Carr and Kemmis (1986, p162)

It is the UK tradition of linking research to bring about the improvement of education-orientated practice that is focused on here. Carr and Kemmis's book was written at a time when teachers were seen as autonomous professionals but with the move to accountability, quality assurance and objective 'measurement', action research has become to many simply another research methodology to be used in teacher training. This, in our view, is to adopt an uncritical stance to action research, in the same way as the concept of the reflective practitioner has sometimes been uncritically accepted. Action research is a broad umbrella term for many different approaches and research methodologies but there are some fundamental principles that are characteristic. Action research means enquiry that is carried out by practitioners into their own practice (where the aim is to improve practice), and not by outside researchers brought in. Action research is by its very essence cyclical, originally described by Lewin (1940) as planning, action, fact-finding about the result of the action, then beginning again. Norton (2001) suggests that an easy way of remembering the process is to use the acronym ITDEM. See Figure 14.1.

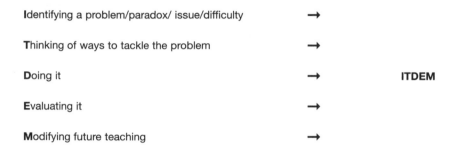

Identifying a problem/paradox/ issue/difficulty	→	
Thinking of ways to tackle the problem	→	
Doing it	→	**ITDEM**
Evaluating it	→	
Modifying future teaching	→	

Figure 14.1 ITDEM: an acronym for the stages in an action research cycle (Norton, 2001)

Action research is collaborative. While it may start as an individual educator's reflective enquiry, it must, if it is to be distinguished from curriculum development or introspective reflection, be open to public scrutiny through dissemination. In research outputs, this would take the form of conference papers and publications such as peer-reviewed journal articles. In sharing good practice within or across an institution, there is a ripple effect which encourages professional bonds and mutual interests among practitioners. In a higher education sector where the emphasis is on communities of practice within subject disciplines, pedagogical action research is one means of cross-fertilisation and is an aspect that lecturers mention as being particularly valuable (Norton, 2005). Finally, action research is constructivist. Owens, in her chapter on problem-based learning (Chapter 4), discusses a socially constructive view of knowledge. The same theoretical arguments she uses can be applied in research where the assumption is that instead of taking a researcher perspective on what is going on (a positivist objective stance where the researcher manipulates the subject and observes the response), there is an acknowledgment that the participants in the research are making their own sense of the research endeavour.

In summary, action research is one means by which university educators can align the goals of improving their students' learning, reflecting on their own practice, but in an active rather than passive way, and meet some of the requirements for continuing professional development. Leitch and Day (2000) consider how action research and reflective practice together can impact on teachers' development. They argue that there has been too little attention paid to the reflective element in the action research process and they suggest that an overemphasis on the rational in reflection has neglected the affective and the role of emotion in understanding and developing a model of action research which facilitates personal and professional change. While Leitch and Day's context is not that of tertiary education, their points apply equally well to the higher education sector (see for example, Zuber-Skerritt, 1992a, b). Kember (2000) pioneered the use of action research in an inter-institutional initiative involving eight universities in Hong Kong. Kember argues that educational development is rarely underpinned by any theoretical rationale but that action research provides an appropriate and enduring framework for evaluating the quality of teaching and learning. There are several examples of an action research approach. Each of the chapter authors in this book highlights a different style of action research but uses their findings to modify practice. This is the enduring effect mentioned by Kember.

Reflective practice through practitioner inquiry and research

Developing reflective practice through inquiry and research highlights the workplace as a learning environment. For higher education the workplace could be the lecture theatre, workshop space, tutorial room or placement setting. The workplace as a learning environment has a number of advantages in that it facilitates some key aspects that fuel reflective practice.

- **Experiential learning.**
- **Theory–practice interaction.**
- **Opportunities for collegiality and collaboration.**
- **Direct links to impact on pupils and their learning.**
- **Taking a risk in a 'safe' environment.**
- **A community of practice.**

Mezirow (1991) identified instrumental learning (skill development), dialogic learning (learning about the organisation and the individual's place within it) and self-reflective learning (promoting understanding of oneself in the workplace and the need for self change) as some important features of learning in the workplace which contribute directly to professional learning.

The value of undertaking inquiry and research into one's practice and the impact on professional learning has yet to be fully appreciated. There are many examples of how practitioners can become researchers evident from earlier days, in Lewin's (1948) work and Stenhouse's (1975) vision of researchers in professional communities. The role of critical friends and critical community is of great importance to the validity and authenticity of practitioner inquiry, research and reflective practice. Collaboration, networking and critical appraisal are key aspects of the inquiry, research and professional learning processes and, we would argue, need to be systematically built into staff development programmes in higher education.

The promotion of approaches that support self-determination, collegiality and partnership are necessary to allow varieties of professional learning to flourish. The twenty-first century professional should be one who undertakes reflection, inquiry and research into the very complexity of learning and teaching. It may be time for a 'wake-up call' for higher education institutions to develop and 'cement' their staff-development approaches for learning and teaching to include opportunities for inquiry, research and reflection. Reflection is an integral and fundamental component of inquiry and research approaches to improving practice as illustrated by a practitioner below:

> *To improve one's practice one needs to continually examine and reflect on courses of action to bring about change. This is a skill that I have used throughout my inquiry to analyse strategies used to stimulate and encourage learning ... Action research has made me want to initiate change, has made me critical of the processes used to bring about change and has led me to question my beliefs in education.*

(Skoyles, 1998, p105)

Conclusion

In this book, we have brought together a number of experienced university teachers who have written about their own practice in working with students from the full range of foundation degrees to postgraduate degrees. Some of the chapters, particularly those to do with e-learning, have been more theoretically and research-orientated but all have had a similar underlying purpose to convey the importance of reflecting on the students' learning experience and thinking through how that might be enhanced.

We have put forward our view in this chapter that developing one's own reflective practice can, and should, take many forms. While acknowledging that such a position might lay us open to those critics who bring charges of passive introspection and comfortable rightness of thought, we believe that it is only through a personal commitment to change that teaching can be improved. Imposing one methodological approach, or insisting on undifferentiated training workshops, is not the way to encourage any of us to change what might often be unconscious but deeply held beliefs about the nature of teaching and learning. Instead, we need to come to change though our own observations and research. In doing this, we are arguing for the same rigour and analytical qualities in pedagogical research and practitioner inquiry that are accepted in all other fields of research. It is our hope that in reading this book, readers will find not only inspiration but practical suggestions for how they might enhance their own teaching, and ultimately improve their students' learning experience and performance.

References

Argyris, C. and Schön, D.A. (1974) *Theory in practice: Increasing professional effectiveness*. San Francisco, CA: Jossey-Bass.

Breslow, L., Drew, L., Healey, M., Matthew, B. and Norton, L. (2004) Intellectual curiosity: A Catalyst for the scholarships of teaching and learning and educational development, in Elvidge, E.M. (ed.) *Exploring academic development in higher education: Issues of engagement*. Cambridge: Jill Rogers Associates.

Brockbank, A. and McGill, I. (1998) *Facilitating reflective learning in higher education*. Buckingham: SRHE and Open University Press.

Carr, W. and Kemmis, S. (1986) *Becoming critical; knowing through action research*. Lewes: Falmer Press.

Cowan, J. (2006) *On becoming an innovative university teacher. Reflection in action* (2nd edition). Maidenhead: SRHE and Open University Press.

Dewey, J. (1910) *How we think*. Amherst, NY: Prometheus Books (1991 edition).

Ellis, A. (1997) A guide to rational living. Hollywood, CA: Melvin Powers Wilshire.

Healey, M. (2003) The scholarship of teaching: issues around an evolving concept. *Journal on Excellence in College Teaching*, 14, 5–26.

Kahn, P., Young, R., Grace, S., Pilkington, R., Rush, L., Tomkinson, B. and Willis, I. (2005) *The role and effectiveness of reflective practices in programmes for new academic staff: a grounded practitioner review of the research literature*. Higher Education Academy literature review report. Available at **www.heacademy.ac.uk/4885.htm** (accessed 28 January 2007).

Kember, D. (2000) *Action learning and action research. Improving the quality of teaching and learning*. London: Kogan Page.

King, P.M. and Kitchener, K.S. (1994) *Developing reflective judgment: Understanding and promoting intellectual growth and critical thinking in adolescents and adults*. San Francisco, CA: Jossey Bass.

Knight, P.T. (2002) *Being a teacher in higher education*. Buckingham: SRHE and Open University Press.

Leitch, R. and Day, C. (2000) Action research and reflective practice: towards a holistic view. *Educational Action Research*, 8 (1), 179–193.

Lewin, K. (1948) *Resolving social conflicts*. London: Harper Row.

Lewin, K. (1951) *Field theory in social science; selected theoretical papers* (D. Cartwright, ed.). New York: Harper & Row.

Masters, J. (1995) The History of Action Research, in I. Hughes (ed.) *Action Research Electronic Reader*, The University of Sydney, online **www2.fhs.usyd.edu.au/arow/o/m01/rmasters.htm#AR%20what** (accessed 17 February 2007).

Meyer, J. and Norton, L. (2004) Editorial. Metalearning in higher education. *Innovations in Education and Teaching International*, 41 (4), 387–390.

Mezirow, V.J. (1991) *Transformative dimensions of adult learning*, San Francisco, CA: Jossey Bass.

Moon, J.A. (2004) *Reflection in learning and professional development*. Theory and practice. London: RoutledgeFalmer.

Norton, L.S. (2001) Researching your teaching: The case for action research. *Psychology Learning and Teaching*, 1 (1), 21–27.

Norton, L.S. (2005) Pedagogical action research (PAR): An evaluation of its effectiveness in engaging busy academics with SOTL. Paper presented at the 2nd Conference of the International Society for the Scholarship of Teaching and Learning (IS.SOTL), Vancouver, B.C., 14–16 October 2005.

Norton, L., Healey, M., Drew, L., Matthew, B. and Breslow, L. (2004) Pedagogical research: a practical approach to going public in the scholarship of teaching and learning. 4th International conference on the scholarship of teaching and learning, London, 13–14 May 2004.

Parker, S. (1997) *Reflective thinking in the postmodern world*. Buckingham: Open University Press. Cited in Knight, P.T. (2002) *Being a teacher in higher education*. Buckingham: SRHE and Open University Press.

Schön, D.A. (1983) The reflective practitioner. New York: Basic Books.

Schön, D.A. (1987) *Educating the reflective practitioner*. Toward a new design for teaching and learning in the professions. San Francisco, CA: Jossey-Bass.

Skoyles, P. (1998) Introducing a vocational course for lower ability students into an academic sixth form. Unpublished MA dissertation, Canterbury Christ Church University College.

Sotto, E. (1994) *When teaching becomes learning. A theory and practice of teaching*. London: Cassell.

Stenhouse, L. (1975) *An introduction to curriculum research and development*. London: Heinemann Educational Books.

Zuber-Skerritt, O. (1992a) *Action research in higher education*. Examples and reflections. London: Kogan Page.

Zuber-Skerritt, O. (1992b) *Professional development in higher education. A theoretical framework for action research*. London: Kogan Page.

Useful further resources

(All the sites below have been accessed 17 February 2007)

Action research websites

Collaborative Action Research Network (CARN)
www.did.stu.mmu.ac.uk/carn/
The Action Research and Evaluation online (AREOL):
www.scu.edu.au/schools/gcm/ar/arhome.html
Action and Research Open Web (AROW):
www2.fhs.usyd.edu.au/arow/
The Action Research Net:
www.bath.ac.uk/~edsajw/
Jean McNiff's website on action research in education:
www.jeanmcniff.com/

Journals which publish pedagogical action research

Action Research
www.sagepub.co.uk/journalsProdDesc.nav?prodId=Journal201642
Educational Action Research
www.tandf.co.uk/journals/titles/09650792.asp
Assessment and Evaluation in Higher Education
www.tandf.co.uk/journals/titles/02602938.asp
Innovations in Educational and Teaching International
www.tandf.co.uk/journals/routledge/14703297.html
Studies in Higher Education
www.tandf.co.uk/journals/carfax/03075079.html

Conferences which accept pedagogical action research studies

Improving Student Learning Symposia (ISL)
www.brookes.ac.uk/services/ocsld/isl/index.html
Higher Education Academy Conference (HEA)
www.heacademy.ac.uk/events/conference.htm
Pedagogical Research in Higher Education Conference (PRHE)
www.hopelive.hope.ac.uk/PRHE/
European Association for Research into Learning and Instruction (EARLI)
http://earli2007.hu/nq/home/
International Society for the Scholarship of Teaching and Learning (ISSOTL)
www.issotl.indiana.edu/ISSOTL/

Index

Added to a page number 'f' denotes a figure and 't' denotes a table.

academic motivation 58
accelerated learning 16–17
accelerated learning planning cycle 17
action inquiry
    assessment 53
    defined 46
    reasons for promoting 45
    and research projects 47–8
action learning
    assessment 53
    defined 45–6
    need for commitment 49
    qualities needed 49
    reasons for promoting 45
action learning sets 46–7
action research, reflective practice through
        144–6
active citizenship 123
active learning, through VLEs 70
administrative issues, supporting students with
        disabilities 134
Aims, Goals and Objectives (AGO) 18
Alternatives, Possibilities and Choices (APC) 18
animated pedagogical agents 86–7
anticipatory duty clause (SENDA) 131–2
artificial intelligence 80, 81
assessment 92–100
    for action learning and action inquiry 53
    effect on quality learning 93
    espoused theory and theory in use 98
    special needs foundation degree 116–18
    student learning 96
    students' understanding of criteria 97
    suggested diagnostic tool 66
    supporting students with disabilities 135
    theoretical background 94–6
    virtual learning environments 70
    see also formative assessment; summative
        assessment
Assessment is learning. The idea of learning without
        some form of assessment is inconceivable 106
Assessment Plus: Using assessment criteria to support
        student learning 97
asynchronous 79
asynchronous e-forums, reflection-on-practice
        26–8

attention-directing tools 18t, 19
audience segmentation 14
autonomy, academic 143–4
AutoTutor 86–7, 88

bandwidth 79
Bayesian networks 83
behaviour/behavioural goals 12, 13, 14, 15
'being reflective' 23, 25
blended learning 71
bugs, in student knowledge 82
business studies, PBL in 35–8

change
    managing 12
    stages of 14f
    see also organisational change
Cheshire Programme Enterprise Group (PEG)
        124
Children and Young People's Partnership
        (CHYPP) 123
CIRCSIM-Tutor project 88
citizenship education 123–4
co-operation, through VLEs 70
co-operative learning 32
coaching see peer coaching collaborations
Cognitive Tutors 85
collaboration 146
collaborative research 145
collegiality 146
communication
    benefits of online 29
    virtual learning environments 70
community
    engagement and participation in 124
    see also learning communities; wider
        community
community of enquiry 22
compiled knowledge 82
computer networks 79
computer-aided instruction (CAI) 81
computer-mediated communication (CMC) 79
Consequence and Sequel (C&S) 18t
Consider all Factors (CAF) 18t
constructivism 31, 103, 145
CORT Thinking programme 18–19

coursework 12
creativity 124, 125
Crick Report (1998) 123
critical appraisal 146
critical evaluation, professional practice 51–2
critical friendship groups 48–9, 53
critical incident analysis 51–2
critical reflection 13, 14t
curricula development
    history and policies 121–2
    post-war reconstructionist 144
curriculum design, humanity as pivotal in 127
'curriculum enrichment' module 104

Dearing Report (1997) 11
decision-making, evidence-informed 144
deep learning 32, 34, 94
deficit approach, to learning 94
Developing Learning Skills module 113–14
    assessment 116–18
Development and Education Programme for
        Daughters and Community (DEPDC) 125
Dewey, John 141, 144
dialogic learning 146
dialogic teaching 83–4
dialogue, formative assessment 108
differentiation 14
disabilities, supporting students with 130–8
    administrative issues 134
    assessment 135
    examples of good practice 135–8
    institutional issues 132
    student support services 133–4
    use of ICT 133
disability, common definitions of 131–2
Disability Advisors 133–4
Disability Discrimination Act (1995) 131
Disability Rights Commission 131
Disabled Students' Allowance 136
discussing 16
diversity 70
domain module, ITS 83

e-forums, reflection-on-practice 26–8
e-learning 68–77
    benefits 70–1
    challenges 71
    key terminology 79
    meeting the standards 68–9
    modes of learning 71–2
    systems development 88

tools for analysis 73–6
    trends in education 69–70
    see also intelligent agents; online learning
e-pedagogy 71
education
    coaching in 50
    new technologies 69–70
emotional intelligence 122
empowerment 70
engagement, in the community 124
enterprise 124
Enterprise Opportunity for All in a World of Change
        124
entrepreneurship 124, 125
espoused theory 98–9
Essay Feedback Checklist (EFC) 98, 99–100
Every Child Matters agenda 121, 122
evidence 144
evidence-informed decision-making 144
Excellence in Schools 124
expectations, communication of 70
explaining 16
extrinsic motivation 59, 107

face-to-face discussions 27t
family expectations, and motivation 59
features dashboard 74, 75f
feedback
    e-learning and ITSs 88
    espoused theory and theory in use 98–9
    general principles 97
    quality 103, 108
    student learning 96
    through VLEs 70
    using ICT to improve 108
    writing tasks 23
FeFiFoFun model 11
file compression 79
First Important Priorities (FIP) 18
force-field analysis 52
formative assessment 102–9
    online 28–9
foundation degrees 111–13
fully online (FOL) learning 73

generative systems 81
Good Learner Inventory 61, 66
group discussion 115–16
group dynamics movement 144
group presentations, assessing 53
group work, PBL 32, 34

Habermas, Jürgen 141
hands-on-teaching 12
Harvard Business School (HBS) 126
health sector, coaching in 50
higher education, changing nature of 9–10
Higher Education Academy (HEA) 1, 11, 120
hints, use of 84
history of curricula development, UK 121–2
humanity, in curriculum design 127

ICT
    pre-course audit of skills 28
    supporting students with disabilities 133,
        137
    to improve formative feedback 108
inclusion, effective 132
informing 16
innovate, ability to 124
Institute for Learning and Teaching (ILT) 11
institutional autonomy 143
institutional issues, supporting students with
        disabilities 132
instrumental learning 146
intelligent agents 80–9
    pedagogical 86–7
    tutoring systems 81–6
intelligent learning systems (ILSs) 87
    and reflective practitioners 87–8
intelligent tutoring systems (ITSs)
    barriers to widespread use 89
    benefits 85
    components 82–5
    development 81–2, 88
    difficulties 85
    screen example 86f
interface module, ITS 85
internet 79, 137
intranet 79
intrinsic motivation 59, 107
involvement, as a tool of learning 122
ITDEM 145
ITS see intelligent tutoring systems

knowledge, bugs in students' 82
knowledge acquisition, through VLEs 70
knowledge generation 126

L2L see learning to learn
lead learners 11
    academics as 10–11
    challenges for 11

learner capacities 63
learner orientation 59, 63
learning
    approaches to 33, 94–5
    constructivist approach 31, 103
    four Rs of 15
    see also action learning; e-learning; learning
        to learn; meta-learning; problem-based
        learning; professional learning; service-
        learning
learning agreements 23–5
learning centres 11
learning communities 79
learning environments 17
    see also managed learning environments;
        virtual learning environments
learning experiences, writing development 23
learning logs 23
learning organisations 11
learning outcomes 13
learning power, building 16
learning profiles, personal 15
learning skills 59, 63
learning styles 114–15
learning support plans (LSPs) 133
learning to learn (L2L) 9–19
    definition 9
    as a future vocational skill 12
    importance of 10–11
    managing change 12
    social marketing and selling 12–15
    strategies 15–16
lecturers 11, 33
lectures, disabled students 136–7
lecturing 11
Lewin, Kurt 144
liberal education 71
lifelong learning 70
looped systems, checking 137

managed learning environments (MLEs) 79
memory, personal reflection 26
meta-cognition 26, 58
meta-learning 58, 114–16
'mind-friendly' learning 16–17
mix-and-match format, e-learning 71
mixed mode (MN) online learning 73
mode dashboard 74, 76f
motivation, for study 58–9
multi-agency approach 121
mutual respect 118

National Committee of Inquiry into Higher
    Education (NCIHE) 103
National Curriculum 123
National Framework for Youth Action and
    Engagement 124
National Learning Mentor Training Programme
    15
networking 146

one-to-one tutoring 83
online assessments 28–9
online learning 26, 79
    see also e-learning
operant conditioning 97
operational practice 11
organisational change, action learning sets 46–7
Other People's Views (OPV) 18
overlay model (ITS) 82

PALs *see* pedagogical agents as learning
    companions
PALS *see* Psychology Applied Learning Scenarios
participation 1, 124
Participation Works 123
partnership 146
passion, and entrepreneurship 125
passive learning 94
'Patchwork Text' assessment 53
PBL *see* problem-based learning
pedagogical agents 86–7
    and reflective practitioners 87–8
pedagogical agents as learning companions
    (PALs) 87
pedagogical module 83
peer coaching collaborations 49–50
peer pressure, and motivation 59
peer tutoring programme 128
peer-support groups, reflection-on-practice
    25–6
PELP *see* Public Education Leadership Project
performance management 11
perseverance 15
persona effect 86
personal autonomy 143
personal learning profiles 15
personal target-setting 25
plagiarism 39–40
Plus, Minus, Interesting (PMI) 18
policies, curricula development, UK 121–2
portfolios, reflective practice 23
PowerPoint 136

practica 122
practitioner inquiry, reflective practice 146
problem-based learning (PBL) 31–40
    learning activity example 38–9
    philosophical rationale 31–2
    plagiarism issues 39–40
    process 34–8
    Professional Standards Framework 32
    theoretical rationale 33–4
professional learning 146
professional practice, critical evaluation 51–2
Professional Standards Framework 1
    assessment and feedback 92–3
    e-learning 68–9
    formative assessment 102
    learning to learn 9
    problem-based learning 32
    reflection-on-practice 22
    reflective practice 140–1
    students' perceptions of themselves as
        learners 56–7
    subject inquiry and knowledge creation
        44–5
    supporting students with disabilities 130
    values for direction 122
Programme Enterprise Group (PEG), Cheshire
    124
programmed learning systems 81
Psychology Applied Learning Scenarios (PALS)
    95
public discussion, reflective process 26
Public Education Leadership Project (PELP)
    124, 126

qualities
    action learning 49
    peer coaching 50
Quality Assurance Agency (QAA) 96
quality feedback 103, 108
quality learning 93
quizzes 70

reflection-in-action 21, 141–2
reflection-on-action 21, 141–2
reflection-on-practice 21–9
    in asynchronous e-forums 26–8
    developing in peer-support groups 25–6
    developing reflective writing 22–3
    self-managed learning agreements 23–5
reflective activity 141
reflective conversation 21, 25, 26

reflective practice 140–7
    criticisms 142
    origins 141–2
    supporting disabled students 137
    ten principles 21
    through action research 144–6
    through practitioner inquiry 146
    in university education 143–4
reflective practitioners 142–3
    learning from intelligent agents 87–8
reflective skills 26
reflective teachers 118
reflective thought 22, 141
reflective writing, developing 22–3
reminding 16
research community (HEA) 11
resilience 15
roles, in PBL process 35

Schön, D.A. 141–2
school block experience (SBE) 107–8
    using ICT to improve formative feedback
        108
Science in Education movement 144
self-authorship 26
self-determination 146
self-development 59
self-esteem 26
self-managed learning agreements 23–5
self-reflective learning 146
selling, L2L 12–15
SENDA see Special Educational Needs and
        Disability Act
service-learning
    choice of model 127
    incorporating at institutions 127
    integrating social enterprise and 126, 127
    learning from other areas 127–8
    throughout the world 122–3
Sharable Content Object Model (SCORM) 87
skill acquisition, through VLEs 70
skills
    for coaching 50
    pre-course audits of ICT 28
    reflective 26
    see also learning skills; soft skills; transferable
        skills; vocational skill
social enterprise 124–6, 127
social loafing 34
social marketing, and selling L2L 12–15
social work, coaching in 50
soft skills 113–14

Special Educational Needs and Disability Act
        (2001) 131
special needs, foundation degree in 112–18
streaming 79
stress, managing 14
structured interdependence 26
student charters 10
student co-operation, through VLEs 70
student model, ITS 82–3, 85
student notices 134
student support services 133–4
student-staff contact, through VLEs 70
students
    development in e-forums 27
    with disabilities, supporting 130–8
    evaluation of learning and teaching 11
    perceptions of themselves as learners 56–66
    personalised views about learning and being
        learners 14
    role as learner 10
    understanding of assessment criteria 97
summative assessments, online 28–9
supportive learning environments 17
surface approach, to learning 33, 94
SWOT analysis 52
synchronous 79
systemic approach
    to assessment 94, 95
    to PBL 33

tablet personal computers 108
target-setting, personal 25
teacher development 145
teacher education, work placement experience
        104–6
teacher-researcher movement 144
teaching, theories of, in HE 33
teaching talk 83
technology-mediated learning (TML) 79
theory in use 98–9
thinking hats 19t
thinking tools 18–19
threaded discussion 79
time on task, through VLEs 70
trainee teachers, work placement experience
        106–8
training 16
transfer of learning 103
transferable skills 32
trips, and disabled students 136
tutor-student interaction 85
tutoring see intelligent tutoring systems; peer
        tutoring programme

uncertainty, modelling students' 83
universities, changing nature of 9–10
university education, reflective practice 143–4

values, in planning educational provision 121
virtual learning environments (VLEs)
    communication and assessment 28, 29, 70, 73
    defined 79
visually impaired students 136
vocational competence, building on 111–18
vocational motivation 58–9
vocational skill, L2L as 12
voice-plus-agent environments 87
voluntary actions 14
volunteering 123–4

web-dependent online learning (WDOL) 72–3
web-supplemented online learning (WSOL) 72
wide-area-networks (WAN) 79
wider community, selling L2L for 13
work experience placements
    students' perceptions 12
    in teacher education 104–6
    trainee teachers 106–8
    value of 103–4
Work Practice module 114
    assessment 116
Wragg, Ted 125

zone of proximal development 108